NEW MATERIAL AS NEW MEDIA

NEW MATERIAL AS NEW MEDIA

NEW MATERIAL AS NEW MEDIA:

THE FABRIC WORKSHOP AND MUSEUM

BY MARION BOULTON STROUD

EDITED BY KELLY MITCHELL, DESIGNED BY TAKAAKI MATSUMOTO

THE MIT PRESS, CAMBRIDGE, MASSACHUSETTS AND LONDON, ENGLAND

First MIT Press edition, 2002

© 2002 The Fabric Workshop and Museum
1315 Cherry Street, Philadelphia, PA 19107
www.fabricworkshopandmuseum.org

Library of Congress Cataloging-in-Publication Data

Stroud, Marion Boulton.

New material as new media: the Fabric Workshop and Museum/
by Marion Boulton Stroud; edited by Kelly Mitchell; designed by
Takaaki Matsumoto.—1st MIT Press ed.

p.   cm.

Includes bibliographical references and index.

ISBN 0-9619760-9-8 (The Fabric Workshop and Museum)

ISBN 0-262-19489-9 (MIT Press)

1. Textile fabrics in art—Exhibitions. 2. Multimedia (Art)–Exhibitions.
3. Installations (Art)—Exhibitions. 4. Art—Pennsylvania—Philadelphia—Exhibitions.
5. Fabric Workshop and Museum—Exhibitions. I. Mitchell, Kelly, 1967– II. Title.

N8251.T4 S77 2003

746—dc21   2002151201

Edited by Kelly Mitchell
Designed by Takaaki Matsumoto, Matsumoto Incorporated, New York
Printed and bound by Toppan Printing Co., Japan

Unless otherwise noted in text or captions, all works are created in collaboration with
The Fabric Workshop and Museum and are part of its permanent collection.

Photography credits

Robert Aidelman: 20 left; Doug Aitken: 20 right, 31–33; Will Brown: 14, 15, 17 left, 18, 19, 21 right,
22, 28, 29, 46 right, 54–59, 61, 68–71, 73–75, 77–79, 81, 110–112, 115–117, 121, 133, 135–137,
144–145, 152–153, 160–161, 163–165, 173, 175, 177, 195–197, 211, 215–220, 223–225, 228,
266, 277, 279 left, 282–283, 285, 286, 295–297, 303–305; John Condax: 13 right; Courtesy
ArtPace, San Antonio, Texas: 16 right; Courtesy the Detroit Institute of Arts: 37, 46 left, 132; Courtesy
Galerie Peter Pakesch, Vienna: 155; Lonnie Graham: 27, 231–235; Paula Goldman: 62; Courtesy of
Haines Gallery, San Francisco, and Dennis Oppenheim: 212–213; Aaron Igler: 16 left, 17 right, 21 left,
38, 39, 53, 91–93, 95, 97, 100, 113, 119–120, 139–141, 143, 151, 158–159, 167, 169, 171,
179–181, 183–185, 190–193, 199, 203–205, 207–209, 227, 237–239, 241–243, 245–247,
253–255, 257–259, 261, 265, 269, 271, 273–275, 279 right, 281; Thibault Jensen, courtesy
Dia Center for the Arts and Sean Kelly: 124–127; Larry Joubert: 300–301; Erik Landsberg: 64–65,
262–263; Julie Marquart, courtesy Venturi, Scott Brown and Associates: 288–289; Vincent Massa: 23
left; Roman Mensing: 291–292; Courtesy Metro Pictures: 154; Tom Meyer: 147–149; Eugene Mopsik:
23 right, 157; Simo Neri: 278 right; Sue Patterson: 278 left; Kira Perov: 293; Tom Powell: 63; Adam
Reich, courtesy Nancy Rubins and Paul Kasmin Gallery: 249–251; Stan Rhys: 200; Oren Slor, courtesy
Dia Center for the Arts: 221; Craig Smith: 67; Matthew Suib: 49, 108–109, 172, 299; Norihiro Ueno:
306–307; Robert Wedemeyer: 123; Graydon Wood: 41–43, 129–131; Dorothy Zeidman: 176.

Contents

Foreword

Anne d'Harnoncourt

*The George D. Widener Director
and Chief Executive Officer
Philadelphia Museum of Art*

How often in life is any of us lucky enough to be present at the launching of an extraordinary new venture and then to watch its progress over so many creative, action-packed years, past the quarter century mark? The Fabric Workshop and Museum gets *younger* every day—full of energy, new techniques, new dreams, with an infinite supply of artists to entice into its peripatetic but always spacious studios and to overwhelm with the skill and ingenuity of its staff. It seems impossible that the whole magic place and everything it has brought into being was once simply a gleam in Marion Stroud's eye—known to all as "Kippy"—but I can testify that it is so.

As Arthur Danto writes eloquently in his essay, fabric is very close to our physical and spiritual roots as human beings. From Joseph's coat of many colors or Penelope's shroud for Laertes, each day's weaving carefully unpicked that night to allow Odysseus time to reach home from his wanderings, is it so far to the mythic realms of the fluttering gowns in Bill Viola's *The Greeting* or Ann Hamilton's sea of horsehair? When the Inca emperor Atahualpa expressed his astonishment that his Spanish conquerors valued silver and gold more than the exquisite textiles woven by his people, he spoke a truth about the preciousness of artistic invention applied to the humblest of materials, which the Workshop bears out today.

Kippy Stroud and the Workshop itself are deeply rooted in Philadelphia, and their extraordinary achievement adds immeasurably to the international cultural stature of the city in the 21st century. The samplers painstakingly embroidered by twelve-year old girls in Colonial Philadelphia, the subdued elegance of a Quaker wedding dress, the striking double-sided coverlets woven in the 19th-century Pennsylvania countryside, Stetson hats and Bill Blass suits—all are testimony to the city's history as a center for textile and clothing production over 250 years. This outpouring of fabric creations makes up the natural backdrop to the Workshop's inventions, as do the jaunty printed potholders and aprons made by inner-city kids at its immediate predecessor, the Prints in Progress program of the late 1960s.

This book can inevitably present only a selection—a fabulous cross section—of the wealth of wonders brought into being at The Fabric Workshop and Museum by over 450 artists from over 30 countries since 1977. Many of those wonders are preserved with great professional care at the Museum, which represents the other half of the Workshop's mission. The most elusive and most precious element of all to be captured in the pages of this book is that extraordinary spirit which emanates from the Workshop, from its incomparable staff and eager apprentices, and above all, from the artists as they embark on their adventures in new directions. It's not going too far to claim that free spirit for Philadelphia, and to say with utter delight, "the adventure begins here!"

Introduction

Mark Rosenthal
Adjunct Curator
Menil Collection, Houston

In Appreciation of The Fabric Workshop and Museum

When I first visited The Fabric Workshop in 1983, I was bewitched by its joyful spirit. The atmosphere of artistic combustion was gripping and intoxicating; derring-do was its modus operandi. At the risk of setting out into dangerous territory, I want to ponder what it means for a *place* to possess joie de vivre, and to note the ingredients for such an entrancing state of being.

The Fabric Workshop and Museum has always been a rather footloose enterprise. Still without a permanent home of its own after twenty-five years, it has nomadically set up shop in three manufacturing buildings, its displacement caused each time by new construction for its neighbor, the Pennsylvania Convention Center. Such settings seem apt, for the Workshop is, itself, a place for manufacturing, in a certain sense. The one constant of this once rough-and-tumble section of the city is the Reading Terminal Market, a vast food hall that is almost as appealing as the Workshop, and which has played a supporting role in making this institution such a wonderful place.

Youthful exuberance fills the air of The Fabric Workshop and Museum, not only because the organization makes extensive use of young interns. Art activity often seems like play, this because the inherently spontaneous approach encourages fresh invention and because the very nature of art making concerns the manipulation by hand of inchoate materials. The fact that so many artists at the Workshop have been young has only added to the devil-may-care attitude. In effect, The Fabric Workshop and Museum claims, "we can do anything, and we have the talent, knowledge, and resources to accomplish what we set out to do."

To look at the roster of artists in any year at the Workshop is to espy today's plenitude of contemporary art. And over the years of its existence, the Workshop has been home to a remarkably fascinating group of individuals, stars caught when still young or when near the pinnacle of their success. Yet the selection process has always been catholic in character, and free of all aesthetic bias or critical theory. Moreover, long before the idea of political correctness took hold in society, The Fabric Workshop and Museum chose artists from an extraordinarily broad spectrum of backgrounds.

This unprepossessing attitude was mirrored by the apprentices, who came from Philadelphia's inner-city neighborhoods as well as from the suburbs.

An important aspect of the Workshop spirit comes from the fact that many of the objects produced there lead a playful double life: on the one hand as artwork, and on the other as life appurtenance. This is not to say the objects made at the Workshop are simply concerned with practical design; no, the point is that all are created by painters and sculptors who play with functionality and appearance, and imbue these with an ebullient, comic, or ironic tone. If Le Corbusier wanted to create a "machine for living," the typical Workshop artist might be said to want to create an artwork for living.

The Workshop functions first and foremost as a laboratory for artistic experimentation. Unlike commercial print shops that seemingly operate in a similar manner, the Workshop is a non-profit organization. Its mission is to provide a place for artists to freely explore and extend their reach or to realize projects that might be beyond their capacity.

Certainly the spirit of The Fabric Workshop and Museum comes from the top, namely from its Founding Director Marion Stroud. She is the presiding force, whose daring attitude and embrace of young artists inspires the institution. It is her character at work: indomitable, energetic, determined, and always respectful of the artist. Her activity has greatly enhanced the cultural life of the city of Philadelphia, where The Fabric Workshop and Museum is a bright light in the firmament of cultural institutions, not only for its exhibition activity, but for providing the vehicle for artists to come to town and contribute to the cultural life of the city. In recent years the Acadia Summer Art Program located in Acadia National Park, Maine, also founded by Stroud, has reinforced the Philadelphia program in substantial ways, prompting new converts and interest.

What started out and succeeded admirably as a laboratory for artists to explore fabric has evolved under Stroud's leadership, so that the *fabric* part of the name became outmoded. The Workshop has collaborated with artists on all kinds of projects outside the realm of fabric alone and now aids artists with every kind of material imaginable beyond Philadelphia, with installations in cities as far-flung as Venice, London,

Dakar, Los Angeles, and New York. From yardage at its start, the Workshop's scope has mightily expanded. In 1987, it began an ambitious exhibition program at both its homeport and in many other cities, where exhibitions have circulated of its collection. Finally, in 1996, the name of the institution became The Fabric Workshop and Museum, acknowledging that the body of works created at the Workshop represents a museum collection that must be cared for and exhibited. The Workshop had grown up!

This was not necessarily a predictable evolution in as much as most alternative space-type institutions founded in the 1970s have fallen by the way side. It is not just a tribute to Stroud that The Fabric Workshop had successfully negotiated the adolescent passages of institutional life; it is a testimony to the mission of the organization. The Fabric Workshop and Museum now has a prominent role in the art world, successfully attracting not only emerging but already highly successful artists, as well as generous funding from traditional sources. The devotees of the Workshop include a veritable who's who from the art world and from the field of architecture.

Though the word *museum* in its name suggests a degree of seriousness and a demonstrated record of accomplishment, The Fabric Workshop and Museum retains its original character. Perhaps a permanent home should remain a distant goal for now, so that its willingness to reinvent itself is unhampered, witness the 1999 Jorge Pardo lobby that has yet to be deemed permanent. The future of The Fabric Workshop and Museum is thus to be determined and, as such, this institution remains a pleasure to behold. In the meantime, the Workshop has aged beautifully, its joie de vivre not just intact but bewitchingly evolved.

Interview with Marion Boulton Stroud

Ruth Fine
Curator of Special Projects in Modern Art
The National Gallery of Art, Washington, DC

Ruth Fine: What was your original idea for The Fabric Workshop? In other words, in 1977 when you started, if you tried to imagine what the Workshop might achieve in its first 25 years, what might you have thought?

Marion Boulton Stroud: I originally thought the Workshop would be about total design, like the studios established in 1881 by William Morris at Merton Abbey with his Pre-Raphaelite friends and their apprentices. They lived on the edge of the River Wandle weaving, dyeing, and printing their own fabrics. They also painted glass and made other decorative arts for household use. I imagined that we would be like that—a William Morris atelier, producing new, fresh fabric designs for home living, fabrics for the world, total decoration coming off the walls with beds, tables, chairs, and curtains.

The model of a contemporary William Morris atelier is still vital and meaningful to me. Around the time the Workshop was started, it was the way artists in New York were living, particularly artists of the Pattern and Decoration movement, who were—not coincidentally—our first artists-in-residence. Many were part of Holly Solomon's gallery. Holly and her husband Horace's house was wild—a Kushner curtain here, a MacConnel screen there, painted chairs. It all came together.

RF: Did you think that this vision was something that was going to endure? Or was your attitude "let's try it and see"?

MBS: I hoped it would fly. The truth is we cast about in many different directions at the beginning before we honed it down to two main programs—a residency for artists, and an apprenticeship for students. Having come from the children's art program Prints in Progress in Pennsylvania, the idea of teaching underserved, urban high school students was paramount to me. The artists then came and proved themselves, and we gained momentum in the residency program with artists who responded to pattern and decoration—and to the idea of fabric—artists like Sam Gilliam (fig. 2), Dale Chihuly, and Richard Tuttle, who came in the early years of 1977 and 1978.

RF: The late 1970s was a time when many artists were starting to work with fabric and decorative imagery.

MBS: Yes, like Kim MacConnel (fig. 3), Robert Kushner, and Tina Girouard. I learned where all the fabric stores in New York were located from Bob Kushner and Ned Smyth

1

2

1. Marion Boulton Stroud, right middle, and Anne d'Harnoncourt, left middle, with Prints in Progress students, west entrance of the Philadelphia Museum of Art, 1977.

2. Marion Boulton Stroud and Sam Gilliam, The Fabric Workshop, 1977.

—there was Weller and Jerry Brown's on 57th Street. It was a thrilling moment when these artists were included in the 1981 Whitney Biennial—they were the stars.

But it wasn't until much later that an artist brought The Fabric Workshop and Museum back to that original vision of total design. In 1999, Jorge Pardo (pp. 214–221) redesigned our public entrance and created a total interior environment for a video lounge and cafe. He took us back to 1950s modernist design, an era in which all the arts were integrated.

RF: I know you were influenced by several organizations and individuals as you envisioned your own space for artists. Can you talk about some of those influences?

MBS: I traveled a great deal in the mid-1970s before starting the Workshop, visiting the design collective Marimekko in Finland and Key West Hand Print, a commercial printer in Florida. Later on, as we got rolling in the late 1970s, I went out to California and visited Gemini G.E.L., the print workshop in Los Angeles, and Crown Point Press, the San Francisco-based print studio and publisher, both of which were working with artists-in-residence.

I deeply admired Kathan Brown at Crown Point Press because she was doing very complicated, experimental prints. Her spirit and her will to make new and interesting works with artists has lingered with me, as has her concept of working with artists as friends—giving them a place to live and spending time with them. The day I met her, she was pasting colored paper on plaster of Paris for a decorative piece with Joyce Kozloff. Kathan had a very bad cold, and I was asking her about non-profit versus for-profit institutions and she said, "We might as well be a non-profit, because we don't make a penny on these labor-intensive projects!" We both laughed at the time.

RF: Speaking of non-profits, how did you fund this vision of yours?

MBS: It can be such a struggle when you're not yet sure of what you're doing, and then so breathtaking when you have even a modicum of success. David Hanks, then curator of American decorative arts at the Philadelphia Museum of Art, gave me early and important grant advice. Amazingly, David believed in me when I described this idea that we had—I still can't believe that he and others had such faith in us. It's incredible how people really want to help if you reach out to them. It is difficult to match the joy of

3

4

3. Kim MacConnel, *Kim's Plaid* (detail), 1978. Pigment on cotton sateen. Width: 50 inches (127 cm).

4. Jacqueline Matisse Monnier, *Moon Pieces (Lexique de Lune)* (detail), 1981. Pigment on viscose rayon challis. Width: 44 inches (111.76 cm).

those early moments when we learned of our first funding.

The 1970s was a period marked by idealistic, even visionary, thinking in the arts, and this was surely reflected in the creative funding initiatives at the National Endowment for the Arts. Among the many vital organizations that started up during this historic period were The Kitchen, the New Museum of Contemporary Art, The Institute of Art and Urban Resources (P.S. 1 Contemporary Art Center), Dia Center for the Arts, and Artists Space. I look back and find it amazing how many creative ventures were begun at that time.

RF: Wasn't The Fabric Workshop started with a grant?

MBS: Two grants, in 1977—one from the National Endowment for the Arts and another from the Pennsylvania Council on the Arts, both of whom have been wonderful supporters of our programs. We've been fortunate to get tremendous funding from the Institute of Museum and Library Services, and many other national and regional foundations and agencies. Also, private supporters and individuals have been generous with us over the years.

RF: What role did your involvement with Prints in Progress play in the idea for The Fabric Workshop?

MBS: I was the artistic director of Prints in Progress for about eight years. Billy Wolf founded the organization dedicated to school age children during the 1960s as part of The Philadelphia Print Club, now called The Print Center. We worked to bring etching, lithography, and silkscreen printing into the public school system. Then, after Lyndon Johnson came into office in 1963, he encouraged Americans to use their talents at home in addition to entering programs like the Peace Corps, so we decided to start print workshops in underserved neighborhoods of the city. We hired artists to teach in our neighborhood print workshops; we got college scholarships for some of our students; we took young artists to visit museum curators, like you, Ruth, at the Lessing J. Rosenwald Collection.

So after printing 5 million t-shirts and Christmas cards at Prints in Progress, we began to think of other ways to expand and keep the artists happy and energized. I was possessed to hire the best African American and Hispanic artists to teach the African American and Hispanic kids in the after-school program. The women artists all loved working with fabric. By that time, I was taking classes at the Philadelphia College of Textiles, now Philadelphia University. We decided to set up a small, three-yard print table in one of the Prints in Progress studios, and the artists and children responded to it. If that hadn't happened, we may not have started the Workshop. It planted a seed for the idea.

RF: Was this the start of your interest in fabric?

MBS: I've always loved fabric, and I've said that fabric is in my genes. I suppose I couldn't escape it. One part of my family is

from a town called Stroud in the southwest of England that was named after them because they ran the town's large textile manufacturing company, which specialized in plain, woven blankets. Interestingly, these blankets were sold to American Indians. My grandmother loved fabric too—she did the interior design for the Cosmopolitan Club in Philadelphia.

RF: How did your family have an impact on your interest in art?

MBS: My maternal grandmother, Marion Sims Rosengarten, certainly influenced me. She had a deep appreciation of the arts as an artist, enthusiast, and benefactor, and even posed for the Philadelphia painter Violette Oakley as the "Muse of Music" for one of Miss Oakley's lunettes for the State Capital in Harrisburg. My grandmother was also a talented draftsman in her own right, and she made caricatures of her contemporaries, such as George Howe, one of my uncles and a Philadelphia architect famous for designing the PSFS Building with William Lescaze. That caricature stands out because she portrayed him with a cigar, onions, and garlic—he looked much more debauched than the dapper gentleman that he was in reality. My grandfather, Frederick Rosengarten—whose family members were manufacturing chemists from Kassel, Germany— supported her comfortably in all her endeavors.

They lived in a spectacular home with a breathtaking view of Fairmount Park. It was designed by her architect brother, Joseph Patterson Sims. His grandson, Patterson Sims, my cousin and now director of the Montclair Art Museum in New Jersey, has been a key advisor to the Workshop throughout the years. My grandmother frequently entertained people like the famous Philadelphia architect Louis Kahn and the renowned composer and conductor Leopold Stokowski—I know I've always had a well-rounded appreciation for her ability to talk to artists. She was very interested in music and founded the children's concerts with the Philadelphia Orchestra, a performance series I attended every Saturday.

RF: Your family certainly has had a long and interesting history of involvement in the arts, which appears to have set the stage for your career. I'm also intrigued by your extensive background in the studio arts. What interested you, and what was your motivation in taking classes?

MBS: I wanted to learn as much as I could about art, and I took many classes at Tyler School of Art throughout the 1970s—etching, lithography, sculpture, ceramics, photography, and painting—and a screenprinting class at the Philadelphia College of Textiles. I have always loved taking photographs. Repetition has always fascinated me, as has the ability to alter images. I loved my lithography class at Tyler—being able to get the subtle nuances you can achieve with an aluminum plate is intriguing. But silkscreen printing has its purpose, and for fabric printing it is one of the best.

5

6

5. John Moore, *Dinner* (detail), 1981. Pigment on cotton upholstery sateen. Width: 55 inches (139.7 cm).

6. Matt Mullican, *Field of Cities* (detail), 1990. Pigment on white cotton upholstery sateen. Width: 50 inches (127 cm).

I do believe that most curators—maybe I'm only speaking for myself here—want to be artists themselves at some level. Curators must have an innate interest in being artists or they wouldn't be interested in what an artist makes. And they certainly have their opinions and criticisms, and they always ask, "How would I have made this, or how would another artist have made this?" The Workshop has been a perfect setting for me to further my understanding of art as well as the artistic process and to participate in it. I have learned so much from the artists who have worked with us—there are times to talk, and times to be silent!

You must know what I mean Ruth, being an artist yourself. Your understanding of art as an artist certainly helps in making you such a wonderful curator. There is a vitality that each role gives the other, though I'm sure it is also a delicate balance. Do you agree?

RF: I have found it useful to have had a studio background, and to have continued working all these years—although I've tried to keep that part of my life private. I'm not sure, though, that most curators are frustrated artists, although some are. I have many colleagues who had liberal arts backgrounds of various sorts before they entered art history. They're devoted to curatorial work intellectually, but with little or no hands-on experience. I get your point, though.

Back to your original conception—making functional objects such as yardage, bags, umbrellas—but the Workshop evolved in a somewhat different direction.

MBS: Yes, it did evolve in a different direction. The artists I wanted to work with wanted to be shown in galleries. They didn't really want to put designs on bed sheets. They often liked that idea in the abstract, but then when you got down to the details, they didn't necessarily want their work altered from the way they saw it on a gallery or museum wall.

RF: So at some point it veered away from making functional objects to making art, in whatever form it might take. When did that happen?

MBS: Immediately. Bob Kushner wanted his project to be a print multiple as well as a cape for a performance. Richard DeVore's early project was very conceptual in nature, with one of his classical ceramic pots placed on top of a pigment print on fabric. Even from the very beginning, things were not always simple printed fabric designs, though yardage and functional objects made from yardage certainly defined us more then than it does now. The major shift away from functional objects came with the shift in the art world toward installations. I was originally naive enough to think Donald Lipski (pp. 174–177) was doing pattern and decoration when he worked with the American flag during his residency in 1990. I've come to see Lipski's work as early installation because he placed the

pieces outdoors and activated entire rooms with these flag balls and other sculptures. It was an adventurous project, and seemed so daring at the time. Now look at the American flag— it has been patterned to death!

I admit I have trouble with installations, or at least with dragging dead trees and other large found objects into galleries. When I started the Workshop, our idea was to make things that a person could use. I don't know how you use an installation, other than to walk through it and to experience it. I find it very difficult that they are taken down and often demolished. In that way, I'm more of a traditionalist. But then again, I love new projects like Leonardo Drew's (pp. 90–93) cast paper installation of found objects.

You have to go with the times you live in, and installations define the art world right now. Our practice has been to follow artists, to let them take the lead. I believe that their intuition is amazing. They hear the tremor of the earthquake before the earthquake comes.

RF: Let me return to something else you just mentioned. Among your first artists were Kushner, who had a bent for the decorative; Gilliam, who had engaged with fabric in his work before coming to the Workshop; and DeVore, who is a ceramic artist. How engaged were you personally with the art/craft questions, and high/low art? Did you actively want to prove frequently held perceptions wrong?

MBS: The question of high vs. low and art vs. craft became irrelevant once we began to work with artists, in my opinion, since their work could be all of these at once. I found that very rewarding. I actively wanted to prove that artists could make repeat yardage, that it wasn't an art form reserved only for the textile industry. Every time we did another repeat yardage I felt completely rewarded, especially when it was with an artist who had never tried it before and came up with a great success, such as John Moore (fig. 5), Jacqueline Matisse Monnier (fig. 4), and Tony Costanzo.

I am always surprised when I get to know artists and learn how many different media they have worked in. There often are no boundaries of high and low. Scott Burton appeared to be a sculptor but he confessed that he had been an abstract painter in his youth. Artists who have experimented with different media seem to incorporate fabric as part of a new work at the Workshop, but I think that if you looked back over their previous works you would often find that they had a latent desire to use fabric, or even attempted to use fabric. Every time we thought we were starting to do something totally new with an artist, we found that they were thinking about it before their experience with us, though perhaps in a different way.

RF: Today, people talk about "prints coming off the walls" as if it's a new concept. Somehow this entered the Workshop's

7

8

7. *Secret Victorians: Contemporary Artists and a 19th-Century Vision*, (curated by Melissa Feldman and Ingrid Schaffner). Exhibited at The Fabric Workshop and Museum, 25 January–7 April 2001. Foreground: Yinka Shonibare, *Nuclear Family*, 1999. Collection of the Seattle Art Museum. Background: Kara Walker, *The Underground Railroad*, 1996. Collection of Penny Pritzer and Dr. Bryan Traubert.

8. Isaac Julien in collaboration with Javier de Frutos, *The Long Road to Mazatlán* (video still), 1999. Four synchronized DVDs projected through three LCD projectors with 10 speaker Surround Sound. 18 minute loop. Exhibited at The Fabric Workshop and Museum, 14 September–20 October 2001. Originally commissioned by ArtPace, A Foundation for Contemporary Art, San Antonio, and Grand Arts, Kansas City, with support from the London Arts Board, the Arts Council of England, and the British Council.

activities almost from the start. Was this part of your original aim?

MBS: No, but the artists we've collaborated with from the beginning all worked four-dimensionally (laughs), so it was never considered other than going to happen. I think our projects were always off the wall, with artists like Scott Burton, Sam Gilliam, and Richard DeVore. They always saw three- or four-dimensionally and now with the pervasiveness of installations this is even more true. It seems to be a conscious aim that a work of art be seen in the round, as opposed to flat yardage that one could "make into anything," which is a myth. If you design a yardage, you have to make it be something—for example, a tablecloth might lead you to use a scale appropriate to a table. You must design for the function of the finished piece. It is impossible to begin a design saying that it will be made into everything—there are very few universal patterns that have developed during our 25 years. Robert Venturi (pp. 284–289), Jun Kaneko, and the late Diane Itter—they all succeeded in doing it, but very few others ever have. Possibly Virgil Marti (pp. 194–197), our reincarnation of William Morris, could make a repeat yardage that could be made into anything, but his would have a conceptual bent. He could revive William Morris-style designs, though he's also been able to come out on top in the world of installation art. He is a very dynamic artist.

Our first artists—Robert Kushner, Sam Gilliam, and Richard DeVore, as examples—certainly did whatever they wanted to do. Gilliam was a print workshop master and he knew exactly what he wanted. He was a genius when it came to arranging fabric and we could never install his pieces the way he did—he painted and sculpted with fabric. Sam was a perfect artist for us to start with. So was Robert Kushner who was looking wildly at the textile industry and making fun of it in a way. They both taught us to work collaboratively. Richard DeVore had an incredible feel for conceptual work. He related fabric to his ceramics, and came up with wonderful ideas.

RF: Did you ever come close to the original vision of a William Morris design studio? Have any of the fabrics created in the residency program been mass-marketed, for instance?

MBS: No. Jun Kaneko's designs for The Fabric Workshop were copied by a manufacturer, or appropriated you could say. That is one of the problems with textiles; you can change almost any colorway or design even slightly and call it your own, and offer it to the mass market without violating copyright laws. It always seemed clear that very few designs were going to get into the mass market, even though every artist who walked in the door was convinced that their design would make a bundle and sell like hotcakes. That's my favorite expression, "This will really sell!" It sells to people in the art world who want a small piece of it, but it doesn't sell to a mass market.

RF: As you mentioned, in order to have a mass distribution you have to work in a certain way, which is not the way that you work. You have to print overseas and follow certain budgetary parameters, and it is my impression that you always give the artists free rein to go in whatever direction they want.

MBS: Probably too free, if we wanted to produce repeat yardage. Early on, we told artists that they had to make yardage. It made more sense in the "decade of pattern" with artists like Robert Kushner, Miriam Shapiro, Kim MacConnel, and Ned Smyth—they were ready and eager to go. Now we're much more adventuresome in the artists we select in terms of their experience with fabric or pattern—it is definitely not a requirement that they have experience working with fabric. We propose it now as experimentation with new materials, which includes all kinds of techniques associated with fabric, but also a lot more. You could say that we've stretched the definition of fabric!

RF: Has the length of an artist's residency changed?

MBS: It was two weeks in the beginning, and it's now two years! (laughs) The creative process takes a little longer these days because we've changed the structure of the collaborative process. In the early years, it was a "real" residency, meaning that artists came for two weeks and worked the entire time with our master printers to make repeat yardage. If we hadn't finished the yardage before they had to go, then we sent them the proofs.

Now the process is more involved. First, an artist makes a site visit so we can introduce them to the archives of past projects and the studios. They also give a slide lecture to our staff and students. This initial step allows all of us to get to know each other—both artistically and personally, which helps in forming the collaborative partnership that we rely on between artists-in-residence and staff. The artist leaves after that first visit, and begins to experiment and send ideas—often via FedEx and fax—and we try them out.

Our staff members also visit artists in their studios, which we didn't do in the early days. We now pick up our sewing machines and cameras and travel to the artist's studio or another location if it's necessary—to San Francisco and Los Angeles, to London. In 1997 and 1998, our Project Coordinator Christina Roberts and then-Associate Director Kelly Mitchell accompanied curator Larry Rinder to Papua New Guinea—that may have been the furthest we have traveled! We invited Larry to curate an exhibition and ended up orchestrating an ongoing international exchange—two staff trips to visit an indigenous tribe called the Maisin (pp. 186–193) who are known for their vivid red and black tapa cloth paintings, and two trips by Maisin artists to Philadelphia. It was an exceptional experience for all of us, and we forged strong ties to these

9

10

9. *Decorative Arts from the Philadelphia Museum of Art* (curated by Jorge Pardo and Kathryn Hiesinger, Curator of Decorative Arts, Philadelphia Museum of Art). Exhibited at The Fabric Workshop and Museum, 22 April–3 July 1999.

10. Charles Juhász-Alvarado, *Jardin de Frutos Prohibidos/ZONA FRANCA (The Garden of Forbidden Fruit/DUTY FREE).* The artist in costume with installation detail. Exhibited at The Fabric Workshop and Museum, 12 July–16 August 2002.

wonderful artists working and painting in their traditional art form, thousands and thousands of miles away from Philadelphia.

The truth is that now it is a very labor-intensive process to do a new project with an artist, and there are often false starts, so we have learned to expect that each new residency will take at least a year, and often a year and a half. This also gives us the time to develop exhibitions from these new residency projects. We are constantly under pressure to exhibit work that we've just completed, and while sometimes time pressure can be good—it adds to the adrenaline and excitement certainly—it also puts tremendous and constant pressure on staff and artists. Because these projects are often very ambitious—sometimes venturing literally into outer space like the space family and shuttle we developed with Yinka Shonibare (pp. 256–259)—it is beneficial to have more time to develop and fabricate them.

RF: False starts seem like they would be a logical part of the kind of experimentation you undertake with artists.

MBS: Yes, we've had a few disappointments. One of the biggest was that Robert Gober's fabric couldn't be water-proofed as he desired. The print was made using Iris printing and at the time the technology simply wasn't there for water-proofing. That has now changed, but of course he's on to another phase. Another disappointment was with Anni Albers. We never completed her project to her satisfaction, and then unfortunately she passed away. Of course, many technical difficulties are eventually solved. Chuck Fahlen's felt piece was like trying to make a sieve hold water, but Project Coordinator Lucy Michels worked her miracles and got it done. As you say, experimentation is a fundamental part of the process.

RF: The Fabric Workshop and Museum (FW+M) has been operating during a period when many boundaries in the arts have changed and expanded. You have contributed greatly to this new way of thinking about art by stretching the definition of fabric, don't you think?

MBS: Yes, I suppose we have. At this point, there has been an endless amount of experimentation and we think that any shred of material in an artist's project makes sense for the Workshop's original concept. Look at Tom Friedman's (pp. 94–97) project—it's photography and it's paper, but paper is fiber, and all of the pieces are carefully woven together. Believe me, we've had some interesting moments trying to explain various projects to skeptics—Steve Izenour's (pp. 286–289) exhibition *Signs of Fun* is a good example. It was very funny explaining to a board member how his work weaves together the highways of America, and therefore relates to fabric. But the truth about his work is that it was pattern and decoration to the hilt. He out-William-Morrised William Morris!

We are very open to new fabrication processes. Our staff enjoys the challenge of learning new techniques, or finding the resources in industry to complement what we can do in the studios. For example, Mary Anne Friel—one of the first project coordinators at the FW+M and she is still going strong—found an industrial felt manufacturer in Boston to make Rachel Whiteread's (pp. 298–301) impressive sculpture, *Untitled (Felt Floor).* And we had the enamel printed on the police badges for Chris Burden's (pp. 60–65) *L.A.P.D. Uniforms* in Lancaster, Pennsylvania, and the uniforms custom-made in Los Angeles. We brought an expert French knotter to the FW+M to make the knots for Marie-Ange Guilleminot's (pp. 118–121) project, *Sea Urchin.* For the most part, though, I have to say that we expanded to new materials by following the wishes of our artists-in-residence. The Workshop has always been artist-driven—in all of our programming—and it really shows through when you look at the incredible diversity of materials we have experimented with over the years. The artists are the ones with the ideas and the intuition. We just have the good sense to follow their lead and reinforce their needs and desires. We will do whatever we can to search for new materials or processes that will satisfy their vision.

RF: With an artist like Mona Hatoum (pp. 128–133), for instance, the project that you completed with her is not made from fabric, though fabric is implicated.

MBS: She was our leap into new materials with her two carpets. We followed her desire to experiment with silicone rubber—the material made by Corning and used for breast implants. She was thinking about her body at the time, and the sculpture is called *Entrails*, and in my opinion, if anything in the body has a relationship to textiles besides hair, it's our intestines. She also made another piece, a carpet, from pins. It was a labor of love and has a wonderful conceptual connection to fabric as a carpet.

Lee Bul's (pp. 156–161) project is an example of another kind. *Live Forever* uses fabric, but only as one component of a much larger piece. It is an effective and important aspect of her futuristic karaoke pods that they are luxuriously uphol-stered and therefore very comfortable to sit in while you sing along to pop songs. This project, by the way, is immensely popular, and is currently touring to six venues throughout the United States and Canada, including the New Museum of Contemporary Art in New York, the Orange County Museum of Art in California, and The Power Plant in Toronto, Canada.

For some artists, it is a big adjustment to think about fabric, even though we're very open about our definitions. And for that reason, it sometimes takes us many years to convince certain artists to work with us—they feel they need to have just the right idea. I think we waited about nine years to work

11

12

11. Lonnie Graham, *In A Spirit House*. Exhibited at The Fabric Workshop and Museum, 20 May–18 July 1993.

12. Ken Dawson Little, *Elements of Progress*. Exhibited at The Fabric Workshop and Museum, 4 January–31 January 1989.

with Chris Burden, and when he was finally ready, it was with an extraordinary idea for L.A.P.D. uniforms. Waiting paid off with him. We also waited for Doug Aitken (pp. 30–35), whose work I first saw four or five years ago. We have been patient and now he has just completed a very ambitious video and sculpture project.

RF: Is the potential of fabric different today than it seemed 25 years ago?

MBS: I've always believed that fabric has unlimited potential, and I still do. Yoshiko Wada was at the FW+M recently and she lectured on shibori. Seeing what contemporary artists are doing with this traditional Japanese dye technique is amazing. There is never an end to learning about other cultures' ways of manipulating fabric, not to mention all of the industrial processes that are used. The possibilities are endless.

RF: What kind of training do your project coordinators have?

MBS: Most of our project coordinators in the early days were printmakers or fabric designers who had silkscreen printing experience. Now many young artists who we hire come with a variety of skills in a variety of media. It doesn't really matter what their background is—some are ceramic artists, some are painters. The important thing is that they are sensitive to the task of working with the artist. They are all artists in their own right. Most of them have their own exhibitions and busy careers as artists above and beyond their responsibilities at the FW+M. I think this diversity of skills brings more to the table with our artists-in-residence. When an artist wants an opinion they have access to a staff with a well-developed sense of their own capabilities, and who complement one another very well.

RF: Your project coordinators must have a major role in the development of the artists' projects.

MBS: They certainly do. The general scenario is that each artist is matched with one of our staff members, who serves as the project coordinator and assists the artist in researching, testing, and then fabricating the new work. There is an incredible range of skills among the artistic staff, which is important because you never know when someone's expertise might transform an artist's work in a new direction. One of the most important factors is that the project coordinator and the apprentices believe that the artist they're working with is one of the greatest living artists. They must give them support and encouragement in every way possible. I used to direct the pairing of artists with staff, but now I try to let staff call the shots because if they're committed to an artist's work it is always a better match. If there is ever any doubt in a project coordinator's mind we take them off the project because there can be no disruption. The project coordinators are sensitive to this, and if they feel they can't please the artist they will step down and

substitute someone else on the project. Our goal is to make it as seamless as possible so that the artists have a good experience and feel that their artistic dreams are realized. Years ago, one of our construction technicians named Annabeth Rosen—who is a great ceramic artist in her own right—was making Ken Little's project. She was designing and sewing a pair of pants, made from American dollar bills. Ken is from Texas, and wears tight blue jeans. Annabeth made them as pantaloons, which she fancied. He said, "I want straight-legged pants," and she said, "I'm not sure I can do it that way." So we put Elizabeth McIlvaine on the job and she was able to make the pants as Ken wanted them.

The artists-in-residence, for their part, pay tremendous homage to our project staff—Chris Burden to Mary Anne Friel, Ann Hamilton (pp. 122–127) to Sue Patterson, Bob Morris (pp. 198–201) to Lucy Michels, who he married and took away from us! Lonnie Graham (fig. 11) married Christina Roberts, his project coordinator, too, so you can see that the artists and staff sometimes work very intimately . . .

RF: Along with the Artist-in-Residence Program, the Apprentice Training Program is central to your original concept for the Workshop, isn't it?

MBS: Most definitely. The program wouldn't exist if I hadn't had my early training at Prints in Progress. The basic idea was—and is, because really this program has not changed except to expand internationally—to offer training for high school, college, and post-graduate students in the industrial skill and expressive art of silkscreen printing on fabric. The high school students work alongside college students, who work alongside the artists-in-residence. It is a wonderful opportunity for young people to develop new skills and also to find their own voice as artists. There is a formal application process, which is obviously a bit more involved for college and post-graduate students than it is for high school students. The college students now come from all over the country and from around the world, and we put them up in our student apartment while they are in Philadelphia. Some of the international students have set up print workshops in their home countries when they go home. One of our printers, Christina Roberts, has gone everywhere to recruit students, including Korea, Japan, and Uganda, and as a result our international scope has expanded greatly.

It is a true apprenticeship in the sense that the students assist in the studios with artists' projects and production printing, and in turn they are trained in silkscreen printing and fabric design. High school students, though, are paid minimum wage because we never want any student to have to choose an after-school job over furthering their education. I feel that the Apprentice Training Program has been part of everything we

13

14

13. Pedro Perez, *I Promise to
Write Poetry*. Exhibited at
The Fabric Workshop and Museum,
16 January–22 February 1992.

14. Viola Frey, *Artist's
Mind/Studio/World*. Exhibited at
The Fabric Workshop and Museum,
4 March–1 May 1992.

do, and we always get more from the experience than we give.

RF: Let's talk about some of the changes that have happened over 25 years. What are some of the key points in the FW+M's evolution?

MBS: First of all, we're bigger. The staff has tripled, at least. In the beginning, I sat in the front office with a secretary and a bookkeeper, and the bookkeeper would get up to sell things from the shop as needed. In the studio, we had two or three printers and one seamstress, maybe two. It's amazing how the staff has grown—we now have 20 staff members—10 in the studio, 10 in the museum and administration—and we still need more time and more energy to get it all done.

There are now so many different facets to the institution— it is both a museum and a workshop. We have a collections management department, with two full-time registrars who handle our permanent collections, including archivally storing each and every object. We also have storage off-site for some of the larger sculptures that have been made, which is another aspect to manage. We have so much more to take care of now that we are a museum. Originally, the number of staff was tiny; now the numbers have grown, but relatively speaking and considering how much we accomplish, we are still small.

RF: Did you ever imagine your atelier—your Workshop—would add the word "museum" to its title? Did that signify a change in the way you defined your mission?

MBS: I believe we are a product of our times and the history of our times. We added the word "museum" because we had a growing collection. We had a history, we had a body of work that was recognizable as a model of making new art and that catalogued the creative process. We felt sure we would have a place in the history of contemporary art. I owe an enormous debt to Kelly Mitchell, our associate director from 1991– 1999, who led our transition and growth from a workshop to a museum. Museums were proliferating during that time, just as alternative spaces had in the 1970s—it is a topic my friend and colleague Michael Brenson raised in his book, *Visionaries and Outcasts*. There was also a generosity of funding to museums at the time, so partly I'm sure we were driven by the possibilities of public funding. Our collection, incidentally, is now over 5,500 objects in a vast range of media, and includes artists like Red Grooms, Roy Lichtenstein (pp. 166–169), Marina Abramović (pp. 26–29), Louise Nevelson (pp. 202–205), Faith Ringgold (pp. 236–239), Vito Acconci, and Carrie Mae Weems (pp. 294–297), just to name a few that haven't come up so far in our conversation.

RF: Do you keep all these objects on-site?

MBS: We have a large storage area on-site for a sizeable portion of our collections, but all large-scale sculptural works or installations are housed off-site in a storage facility.

RF: I can imagine the practical and logistical issues involved with a collection like yours must be staggering. Have you had conservation problems?

MBS: Is there a museum in the world that hasn't had problems? There are always moments of panic, but the one thing you learn is not to act on that panic. The first lesson of art handling is to decide before you pick up a work of art where you will put it down. We don't have a conservator on staff, but we have used outside consultants to assist with questions or problems we have had, and we've also relied on the project staff who, because they are the original fabricators of the pieces, often know the most about how to address a problem.

We are also constantly expanding and improving our collections storage areas, and have been very fortunate to receive conservation funding from the Institute of Museum and Library Services for many years. They have helped us to upgrade our storage areas with new shelving, fire suppression sprinklers and UV filters on lighting fixtures, and also to re-house large portions of the collections including our artists' mylars, photography collection, video collection, and unique collection of Artist Boxes that document the creative evolution of each artist's project.

RF: Are you conscious of potential conservation issues as artists explore materials for their projects?

MBS: We haven't limited an artist's choice of materials that I can recall, and the jury is still out on the long-term reliability of materials like hog intestine, which we used with Miroslaw Balka (pp. 36–39) in a series of sculptures. One of our biggest debates was with Robert Venturi (pp. 284–289) over whether we could Scotchgard™ his fabric. This process gives fabric a longer shelf life, but Bob didn't want it done. We went to U.S. Testing and had samples of his fabric hammered and pummeled and put under ultraviolet lights to make sure it wouldn't fade without Scotchgard™. After many tests and many changes to the pigments, we were able to satisfy Bob's desire. It has ended up in museum collections such as the Montreal Museum of Fine Arts and the Philadelphia Museum of Art.

RF: Even before you became a museum, you had initiated an exhibition program. How did that come about?

MBS: Paula Marincola—a talented curator and former Board member who is now director of the Philadelphia Exhibitions Initiative at The Pew Charitable Trusts—said to me, "You have to exhibit work; you can't just make it!" I have to credit her for lighting the fire under us for our first exhibitions.

Our first exhibition was a small show of self-taught artists including the Reverend Howard Finster and Willie Stokes. This was in 1984 and we were in a building at 1133 Arch Street. We put a crummy carpet down on the floor and curtains over

15

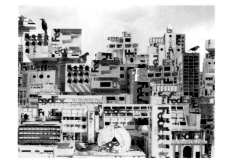

16

15. Robert Venturi and Denise Scott Brown with *Queen Anne Chair* (left), 1979, and *Empire Chair*, 1979. Denise Scott Brown wears the dress she designed from *Grandmother* fabric.

16. Doug Aitken, *Plateau*, 2002 (detail). Fujitran print mounted on plexiglass in aluminum lightbox. 122 x 52 ¼ x 14 inches (309.88 x 132.72 x 35.56 cm). Edition of 6.

the windows and began to hang things on the walls. There were leaks in the ceiling and the lights weren't very good, but it was a start. When we moved to 1100 Vine Street in 1987, we designed an exhibition space with the help of the architect Mark Thompson, though most of the space then went to the studio and archives. Our first show there was scheduled to open on New Year's Eve with a Texas chili party for Ken Little. The floor was a disaster and I asked Ken if he minded having a tar floor, which obviously he did, so we put down birch plywood flooring and painted it. It was a beautiful exhibition of Ken's work including *Bread Couple*, *Buck and Doe*, the money suit and dress I mentioned earlier (fig. 12).

Now, in our space at 1315 Cherry Street, we have two large exhibition galleries with a third space that we use for public events or exhibitions. Our first show in this space was created by Felix Gonzalez-Torres (pp. 106–113) in 1994. He was one of the most generous, upbeat human beings I've ever known, with the brightest eyes that saw the good in humanity. He did so much for us. When we invited him to do an exhibition, he came to our new and only partially renovated space and he said, "I don't need a gallery to do a show, I'll do it right now." The next thing we knew, he was installing mirrors, clocks, a pile of Baci candy, lovely blue curtains, and a portrait of the Workshop. The pieces were scattered about—the candy was outside the men's room, the lights were on the large meeting table, the clocks were in the office, and the curtains were in the space that would later become the gallery. The place came to life with his generosity. He was so inquisitive, but he saw the beauty of a bird in the sky or of a light bulb; he saw the perfection in man-made objects that symbolized life and vitality. And our visitors really got to know our new space because they had to explore it to find the artwork.

RF: Now that you're well established on Cherry Street, how does the exhibition program work?

MBS: Usually, two shows are on view at any given time for a two-month period, though we have had large-scale exhibitions that use all of the galleries, like Ellen Lupton's inventive show called *Comfort Zone*, and Thelma Golden's (pp. 98–105) 1999 exhibition, *Cut on the Bias: Social Projects of the 90s from the Permanent Collection*. We're working up to showing three simultaneous exhibitions with the addition of a new, versatile space where we've begun installing large-scale video projection works. We've just installed Lorna Simpson's (pp. 264–267) *Call Waiting*. In addition to the exhibition galleries, we now also utilize the Jorge Pardo (pp. 214–221) video lounge for exhibitions of single-channel videos, showing works that complement the other exhibitions. For example, we screened Charles and Ray Eames' *Power of Ten* in conjunction with Steve Izenour's (pp. 286–289) exhibition in 2001.

In selecting exhibitions, I am constantly looking at the progress of projects in the studios. As they finish, or near completion, they are considered as possible exhibitions, and depending on the project we either show it on its own or in tandem with other related works by the artist. I've noticed that artists are always willing to fill a gallery! For Tom Friedman's (pp. 94–97) exhibition, we showed his new project along with ten or so other pieces to give our audiences a larger context in which to view his work. Bert Long brought in cotton, watermelons, an old plow, and painted the walls midnight blue. He also gave an incredible public performance wearing a Klan costume on the night of the opening.

RF: You mentioned Ellen Lupton, a curator of design at the Cooper-Hewitt Museum in New York, and Thelma Golden, exhibitions director at The Studio Museum in Harlem. Do you often work with outside curators?

MBS: We've had a guest curator program since the early 1980s—it's the same program under which we invited you, Ruth, to curate an exhibition from the permanent collection in 1990. The early exhibitions in this series were wonderful. Patterson Sims called me and said he had an idea for an umbrella show with contemporary artists. He was living in Seattle at the time, and must have been inspired by the amount of rain there. I recall that you wanted to bring the whole collection out for your show *Let's Play House*. I dare you to try that today!

Other curators have gone in totally different directions, like Larry Rinder (pp. 230–235) who organized the international exchange with an indigenous tribe in Papua New Guinea (pp. 186–193), as I've already mentioned. And Mary Jane Jacob, whose exhibition from the collection blossomed to include the commissioning of many new works in our residency program. Eventually it became a traveling exhibition called *Changing Spaces* that went to venues all over the United States and Canada in 1997 and 1998. And now, as we celebrate our 25th anniversary, we are touring another major exhibition organized by Paolo Colombo, one of our advisors, to Geneva, Switzerland, and Sydney, Australia.

RF: Have you ever exhibited shows of works produced outside The Fabric Workshop and Museum?

MBS: We have borrowed shows, but only exhibitions that relate very closely to our objectives. In 1999, we borrowed an exhibition of contemporary tapestries called *Threads of Dissent*. It was curated by Jennifer Gross who is now at Yale Art Gallery but was then at the Isabella Stewart Gardner Museum in Boston. We also borrowed a wonderful traveling exhibition of contemporary art with nineteenth century sensibility, organized by Ingrid Schaffner and Melissa Feldman, called *Secret Victorians* (fig. 7). That show included some fantastic

17

18. Virgil Marti, *Bullies* (detail),
1992/2001. Fluorescent ink and
rayon flock on Tyvek. Width: 55 inches
(139.7 cm).

17. Hella Jongerius, *Mobile Dreaming*,
2001. Polyester, wool, and flexothane.
54 x 84 x 6 inches (137.16 x 213.36
x 15.24 cm).

fabric-related pieces like Yinka Shonibare's (pp. 256–259) *Nuclear Family*.

RF: What else has changed? It strikes me that you have a much more international program now than you used to, don't you?

MBS: Yes, we're not afraid to call Korea, or Germany, Africa, or Australia, or anywhere in the world for that matter. One day a few years ago, we had three artists from the Maisin tribe of Papua New Guinea (pp. 186–193), Marie-Ange Guilleminot (pp. 118–121) from France, and Jim Hodges (pp. 134–137), who lives in New York, in our studios all on the same day. It was wonderful. Now it's the norm for us to have several international artists on our roster each year.

RF: Does that mean that you're traveling more to look at artists' work?

MBS: I do travel frequently—to New York and to the West Coast especially, and internationally as well. I make it a point to go to international exhibitions like Documenta, the Venice Biennale, and other major shows and biennials. Mary Jane Jacob, an independent curator who has organized many impressive exhibitions in addition to our *Changing Spaces*, has been instrumental in dragging me around the world to see and meet new artists. I have always loved visiting artists in their studios, but I don't do it as much as I used to, probably because artists are traveling so much themselves these days and they come to us, too.

RF: Do local and regional artists still fit into your programming? Promoting them has always been a part of your mission, too, hasn't it?

MBS: Oh yes, we always have local artists in the Artist-in-Residence Program. I feel that their work compares so well with international artists, and yet outside the city they get very little recognition. Younger artists like Virgil Marti (pp. 194–197), Tristin Lowe (pp. 178–181), Gabriel Martinez, and Sue Patterson are all wonderful talents, and Philadelphia is also home to well known, established artists such as Moe Brooker, Sidney Goodman, and Edna Andrade. Of course, I'm only mentioning artists who have done projects with us, so there are many others. I'm sure that Thomas Eakins had the same problem—he had very little recognition outside Philadelphia during his lifetime. I find it very difficult to watch Philadelphia artists get such limited exposure in the Whitney Biennial and other international biennials.

RF: Plus, there are so many good art schools in Philadelphia. Do you interact with them at all?

MBS: Absolutely. There is a density of art schools to draw from, and they all send students to our Apprentice Training Program. Tyler School of Art, Moore College of Art, the Pennsylvania Academy, which is right next door, University of

the Arts, and the University of Pennsylvania, which has a graduate program in fine arts that is very dynamic—they are our best sources of young staff.

RF: How do you discover new artists, locally and internationally? Has the process of selection changed at all?

MBS: We can only work with approximately ten artists each year, so we have to be very selective. Primarily, we look for artists who are ready for us—in the sense that they need and want the kind of artistic support and experimentation we can provide, and who are open to the process of collaborating with our staff. I often get to know the artists before I invite them to do a residency, but it is not essential. We are concerned with an artist's work first and foremost. I care about diversity, and I want to have a range of media.

As for discovery, we have a wonderful Artist Advisory Committee, and they have been magnificent and absolutely instrumental in selecting artists. They are sent questionnaires three times a year, and they all make great recommendations. Advisory Committee members like Lisa Phillips, Paul Schimmel, Francesco Bonami (pp. 44–47), Paolo Colombo, Robert Storr (pp. 276–279), and John Ravenal have introduced new artists to us. I really cannot praise them enough. Artists also recommend other artists. I try to keep in close contact with curators, museum directors, and artists who are all great sources of information and ideas. There is an extended committee too— an informal network of curatorial and museum support that has been very successful.

RF: Has the Acadia Summer Art Program (A.S.A.P.) that you developed in the early 1990s also helped you with this? Tell me more about that program.

MBS: Yes, A.S.A.P. has expanded my network of colleagues tremendously. It gives me the chance to meet new artists and curators who come to Mount Desert Island, Maine, for a relaxed residency over the summer. It is not connected to the FW+M in any way, except that I founded and direct both organizations, and the staff of both hopefully benefit from one another. Each program has its own integrity. I invite the FW+M staff to A.S.A.P. on their vacations, which allows them to meet other artists and curators on an informal basis. I never expected to run a camp (laughs), but that's just what I'm doing. It's not an art colony in the traditional sense, just as the FW+M is not about traditional residencies. It is very informal and my main goal is to provide artists, curators, critics, museum directors, and distinguished scholars from other fields with a place where they can relax in a beautiful setting and in the company of other people who are interested in sharing their ideas.

RF: You seem to have maintained a casual sense of relationship with people. However, the Workshop couldn't have

19

20

19. Jene Highstein, *Great Manis*. Foreground: two *Anti-Lamps*, 1989. Background: *Great Manis*, 1989 (through doorway). Exhibited at The Fabric Workshop and Museum, December 1989–April 1990.

20. Ecke Bonk, *Chess Jacket (Checkett)*, 1987–1991. Pigment on Gore-Tex fabric with plastic chess pieces. 39 x 70 inches (99.06 x 177.8 cm). Edition of 32.

survived without a tough business sense. Is that part of your role, or do you have other people who handle that?

MBS: We always work through the arrangements of each artist's residency with the artist or with their dealers. It is wonderful when we can recoup some of the costs of the materials—which at times can be outrageously expensive, like Jana Sterbak's (pp. 272–275) woven metal fabric. The artists and their dealers have often been very generous in that respect. I handle some of these negotiations, but my associate directors and other staff are helpful in steering us towards what we hope will be a win-win situation for us and for the artist. By any means necessary, we come to an amicable agreement. The big question now is with installations, where the artists want to take the entire work with them and we want one for our archives. Because we are a museum, there is a push and pull here. All museums are experiencing this phenomenon, so we are all in the throes of working through these issues.

RF: You have some close friendships with museum professionals; how have they impacted your vision for the FW+M, if at all?

MBS: They have been vital to the vision of the Workshop. My constant questioning and their patient answering have helped me in more ways than I can describe. They have been advisors as we have evolved from a workshop into a museum, which officially happened in 1996 with the addition of the word "museum" to the title of The Fabric Workshop. My friend Anne d'Harnoncourt has been par excellence, offering her guidance on many museum policies that we have established, such as accessioning and deaccessioning, and also Board development and staffing. She is a treasure. Innis Shoemaker, Curator of Prints, Drawings and Photographs at the Philadelphia Museum of Art, has also been a wonderful advisor on every topic of collections management you can imagine. Susan Lubowsky Talbott has given me consistently excellent advice for years, ever since her early days at the NEA. Patterson Sims has advised on museum policy, and also made great recommendations for exhibitions. Mark Rosenthal has held our hand through the development of various collections policies, and he has been a wonderful artistic advisor. Thelma Golden and Paula Marincola have been extraordinarily helpful with artists and exhibitions. Steve Bruni, director of the Delaware Art Museum, has reviewed new management structures as they've emerged. I am absolutely reverential of Robert Venturi (pp. 284–289) and have appreciated the encouragement he has extended to us through the years. One of his principal architects, Steve Izenour (pp. 286–289), was a dear friend to me and in addition to serving on our Board until his death in 2001, he designed the stairway between our two floors. Also, the architect Richard Gluckman and his staff have been critical

in designing our galleries with hidden hardware and beautiful lighting systems. There are many others—just look at the list of our Board of Directors and Artist Advisory Committee!

RF: How do you juggle your many roles?

MBS: I love being involved in all aspects. I am similar to Anne d'Harnoncourt in that regard—and I agree with her that toilet paper should roll over the top in the bathrooms! I care about the smallest details like the hallway being a specific color of white. You channel your energies into the things that will bring the whole together and lend something to the symphony. A sense of satisfaction can be very remote, and I often think, "Well, I suppose I played a part in all of this." It's a wonderful feeling to stand outside of it and have it all happen in front of your eyes.

RF: Like an orchestra conductor?

MBS: No, like the person whose job is to pull the curtain closed when the show is over. You're standing off to the side and you can feel it all working. It's wonderful. If it's done right, your involvement at that moment is nil, you're simply there.

One of the most satisfying moments when I felt no sense of doing, but was simply a participant in an incredible occurrence, was the night of Louise Bourgeois' (pp. 52–59) performance at the Workshop. She brought a magician and several handsome men with her, and chose some of our staff to participate in a 22-minute performance. She brought the world with her. She herself sat in silence, next to a column, hiding. She must have felt some satisfaction, but truthfully it was hard to tell. She had lent us her sculpture entitled *Fears*, which was installed in the middle of her installation with the text about a woman waiting for a man to come home.

We had our own fears that night! Louise wouldn't say whether or not she would come to the performance. She told me to cancel the limousine that we had arranged for her. She kept us on pins and needles not knowing if she would come or not. We did send the limousine to New York for her, but I didn't know for sure if she had come until I was told that she was rehearsing, which they did only once! It was an incredible evening and Louise was wonderful beyond belief. Moments like those are very memorable.

RF: They're the best; they make any problems involved worthwhile. I must say, however, that I think the analogy with an orchestra conductor is more apt than with the person who closes the curtain. But anyway, what are some of the highlights of the projects you've done at The Fabric Workshop and Museum?

MBS: I consider every project we have done beneficial in some way. There are a number of highlights, of course, but I hate to single out one and not mention them all. There are certain projects—like Maria Fernanda Cardoso's (pp. 66–71) *Flea Circus*—that surprised me in terms of how deeply audi-

21

22

21. Louise Bourgeois at The Fabric Workshop and Museum, December, 1992.

22. Marion Boulton Stroud and staff of The Fabric Workshop and Museum, with artist-in-residence David Chung, 1995.

ence members responded to them as works of art and culture. Maria Fernanda had been working with the fleas for a while, and we helped her to give form to her fascination. We made a tent and produced a movie that she made with our staff and with her husband, Ross Harley. So many wonderful things came out of that project, much of which she could not have realized without us, nor could we without her obviously. I admit I doubted the relevance of this piece at the time, and it was my own foolishness because the project worked beautifully. We gave several performances to hundreds of visitors, and also showed the live performance on satellite monitors for the overflow crowd. Maria Fernanda has gone on to perform and exhibit the piece in New York, Paris, and Sydney.

Also, because of my personal interest in conceptual art, I think that Chris Burden's (pp. 60–65) project, *L.A.P.D. Uniforms*, is magnificent. We waited for years to get Claes Oldenburg (pp. 206–209) and Louise Bourgeois (pp. 52–59), and their projects are both spectacular. Maybe we'll still get to work with Robert Rauschenberg and Jasper Johns—hopefully they'll need us in some way!

RF: When you look back over these twenty-five years, and everything that the Workshop has contributed to the field, what are you most proud of?

MBS: I feel very humble. I can never quite believe I'm a part of this vital enterprise. I'm not always sure whose idea all of this was originally, and I'm not completely convinced it was mine at all!

I also have the "glass half empty/glass half full" syndrome—there has always been so much to do and I think about how much we haven't done, and then I turn around and feel overwhelmed by how much we have accomplished. So many people have given their lives, ideas and energy, and worked harder than you can imagine making all that we have accomplished possible. And, of course, it's to the artists that I feel the most indebted.

I know we have been a tremendous resource in the textiles field, and that makes me happy. And I know that our ideas have provided the inspiration for other art workshops and print workshops—in London and Ghana, for example. I find it unbelievable that the word has spread internationally. I am amazed when I speak with an artist in another country, such as Do-Ho Suh in Korea, who just told me: "Yes, I know the FW+M and the work that you've done! I'd love to try it." This is a source of great satisfaction for us.

RF: What has changed the most since you started The Fabric Workshop, and what is still the same?

MBS: The vitality is still there. Working with and following the lead of artists is still the foundation of our mission. The staff is still excited about what they're doing, and the newcomers

are still coming in the door with a real sense of belonging to this place. It's amazing that what began as a modest workshop is now a museum with an established exhibition program—in the early days, we never dreamt about that. If we put a silk scarf up on the wall, we felt we had accomplished a lot! To see the galleries and the professionalism of the exhibitions is very rewarding.

At the same time, the FW+M's uniqueness is about the studio, and the art that we make with artists. This is what we feel we must keep intact. We want to continue to be a living museum. We recently developed our web site, though we don't know yet if we will do any web-based artists' projects, but I suppose if an artist proposed it, we would do it. We rarely say no! Our permissiveness has been wonderfully productive, not to mention challenging, but you owe it to yourself if you're on the cutting edge to go further each time.

RF: Would you like to see it go on for another fifty or a hundred years?

MBS: Of course! I see the museum 50 years from now—when I have been dead for quite a while—still responding to the needs of artists of the times. Philadelphia audiences have been superbly responsive, and I hope that we will continue to introduce them to contemporary art trends from around the world. We are an artist-driven organization, and we will always be so. We also provide a record of the history of our time. I hope that the FW+M will have a building of its own, and that we will be able to show the permanent collection on a continual basis.

It's what I see in the FW+M's future. Most important, I see it ongoing, as a creative process.

21

22

21. Louise Bourgeois at The Fabric Workshop and Museum, December, 1992.

22. Marion Boulton Stroud and staff of The Fabric Workshop and Museum, with artist-in-residence David Chung, 1995.

ence members responded to them as works of art and culture. Maria Fernanda had been working with the fleas for a while, and we helped her to give form to her fascination. We made a tent and produced a movie that she made with our staff and with her husband, Ross Harley. So many wonderful things came out of that project, much of which she could not have realized without us, nor could we without her obviously. I admit I doubted the relevance of this piece at the time, and it was my own foolishness because the project worked beautifully. We gave several performances to hundreds of visitors, and also showed the live performance on satellite monitors for the overflow crowd. Maria Fernanda has gone on to perform and exhibit the piece in New York, Paris, and Sydney.

Also, because of my personal interest in conceptual art, I think that Chris Burden's (pp. 60–65) project, *L.A.P.D. Uniforms*, is magnificent. We waited for years to get Claes Oldenburg (pp. 206–209) and Louise Bourgeois (pp. 52–59), and their projects are both spectacular. Maybe we'll still get to work with Robert Rauschenberg and Jasper Johns—hopefully they'll need us in some way!

RF: When you look back over these twenty-five years, and everything that the Workshop has contributed to the field, what are you most proud of?

MBS: I feel very humble. I can never quite believe I'm a part of this vital enterprise. I'm not always sure whose idea all of this was originally, and I'm not completely convinced it was mine at all!

I also have the "glass half empty/glass half full" syndrome—there has always been so much to do and I think about how much we haven't done, and then I turn around and feel overwhelmed by how much we have accomplished. So many people have given their lives, ideas and energy, and worked harder than you can imagine making all that we have accomplished possible. And, of course, it's to the artists that I feel the most indebted.

I know we have been a tremendous resource in the textiles field, and that makes me happy. And I know that our ideas have provided the inspiration for other art workshops and print work-shops—in London and Ghana, for example. I find it unbelievable that the word has spread internationally. I am amazed when I speak with an artist in another country, such as Do-Ho Suh in Korea, who just told me: "Yes, I know the FW+M and the work that you've done! I'd love to try it." This is a source of great satisfaction for us.

RF: What has changed the most since you started The Fabric Workshop, and what is still the same?

MBS: The vitality is still there. Working with and following the lead of artists is still the foundation of our mission. The staff is still excited about what they're doing, and the newcomers

are still coming in the door with a real sense of belonging to this place. It's amazing that what began as a modest workshop is now a museum with an established exhibition program—in the early days, we never dreamt about that. If we put a silk scarf up on the wall, we felt we had accomplished a lot! To see the galleries and the professionalism of the exhibitions is very rewarding.

At the same time, the FW+M's uniqueness is about the studio, and the art that we make with artists. This is what we feel we must keep intact. We want to continue to be a living museum. We recently developed our web site, though we don't know yet if we will do any web-based artists' projects, but I suppose if an artist proposed it, we would do it. We rarely say no! Our permissiveness has been wonderfully productive, not to mention challenging, but you owe it to yourself if you're on the cutting edge to go further each time.

RF: Would you like to see it go on for another fifty or a hundred years?

MBS: Of course! I see the museum 50 years from now—when I have been dead for quite a while—still responding to the needs of artists of the times. Philadelphia audiences have been superbly responsive, and I hope that we will continue to introduce them to contemporary art trends from around the world. We are an artist-driven organization, and we will always be so. We also provide a record of the history of our time. I hope that the FW+M will have a building of its own, and that we will be able to show the permanent collection on a continual basis.

It's what I see in the FW+M's future. Most important, I see it ongoing, as a creative process.

Marina Abramović

About the artist

Yugoslavian, born 1946, lives in Amsterdam

Marina Abramović was born in Belgrade, Yugoslavia (now Serbia). She studied at the Academy of Fine Arts, University of Belgrade, from 1965–1970, and continued her studies at the Academy of Fine Arts, University of Zagreb, from 1970–1972. Abramović first became known for her performance and video projects exploring the possibilities and limits of the body and mind, themes that remain paramount in her work. Her 12 years of collaboration with the artist Ulay ended during their 1988 project, *The Great Wall Walk,* in which each artist walked from opposite ends of the Great Wall of China; after two months of walking, they met, for the last time, at the wall's center. Abramović's work has been exhibited widely in the United States and Europe. In 1997, she won the International Award at the Venice Biennale for her video installation and performance *Balkan Baroque.* A major one-person traveling exhibition was organized by the Museum of Modern Art, Oxford, in 1995, and traveled to Denmark, Germany, Holland, Belgium, and Australia.

About the work

Expiring Body is an ambitious series of related videos made up of two parts: *The Body* and *The Diary.* They are based on Abramović's travels to Sri Lanka and India in 1998, where she searched for and met people whose meditative practices allow them to experience extreme states of body and mind. Abramović has traveled extensively over the course of her career, often to remote areas to learn from primitive cultures. In her own words:

> When I was in Tibet, or when I lived among the Aborigines in Australia, or when I learned some of the Sufi rites, I understood that these cultures have a long tradition of techniques of meditation which lead the body to a border-line state that allows us to make a mental leap to enter different dimensions of existence and to eliminate the fear of pain, death, or the limitations of the body. In the Western world, we are so full of fears . . . that we have never developed techniques that can push back physical limits. (*Marina Abramović: Performing Body,* Studio Miscetti and Zerynthia, Rome, 1998*)*

Expiring Body: The Body is Abramović's own version of the *Cadavre Exquis.* For this large-scale video installation, she mixed the head, torso, and feet of three different bodies from three different cultures. The top video, or the head, is her brother Velimir Abramović, a philosopher in Yugoslavia, discussing topics such as time, space, energy, and the alpha state of mind and death. The middle video, or the torso, is an African man in Amsterdam performing a Voodoo dance ritual. The lower video, or the feet, is footage of a fire walking ceremony in Sri Lanka.

Expiring Body: The Diary comprises five videos, each depicting people with special psychic powers involved in ritualistic acts. The acts are often repetitive—such as a Tibetan woman prostrating herself over and over again—and all capture the performer entering another state of consciousness.

At the end of her residency in 1998, Abramović presented a lecture and perform-ance, titled *Expiring Body: Performing Body,* in which she presented her own early video works and those of other artists who have affected her thinking and way of working.

Still images from *Expiring Body: Performing Body,* a lecture and performance, 4 December 1998, Philadelphia.

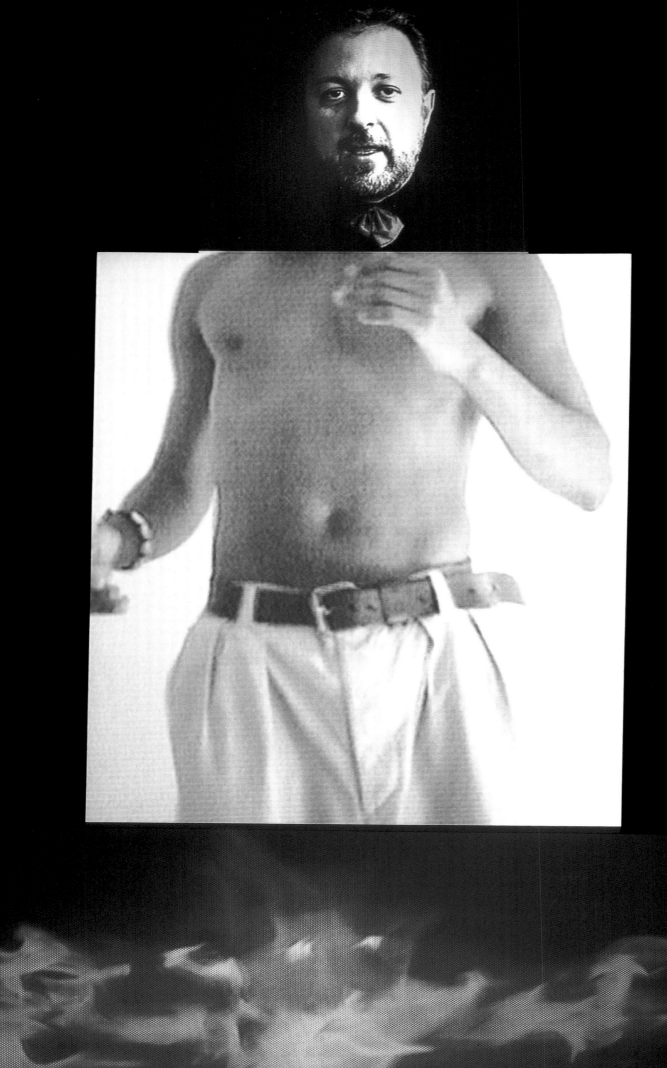

Expiring Body: The Body, 1998 (left). Video installation in three parts. Dimensions vary with installation. Edition of 3.

Expiring Body: The Diary (Lama Tulku Trichen), 1998 (above). Video installation in five parts. Dimensions vary with installation. Edition of 3.

Doug Aitken

About the artist

American, born 1968, lives in Los Angeles

Born in Redondo Beach, California, Doug Aitken received his BFA
from the Art Center College of Design in Pasadena in 1991. In the
1990s Aitken became known for his video installations, which involve
a productive cross-pollination of styles borrowed from television
advertising, Hollywood cinema, experimental and documentary film,
as well as the music video genre—a blend he refers to as "pure
communication." Aitken was awarded the Larry Aldrich Foundation
Award in 2000, and the International Prize at the Venice Biennale in
1999. His work has appeared in solo exhibitions at venues such as
the Centre Georges Pompidou, Paris (2002); the Serpentine Gallery,
London (2001); and the Museum of Contemporary Art in Los Angeles
(2000). Major group shows include *Let's Entertain* (organized by the
Walker Art Center, Minneapolis, 2000); the Biennale of Sydney 2000
(Museum of Contemporary Art, Sydney); and the 1997 and 2000
Whitney Biennials (Whitney Museum of American Art, New York).

About the work

Doug Aitken's collaborative project with The Fabric Workshop and Museum (FW+M),
Interiors, comprises a series of filmic narratives projected onto an architectural fabric
structure. Shot in locations around the world, the constituent narratives initially appear
to be unrelated. One sequence depicts a businessman in a Tokyo penthouse at sunset
talking to himself, another portrays an African American man wandering around a
bombed out neighborhood in Los Angeles. As the viewer moves through the installation,
the rhythms in the sound element of each narrative grow increasingly synchronized.
Eventually, the sound components of each join into one rhythm, growing faster and
faster into a moment of complete visual and aural transformation. The moment passes,
and the sound for each segment falls back into its own disparate, random rhythm,
but the individual stories are each affected and changed by the temporary alignment.
Interiors offers flashing moments of order in an ever-changing world.

Each of these narratives is fictional, and carefully scripted and arranged by
Aitken. For example, the man in the Tokyo penthouse is actually an auctioneer from the
Tokyo fish market; the African American man is in reality a member of the hip-hop duo,
Outkast; another segment takes place in a vast, symmetrical helicopter factory and
shows a performance choreographed by a professional dancer. These rich, saturated
environments are vividly portrayed in the striking imagery for which the artist is known.

While at the FW+M, Aitken experimented with a wide array of reflective, transparent,
and opaque materials, which were stretched onto a variety of architectural forms.
These fabric-covered shapes were used in the filming of the piece to achieve special
visual and lighting effects; they are also a part of the final installation, serving as the
scrims onto which the videos are projected. These sculptural experiments allowed the
artist to continue his ongoing conceptual explorations while breaking out of conventional
narrative structure and the bounded two-dimensional frame. Moving through the physical
installation, visitors actively participate in the poetic construction of various themes
that run through this work, including ideas about mapping, navigation, and placing
oneself in new realities.

Interiors, 2002. Production images. Dimensions vary with installation.

Interiors, 2002 (above and facing page). Production images. Dimensions vary with installation.

Conceptual sketch for development of warped screens, 2002 (following pages). Composite digital illustration.

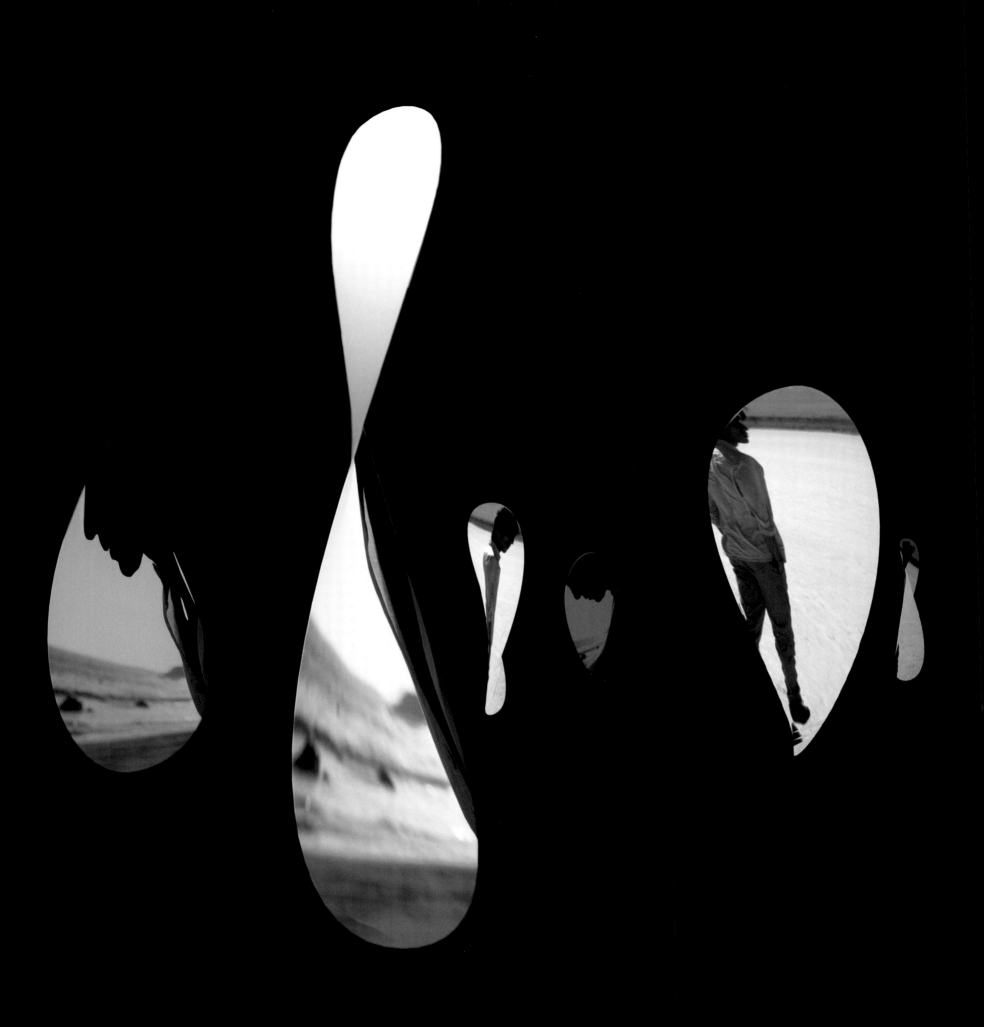

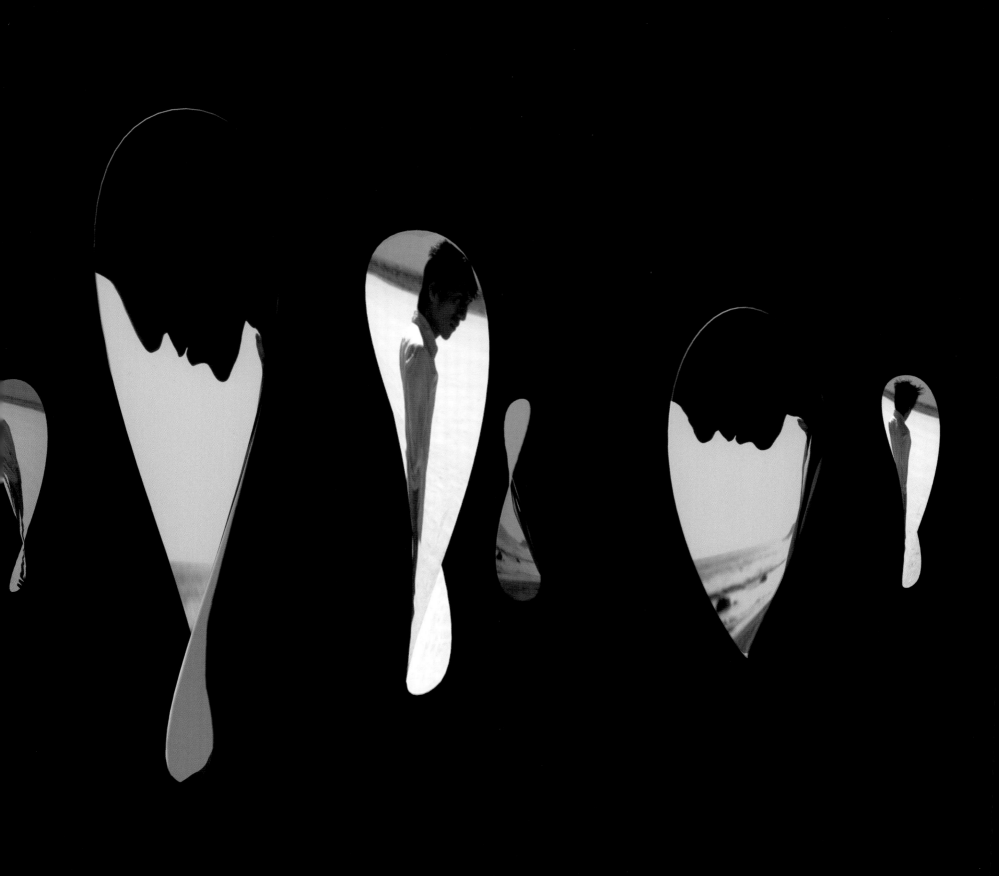

Miroslaw Balka

About the artist

Polish, born 1958, lives in Warsaw, Poland

Miroslaw Balka was raised in a small town outside Warsaw, and his artwork often draws on memories of his childhood home, which is now his studio. He studied art at the Academy of Fine Arts in Warsaw, earning his degree in 1985. Balka's work has been the subject of many one-person exhibitions, including shows at The National Museum of Art in Osaka, Japan (2001); the Tate Gallery, London (1995); and the List Center for the Visual Arts at the Massachusetts Institute of Technology in Cambridge, MA (1993). In 1993, he was selected to represent Poland at the 45th Venice Biennale.

36

About the work

Miroslaw Balka has a gift for making art of highly symbolic content from the most humble of materials, and he continued in this vein at the FW+M by creating a series of related sculptures made primarily from hog intestines.

Like many of Balka's works, the form of *2 x (Ø60 x 190)* relates to the human body—specifically, to Balka's body, as the diameter of each of these cylindrical columns equals the artist's shoulder width. Each column in the pair is fabricated from hog intestines that were dried, cut into small squares, rehydrated and layered repeatedly until a strong skin formed. This labor-intensive technique is based on an Inuit process for creating waterproof garments from seal gut. Inside the columns, Balka placed hundreds of inflated dried intestinal lengths, which are just visible through the translucent shell. Transformed by the artist, this most base material becomes pristine and, with light directed onto the columns, luminescent.

The sculpture *250 x 190 x 67* is also made from hog intestines, though in this case the tubes of natural material remained uncut, allowing them to shrink into long strands as they dried. When moistened, the strands were pliable enough to hand-knot (the same technique used to make snowshoes) into the final form. The height of the sculpture is equal to Balka's own height with his arms outstretched above his head, and the width measures the distance of his outstretched arms. The finished form resembles a net, though unlike a net it defines a fixed shape.

A third sculpture, *203 x 97 x 7*, is a bronze cast of a puddle, filled with salt. The autobiographical reference in this piece is the volume of the salt, which equals the water weight of the artist's body. Balka's use of this material highlights the importance of salt in maintaining the fragile, life-sustaining balance of water in our bodies.

250 x 190 x 67, 1998 (detail). Hog intestine, aluminum, and newspaper. 98 $\frac{1}{2}$ x 74 $\frac{3}{4}$ x 26 $\frac{3}{8}$ inches (250 x 190 x 67 cm). Edition of 2.

2 x (Ø60 x 190), 1997 (above, left background). Hog intestine and aluminum. 23 ⅝ inches (60 cm) in diameter x 74 ¾ inches (190 cm). Edition of 2. *203 x 97 x 7*, 1998 (above, right foreground).
Bronze and salt. 80 x 38 ¼ x 2 ¾ inches (203 x 97 x 7 cm). Edition of 2.
2 x (Ø60 x 190), 1997 (facing page). Hog intestine and aluminum. 23 ⅝ inches (60 cm) in diameter x 74 ¾ inches (190 cm). Edition of 2.

Barbara Bloom

American, born 1951, lives in New York City

About the artist

Barbara Bloom studied art at the California Institute of the Arts in Valencia, CA, earning her BFA in 1972. For many years, Bloom lived abroad in Holland and Germany, and began exhibiting early in her career with solo shows in Europe and the United States. In 1993, she was commissioned by the MAK-Austrian Museum of Applied Arts in Vienna to participate in their inaugural exhibition, an intervention using the museum's permanent collection. Her subsequent sculptural installations, *The Reign of Narcissism* and *Pictures from the Floating World*, have traveled extensively, including to museums such as the Museum of Modern Art in New York (1999), the Serpentine Gallery in London (1990), and Kunsthalle Zürich (1990). In 1989, Bloom was honored with The Louis Comfort Tiffany Foundation Award, and, in 1988, the Due Mille Prize at the *Aperto* of the Venice Biennale.

About the work

Created in collaboration with the FW+M, *Pictures from the Floating World* is a set of two folding screens—one too short to be used comfortably, the other too tall. Bloom's reference to the term "floating world" reflects a medieval Buddhist belief in the fleeting quality of the material world and its predictability as a source of suffering in life.

The screens are fabricated in the traditional Japanese style, with wooden frames and leather hinges. The four panels are made from silk, dyed the color of tea, and printed with images of classic Ukiyo-e prints—known as floating world prints—first produced in 17th century Japan. They are erotic images depicting men and women copulating; on the taller of the two screens, Bloom heightens their mystery by printing the erotica in pigment matching the color of the silk. Bloom then added black censorship dots and red blush to the cheeks of carefully selected male and female figures. The effect is a subtle image, visible only when the screen is lit from behind; otherwise, a repeating pattern of black and red dots is all that can be seen. This subtlety combined with the small scale of the images forces viewers to peer closely, acting as voyeurs to these intimate scenes. The shorter screen also depicts erotic images, which are silkscreen printed on silk in a soft palette of light pink, purple, green, and brown, also on a tea-colored background.

Bloom later created a larger installation also titled *Pictures from the Floating World*, of which the two screens were a part. Other components included a wooden Japanese bridge, which stretched over a painted red floor with plaster casts of male and female heads "floating" by. On top of the bridge, Bloom placed a vitrine holding grains of rice, each printed with a minute erotic image, visible only with the magnifying lens provided.

Pictures from the Floating World (tall screen), 1995 (detail). Pigment on silk, mahogany, and leather. 84 x 20 inches (213.36 x 50.8 cm). Edition of 5.

Pictures from the Floating World (short screen), 1995. Pigment on silk, mahogany, and leather. 54 x 18 inches (137.16 x 45.72 cm). Edition of 5.

Pictures from the Floating World (tall screen), 1995. Pigment on silk, mahogany, and leather. 84 x 20 inches (213.36 x 50.8 cm). Edition of 5.

Francesco Bonami

About the author

Italian, born Florence 1955, lives in Chicago

Francesco Bonami is the Manilow Senior Curator at the Museum of Contemporary Art, Chicago, and the Director of Visual Arts for the 50th Venice Biennale (2003). His exhibitions at the Museum of Contemporary Art include *Age of Influence: Reflection in the Mirror of American Culture* (2001); *Short Century: Independence and Liberation Movements in Africa, 1945–1994* (2001); and *Examining Pictures* (1999). In 2001, he organized *Uniform: Order and Disorder* for P.S. 1 Contemporary Art Center in New York, and served as consulting curator for an exhibition on Arte Povera for the Walker Art Center, Minneapolis, and the Tate Gallery, London (2001). Bonami is also the director and curator of Fondazione Sandretto Re Rebaudengo per l'Arte in Turin, Italy, and the artistic director of Pitti Discovery in Florence, Italy. A writer and critic, Bonami served as the United States editor for *Flash Art International* from 1990 until 1997, and contributes regularly to contemporary art journals and publications. He is a member of the FW+M's Artist Advisory Commitee.

Do you remember? Do you remember? Do you remember?
Miroslaw Balka and Felix Gonzalez-Torres

History, whether private or public, is based on memory—a warped memory mostly, but memory still. There is not, however, one form of memory that gives rise to history; instead there are many different kinds of memory, each of which defines our relationship to time.

Two artists come to mind who define memory in extremely different, though not opposite, ways. The first artist is Miroslaw Balka (pp. 36–39), whose work constantly digs into the field of memory. With each new work he goes deeper and deeper, attempting to discover why memory is an open wound that cannot be healed with time. The further down he goes, the fresher the wound becomes. Balka opens the scar of time and sinks his eyes into the darkness of his personal history to the point where it blends into the history of his family, and then blends again into the history of his people, and deeper down into that of his country, and deeper still into the history of Europe, and finally the hole arrives at a dead end and Balka stops. The resulting artwork appears as another kind of memory—a memory transformed, changed by the soil of time, the moistness of pain and the texture of oblivion.

The second artist is Felix Gonzalez-Torres (pp. 106–113), whose treatment of memory is much more American. What distinguishes this kind of memory? It is not European or Asian, but decidedly North American, even though the artist was born in Cuba, later growing up and working in the United States and, sadly, dying there at a very young age. Rather than looking back at the past, this memory looks into a present that is no longer, a present that will no longer be what it was. It looks into the now and projects it into the future and into a longing that has less to do with the past than the impossibility of experiencing again and again the beauty of the now. It celebrates and mourns the tenderness of the moment that could be but is not infinite, sweet and deep at the same time. Felix Gonzalez-Torres builds up his own memory into a future that eludes him. He does not, like Balka, search inside; he searches outside, capturing the elements of life that are not superficial but that adore the intensity of the surface.

Felix Gonzalez-Torres does not care about a larger history but seeks a history con-structed around images and flashes of love and intimacy, moments where the private succeed in devouring the public or in transforming tragedies into extended experiences and new alibis for enlightenment.

Miroslaw Balka and Felix Gonzalez-Torres belong to different histories, different universes—the old world and the new world—yet both long for the other's perspective. The Polish artist's craving is for a present purified by history, the Cuban artist's is for a personal yet elusive future from which to look backwards at a personal past trans-formed into an historical moment. Both fail in their desires, and both remain attached to their human destiny, anchored into the mishaps of geography and society. They are both victims of the collapse of the system they relied upon.

Miroslaw Balka survived the overwhelming disaster of Communism. He resists producing work that simultaneously shapes the spaces of a new reality and reveals the scars of the past, brutally swiping away those scars that for so many years resisted this old time ideology. The rust, the smoke, and the burned paper in Balka's work all represent a form of resistance against blind destruction—against unconditional rule and a society that chews the future with jaws of a utopian ogre. Miroslaw Balka's spaces are not empty; they are abandoned and evacuated. They are carcasses of monuments to un-human folly. "It's time to go, it's time to leave," each of Miroslaw Balka's works seems to echo. Yet he stays within the borders he defines for himself. Memory, the old world's memory, is a vast continent folded inside the citizen soul. The citizen Balka wants to unfold this land inside his mind and soul, and his work is a beautiful exercise in frustration because no matter how careful he is, the memory of the continent will never be smooth, plain or clear. Always, ugly creases of the past will appear on the surface, spoiling the expectation of a present finally ready to become its own future. Miroslaw Balka, however, is not delusional. He knows that his work's purpose is not to build the future but to preserve and restore over and over the façade of a dissolved utopia. He is a worker deprived of his working class, which he tries to remember through the labor he puts into his art, the space he tries to rebuild in order to host out-of-focus memories and banal dreams. And while he diligently

Miroslaw Balka, *250 x 190 x 67*, 1998 (left). Hog intestine, aluminum, and newspaper. 98 $\frac{1}{2}$ x 74 $\frac{3}{4}$ x 26 $\frac{3}{8}$ inches (250 x 190 x 67 cm). Edition of 2.

Felix Gonzalez-Torres (right). Foreground: *"Untitled" (A Corner of Baci)*, 1990. Baci chocolates, individually wrapped in silver paper, endless supply. Dimensions vary with installation. Ideal weight: 42 lbs.

Private collection. Background: *"Untitled" (Perfect Lovers)*, 1987–1990. Wall clocks. 13 $\frac{1}{2}$ x 27 x 1 $\frac{1}{4}$ inches (34.29 x 68.58 x 3.18 cm) overall. Edition of 3. Private collection.

reassembles the pieces of his past into drawings, boxes and walls, he slowly approaches some kind of closure where he finally comes to terms with the idea that what he believes to be the present is nothing but an extended past with no expiration date.

Felix Gonzalez-Torres suffers from a different form of deprivation. It is not history or class that are denied him, but the opportunity simply to experience the heroic aspects of life. Under the threat of sickness, all becomes a domestic affair. Nothing appears relevant beyond the end of the day, which could easily be the end of everything else. His posters, his clouds, his birds, his sand—each is but a milestone in a twenty-four hour journey. To remember any of these fragments is to remember that each day has the weight of a century for all of us, not just for those whose lives have been shattered by an unpredictable disease, the dark side of love, or the black hole of human bonding. The curtains we pass through and the beads we touch are the reminders of the threshold that people are doomed to go through over and over, with all of their hopes and despairs.

Both Miroslaw Balka and Felix Gonzalez-Torres, from opposite places, understand that the forms of time give shape to human experience. They see time as a universal pattern of synchronous events—the individual and history, the person and the awareness of his finitude. Both artists make self-evident with their works that concepts of past, present, and future are not universal. They collapse under several and random circumstances—in Balka's work, under the weight of historical transformation and social decay, and, in Gonzalez-Torres' work, under the weight of bodily transformation and decay. While Miroslaw Balka looks at his country as the representation of history, Felix Gonzalez-Torres observes the history of his own body. Both understand that memory will last as long as those two kinds of histories survive; then somewhere someone else will start from scratch, another country, another life.

Christine Borland

About the artist

British, born 1965, lives in Glasgow, Scotland

Christine Borland was born in Darvel, Ayrshire, Scotland. She trained at the Glasgow School of Art, earning a BA in 1987, and at the University of Ulster in Belfast, where she received a graduate degree in art in 1988. Borland's work has been exhibited internationally, including solo shows at the Contemporary Arts Museum, Houston (2002), and Skulptur Projekte III in Münster, Germany (1997). In 1997, she was a finalist for the coveted Turner Prize, sponsored by the Tate Gallery, London. The work created during Borland's residency at the FW+M toured in the United States and Canada as part of a solo exhibition organized by York University Art Gallery in Toronto (2000).

About the work

Christine Borland often looks to science, or uses scientific theory, to investigate social, historical or political realities, and her two related projects created at the FW+M continued this interest. In *Bullet Proof Breath* and *Nephila-Mania*, Borland explored recent scientific research into spider silk, specifically the silk of the golden orb weaver spider, whose scientific name is "Nephila."

The title *Bullet Proof Breath* refers to the tremendous strength of the golden orb weaver's silk, and its potential as a material for bullet-proof vests. Despite the seemingly delicate nature of spider silk, under specific conditions it defies its size and weight and demonstrates tensile strength greater than any other man-made or natural material. A representation of a bronchial tree made from glass is the primary form of *Bullet Proof Breath*, with clusters of its fragile branches wrapped with spider silk. The delicacy of the bronchial tree contrasts with the actual strength of the silk, alluding to the protection science hopes to coax from this natural phenomenon, but also to suffocation as this anatomical form connected to the breath is tightly bound.

Nephila-Mania is a set of video projections depicting the silking process of the large golden orb weaver spider, created by the artist and the FW+M in collaboration with scientists affiliated with a laboratory researching spider silk. The title alludes to 16th and 17th century Southern Italian folklore, when "dancing-mania" afflicted those bitten by a spider. The legend suggests that people infected with this mania danced from town to town, believing that death awaited them once they stopped. The dance was named the tarantella because the belief at the time was that the malady was caused by tarantulas, though in fact the culprits were black widow spiders. The audio track for Borland's video is traditional tarantella music.

Bullet Proof Breath, 2001 (detail). Glass and spider silk. 14 x 12 x 10 inches (35.56 x 30.48 x 25.4 cm). Edition of 4.

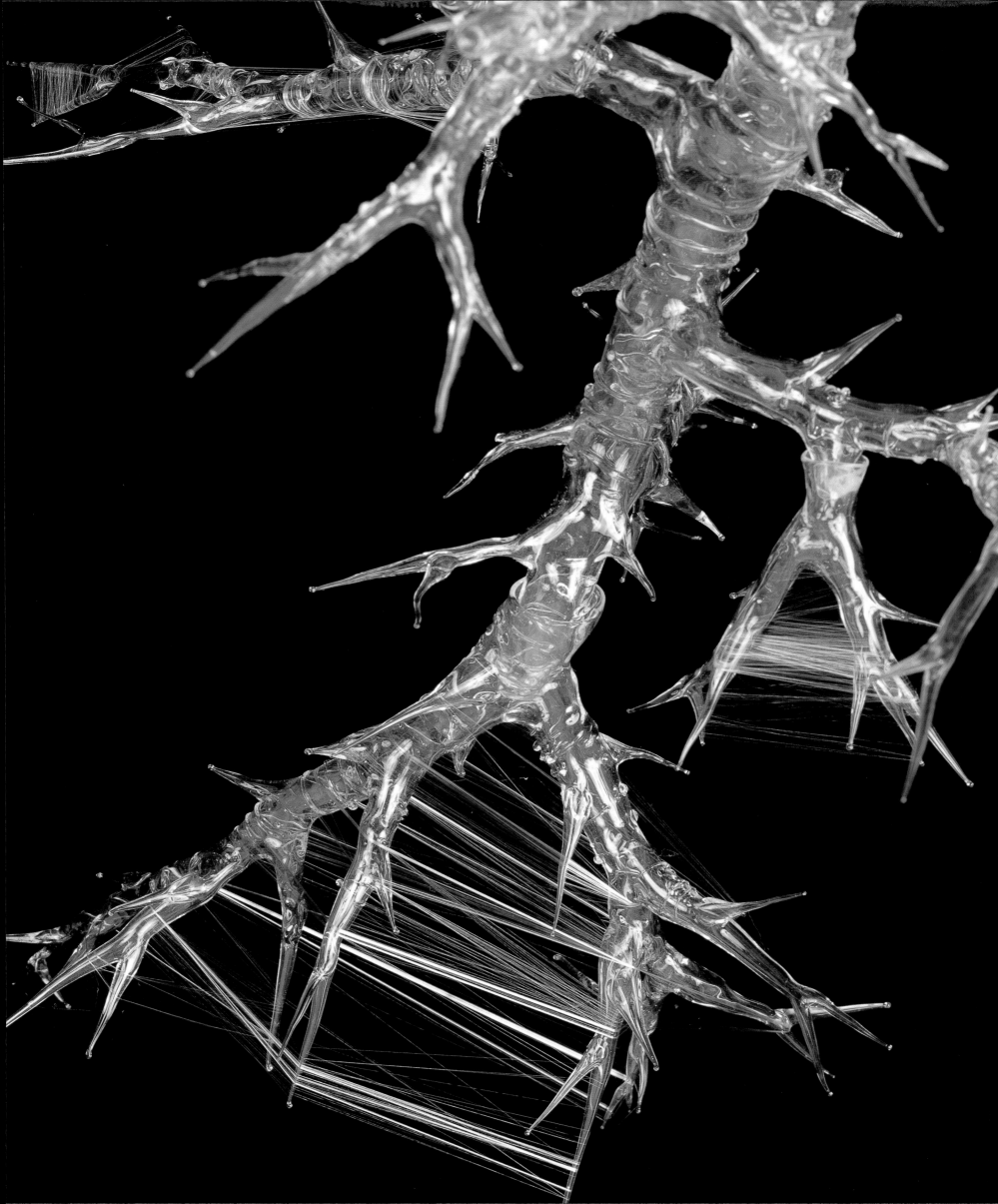

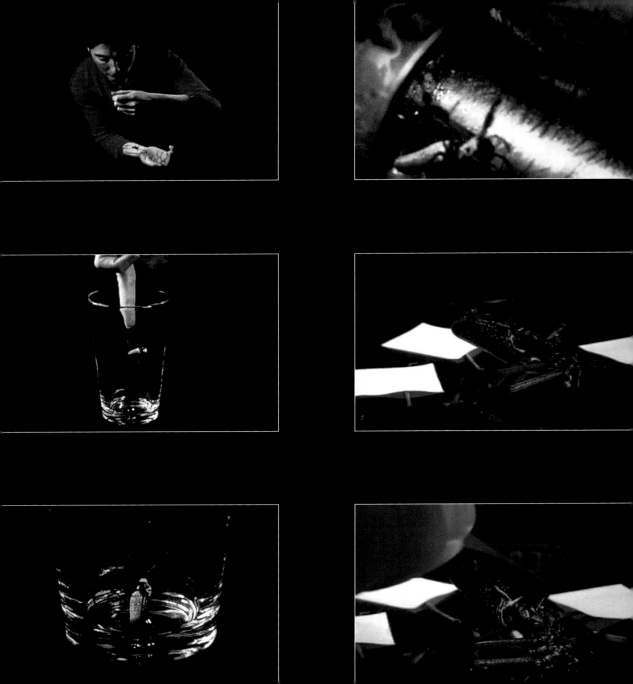

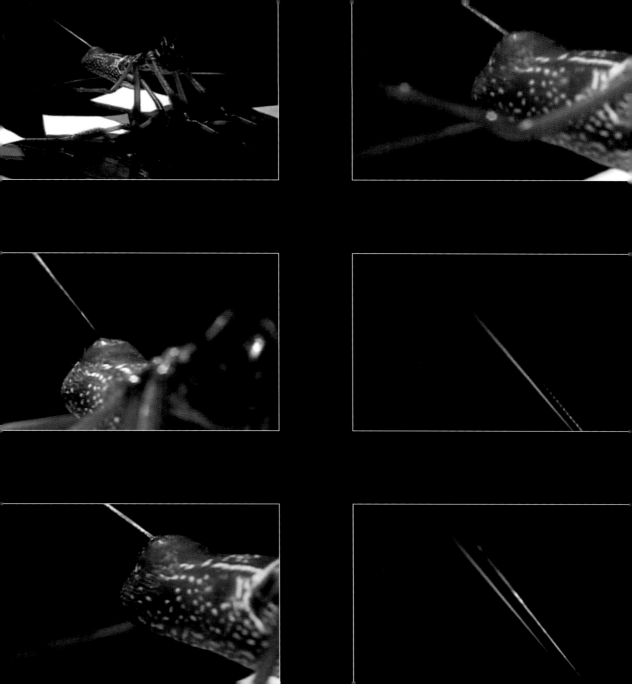

Louise Bourgeois

About the artist

American, born France 1911, lives in New York City

Louise Bourgeois was born in Paris, and grew up working in her
family's tapestry restoration shop. She studied art at many schools
in Paris before immigrating to the United States in 1938, continuing
her studies at the Art Students League of New York. Over fifty
years, Bourgeois has established herself as one of the twentieth
century's most accomplished and acclaimed sculptors, and one of
the few women of her generation to gain international attention.
In her work, she has consistently experimented with a range of
media (rubber, stone, bronze, wood, fabric) to symbolically explore
themes of a personal nature—desire, loss, cruelty, memory, sexuality,
and love. Bourgeois had her first individual exhibition in New York
in 1945 (Bertha Schaefer Gallery), and since that time has had hundreds of one-person exhibitions. In 1982, the Museum of Modern
Art, New York, organized a retrospective exhibition that traveled to
venues throughout the United States, and in 1993, she represented
the U.S. at the Venice Biennale. Bourgeois has been recognized
with eight honorary doctoral awards, and in 1999 she received the
Golden Lion award at the Venice Biennale.

52

About the work

In 1991, the FW+M invited Louise Bourgeois to participate in an exhibition of artist-designed scarves. Inspired by the vastness of the 75-foot long print tables in the FW+M's studio, Bourgeois decided to make a "scarf" of enormous proportion that would eventually wrap the walls of a spiral exhibition space in much the same way a scarf wraps around a neck.

Bourgeois selected a story that she had written in 1947 to print in red pigment on white cotton voile:

> *A man and a woman lived together. On one evening he did not come back from work. And she waited. She kept on waiting and she grew littler and littler. Later, a neighbor stopped by out of friendship and there he found her, in the armchair, the size of a pea.*

For the installation of *She Lost It*, Bourgeois placed a sculpture—a wooden ball with metal shackle, inscribed with the word "Fears"—midway through the spiral exhibition space. Circling through the gallery, one reaches the end of the story and the end of the spiral at the same time, which adds to the psychological poignancy of the installation's themes of love, loss, abandonment, and fear.

Printed on cotton gauze, another version of *She Lost It* was used for a one-time performance held at the FW+M in 1992. Choreographed by the artist, the performance began with models (staff members and friends of the artist) parading across the stage to contemporary dance music wearing slips and undergarments embroidered with text written by Bourgeois. A figure enshrouded in the gauze "scarf" came onto the stage, and with the assistance of the models, his shroud was slowly unwrapped so that it could be read by the audience before being rewound around an embracing couple. At the performance's end, the couple stood wrapped in the narrative, and the original figure was revealed as a man holding a pea in his hand.

She Lost It (scarf), 1992 (detail). Acid dye on China silk. 72 x 20 inches (182.88 x 50.8 cm). Edition of 150.

A MAN AND A WOMAN

LIVED TOGETHER. ON ONE EVENING

HE DID NOT COME BACK FROM WORK,

AND SHE WAITED. SHE KEPT ON WAITING

AND SHE GREW LITTLER AND LITTLER.

LATER, A NEIGHBOR STOPPED BY OUT OF

FRIENDSHIP AND THERE HE FOUND HER, IN

THE ARMCHAIR, THE SIZE

OF A PEA.

LB.

Still images from *She Lost It*, a performance at The Fabric Workshop and Museum, 5 December 1992 (above). Pigment on cotton gauze. 19 x 1,978 ½ x 8 inches (48.26 x 5,025.39 x 20.32 cm).
Collection of Museum of Modern Art, New York.
Installation of *She Lost It* at The Fabric Workshop and Museum, 1992 (right). Pigment on cotton voile. 19 x 1,978 ½ x 8 inches (48.26 x 5,025.39 x 20.32 cm). Edition of 6.
Fears, 1992 (following pages). Wood and iron. Diameter: 30 inches (76.2 cm). Collection of the artist.

N THE ARMCHAIR, THE SIZE OF A PEA.

Garments from the performance of *She Lost It*, 1992. Embroidery on cotton, tulle, and nylon. Dimensions vary with installation. Collection of the artist.

Chris Burden

About the artist

American, born 1946, lives in Topanga, California

Raised in California, Chris Burden earned his BFA in 1969 at Pomona College in Claremont, California, before completing his MFA in 1971 at the University of California in Irvine. During the 1970s, Burden created performances of simple, yet often extreme, acts that challenged the cultural preconceptions of the day and transformed the stage of contemporary art making practice: no longer were artists limited to the realm of painting and sculpture. These performances—among them *Five Day Locker Piece*, *Shoot*, and *Doorway to Heaven*—form the artist's early career, while he later went on to produce significant sculptural and installation projects. Among the venues for his numerous solo exhibitions are the Orange County Museum of Art (2000), the MAK-Austrian Museum of Applied Arts in Vienna (1996), and the Brooklyn Museum of Art (1991). He has also been included in major group shows such as *Sunshine and Noir* (organized by the Louisiana Museum, Denmark, 1997) and *Helter Skelter* (Museum of Contemporary Art, Los Angeles, 1991).

About the work

L.A.P.D. Uniforms is an edition of thirty Los Angeles Police Department uniforms, fully equipped with regulation belt, holster, baton, handcuffs, 92F Beretta handgun, and a copy of the official badge. After extensive research, the artist and the FW+M designed an enlarged prototype for the edition of wool uniforms, which were then custom-made by the company that manufactures the L.A.P.D.'s actual shirts and pants. Designed to fit a seven feet four inch officer, the uniforms are installed with the outstretched sleeve of one uniform almost touching the next, as they circle the perimeter of the exhibition space. The viewer is engulfed by the physical presence of these symbols of authority and power.

Burden proposed this project soon after the Los Angeles riots of 1992, which were precipitated by the acquittal of Los Angeles police officers accused of unnecessarily beating Rodney King—an event captured on videotape and played repeatedly on television news programs throughout the world. While *L.A.P.D. Uniforms* offers commentary on a specific event in recent American history, it also provides a vehicle for more general questioning about the nature of authority.

Chris Burden often exhibits *L.A.P.D. Uniforms* with another sculptural work, *America's Darker Moments*, which he created in 1994 after his residency at the FW+M. This pentagonal vitrine encapsulates miniature, painted tin castings that look very much like toys. The five vignettes depict significant moments in American history, where violence played a significant role—the John F. Kennedy assassination, the killings of students at Kent State University by National Guardsmen, the My Lai Massacre in Vietnam, the bombing of Hiroshima, and the murder of Emmett Till at the start of the Civil Rights era.

L.A.P.D. Uniform, 1993 (detail). Wool serge, metal, leather, wood, and plastic. 88 x 72 x 6 inches (223.52 x 182.88 x 15.24 cm) each. Edition of 30. Collection of The Fabric Workshop and Museum and the Los Angeles County Museum of Art.

America's Darker Moments, 1994 (detail, above). Figures: cast tin with enamel. Vitrine: wood, plexiglass, glass, and florescent lights. 56 ½ x 36 ½ x 36 ½ inches (143.51 x 92.71 x 92.71 cm). Edition of 3. Collection of Yale University Art Gallery.

L.A.P.D. Uniform, 1993 (facing page). Wool serge, metal, leather, wood, and plastic. 88 x 72 x 6 inches (223.52 x 182.88 x 15.24 cm) each. Edition of 30. Collection of The Fabric Workshop and Museum and the Los Angeles County Museum of Art.

Installation of *L.A.P.D. Uniforms* and *America's Darker Moments* at Gagosian Gallery, New York, 1994 (following pages).

Maria Fernanda Cardoso

About the artist

Colombian, born 1963, lives in Sydney, Australia

After completing an undergraduate degree in visual arts and architecture in Bogotá, Colombia, Maria Fernanda Cardoso came to the United States to pursue graduate training in sculpture, first at the Pratt Institute in New York (1987–1988) and then at Yale University (MFA, 1990). She is most well known for her performances and installations of the *Cardoso Flea Circus*, a project she fully developed in collaboration with the FW+M. In addition to her 1996 performance at The Fabric Workshop and Museum, Cardoso has presented the *Cardoso Flea Circus* at the Sydney Opera House (2000), Centre Georges Pompidou in Paris (1998), and the San Francisco Exploratorium (1995–1996).

About the work

Several years before realizing the idea of the *Cardoso Flea Circus*, Maria Fernanda Cardoso began researching the history of flea circus performances and teaching herself the lost art of training fleas. Popularized in the nineteenth century, flea circuses were novelty performances staged for small groups of onlookers; two varieties are documented—one that used "sleight of hand" to create the appearance of real fleas, and a second that used actual fleas. Cardoso, whose past sculptural investigations have often been inspired by the animal or once-living world (using such material as shells and bones), was interested in raising and training live fleas.

At the FW+M, Cardoso created the "big top" tent to heighten the performative aspects of the circus while also allowing for a sculptural installation to remain after the initial performance was over. Constructed from a variety of fabrics—canvas, taffeta, silk, rayon, cotton, and polyester—the tent is highly decorative and is embellished with painted portraits of the famous flea performers. A plexiglass arena, which serves as the staging ground for the fleas' performances, is equipped with props such as cannons, netting, tall ladders with thimbles of water, and tightropes.

When performing *Cardoso Flea Circus*, Maria Fernanda Cardoso, dressed in circus attire, leads her fleas through a series of daring tricks, all of which are designed to accentuate the fleas' natural responses to heat, light, and breath (carbon dioxide). The compelling acrobatic efforts of the fleas include dancing, tightrope walks, high dives, and weightlifting.

Cardoso and her husband, video and filmmaker Ross Harley, created a video of the circus with the FW+M, which serves as a stand-in for the live performance and provides close-up views of the fleas performing their tricks.

Cardoso Flea Circus, 1996 (detail). Acrylic and oil on cotton canvas, pigment on nylon taffeta, various fabrics, steel, brass, video, various props, and fleas. 96 x 116 inches in diameter (closed) (243.84 x 294.64 cm). Edition of 2.

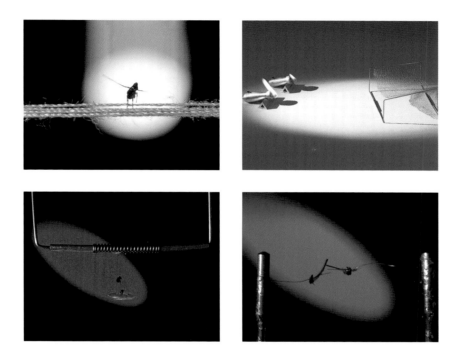

Maria Fernanda Cardoso performing *Cardoso Flea Circus* at The Fabric Workshop and Museum, 6 December 1996 (preceding pages).

Still images from the performance of *Cardoso Flea Circus* (above).

Mel Chin

American, born 1951, lives in New York City and Burnsville, North Carolina

About the artist

Mel Chin was raised in Houston, Texas, the first generation of his family born in the United States. Of Chinese descent, he grew up in a predominantly African American and Latino neighborhood and worked in his family's grocery store. He began making art at an early age and earned his BA from Peabody College in Nashville, Tennessee, in 1975. Chin is best known for undertaking collaborative and cross-disciplinary artistic investigations into political and often ecologically-charged topics. For example, in 1991 Chin worked with a group of scientists to create gardens of plants that draw heavy metals from contaminated areas to make *Revival Field*. His numerous one-person exhibitions and innovative projects have been sponsored by List Center for Visual Arts at the Massachusetts Institute of Technology, Cambridge, MA (2000); the Metro Transit Authority, New York City (1995–1997); the Headlands Center for the Arts, Marin County, CA (1994–1999); the Walker Art Center, Minneapolis (1990); and the Hirshhorn Museum and Sculpture Garden, Washington, DC (1989).

72

About the work

During 1991–1992, Mel Chin worked with the FW+M to complete his ambitious installation *Degrees of Paradise*, which was first exhibited at the Storefront for Art and Architecture in New York. As is typical for Chin, the artist worked with a diverse range of collaborators to realize this project, including scientists, computer programmers, and traditional hand-weavers in Turkey. The title references Dante's *Commedia* and the "complex vertical geography of the ascent from earth to heaven . . . [which was] earlier prominent in the Arabic and Persian traditions . . ." (Thomas McEvilley, *Soil and Sky*, The Fabric Workshop and Museum, Philadelphia, 1993).

For the installation, two triangular-shaped rooms were constructed opposite one another. A small drawing on slate of an unfolding lotus serves as the fulcrum between the rooms, in which two divergent yet complementary sculptural installations are suspended from the ceiling. On one side, Chin hung fourteen video monitors that display multi-dimensional fractal images chronicling the world's weather mapped for one full day as recorded by scientists at McGill University. The images appear in a triangular format on the monitors, a looped display of clouds moving across a blue sky. On the ceiling of the other room hangs a hand-knotted Kurdish wool carpet made by women in Damlacik, Turkey, during the beginning of the Gulf War—the influence of which can be detected in a helicopter form hidden in the design. The carpet depicts the women's interpretation of the scientific satellite mappings, samples of which were given to them in still format.

The elements of *Degrees of Paradise* represent Mel Chin's first explorations into the subject of ozone depletion, and provided the basis for a larger installation called *The State of Heaven*. *Degrees of Paradise* was included in an exhibition of Chin's work, co-sponsored by the FW+M and Swarthmore College in 1992.

Installation of *Degrees of Paradise* at The Fabric Workshop and Museum, 1992 (right).

Following pages: *Degrees of Paradise* (video), 1991 (left). Video monitors and computers. 96 x 276 x 144 inches (243.84 x 701.04 x 365.76 cm) and *Degrees of Paradise* (carpet), 1991 (right).

Wool and cotton. 96 x 276 x 144 inches (243.84 x 701.04 x 365.76 cm). Collection of the artist.

Willie Cole

About the artist

American, born 1955, lives in Mine Hill, New Jersey

After studying for a year at Boston University's School of Fine Arts,
Willie Cole went on to earn his BFA from The School of Visual Arts,
New York (1976). He continued his studies at The Art Students
League of New York from 1976–1979. Cole's work consistently draws
on issues of African American identity, often through the use of found
or domestic objects that imply larger social meaning after their
manipulation and transformation by the artist. One-person exhibitions
have been organized by the Bronx Museum of the Arts in New York
(2001), the Miami Art Museum (2000), and the Museum of Modern
Art, New York (1998). In 1995, Cole was honored with The Louis
Comfort Tiffany Foundation Award.

About the work

Created as a site-specific work for the exhibition *Prison Sentences: The Prison as Site/
The Prison as Subject* at Philadelphia's now-abandoned Eastern State Penitentiary
(organized by independent curators Julie Courtney and Todd Gilens), *5 to 10* is Willie
Cole's poignant examination of the futility and loss that accompanies imprisonment.
The installation gains its power from the simplicity of the materials—used and broken
playground equipment—which are placed in suggestive arrangements: a swing set
leans against the prison wall, the row of swings pressed to the hard stone as if in a
firing line; a series of basketball nets are hung 30 feet high on the prison's outer
wall, across from the prison's former Death Row and far too high to ever be used for
play; a sandbox is littered with pairs of children's sneakers, turned sole-side up.

Cole's initial idea for the project came when he saw a newspaper article chronicling
the story of a child's murderous act. The use of basketball nets and sneakers suggests
a cultural critique of the often hopeless but common dream among America's youth—
especially poor African American youth—to be "discovered" as the next star athlete.
By conflating relics of childhood with the idea of imprisonment, Cole offers commentary
on lost innocence and hopelessness that plague more than just the inmates confined
to a prison's walls.

5 to 10, 1995. Installation at Eastern State Penitentiary, Philadelphia. Playground equipment, basketball hoops, and children's sneakers. Dimensions vary with installation.

5 to 10, 1995. Installation at Eastern State Penitentiary, Philadelphia. Playground equipment, basketball hoops, and children's sneakers. Dimensions vary with installation.

5 to 10, 1995. Installation at Eastern State Penitentiary, Philadelphia. Playground equipment, basketball hoops, and children's sneakers. Dimensions vary with installation.

Arthur C. Danto

About the author

American, born 1924, lives in New York City

Arthur Danto is a philosopher and art critic. In 1992 he was named the Johnsonian Professor Emeritus of Philosophy at Columbia University, where he has taught since 1952. Since 1984, Danto has been art critic for *The Nation*, and, since 1998, he has served as a contributing editor for *Artforum*. Well known for his work in aesthetics and art criticism, Danto has written numerous books, including: *The Madonna of the Future: Critical Essays in a Pluralistic Art World* (2000); *After the End of Art* (1996); *Encounters and Reflections* (1990, winner of the National Book Critics Circle Prize in Criticism); and *The Philosophical Disenfranchisement of Art* (1986). Mr. Danto has received numerous honors for his work in art criticism including the Frank Jewett Mather Prize for Criticism from the College Art Association (1996), a "Literary Lion" award from the New York Public Library (1993), and the George S. Polk award for criticism (1985). The following essay was first commissioned by The Fabric Workshop and Museum during the North American exhibition tour of *Changing Spaces*, organized by consulting curator Mary Jane Jacob.

Reflections on Fabric and Meaning: The Tapestry and the Loincloth

The two objects conjoined in my subtitle might appear to have in common little beyond the fact that both are fashioned in cloth, and that each conveys a set of meanings derived from the role it plays in forms of life each helps define. The loincloth, as a minimal garment, is probably as old as clothing itself, given the meaning of what it covers—the first garments were handfuls of leaves, according to the Biblical account, hiding the genitals. "All clothing from every nation and age," wrote the architect and philosopher of art, Gottfried Semper, "can be traced back to three basic forms or elements: namely, the loincloth as the earliest, the shirt, and third, the wrap."[1] I shall concern myself with a relatively late exemplar, the loincloth adopted in the spirit of protest by Mohandas Gandhi in his struggle for Home Rule in India. The tapestry, as a woven picture, also has credentials ancient enough that Helen of Troy, when we first glimpse her in the *Iliad*, is weaving images of heroes, a pictorial text not unlike the verbal text of the *Iliad* itself in which we read about it. And Helen must have been working on the kind of *haute-lisse* loom pictured on Greek vases, where the female weaver is conventionally identified as Penelope, who, unlike Helen in all other ways as well, is weaving a non-pictorial garment as fraught with meaning as the loincloth was to become—a shroud for her father-in-law, Laertes. But I shall concern myself with one of the masterpieces of tapestry, a late work of Raphael. *The Acts of the Apostles* (1515–1516), has, in addition to the range of meanings it conveys through the form of life to which tapestries belonged—the life of princes and of papal majesty—a set of meanings the loincloth altogether lacks, since the latter, like the shroud, is character- istically without pictorial content (the Shroud of Turin, bearing the alleged image of Jesus, is a special case). Raphael's work is a piece of narrative art, illustrative of episodes in the life of Jesus, Peter, Paul and others, as recounted in the New Testament. It has meaning as picture and as cultural object, whereas the loincloth (or shroud) has meaning as cultural object only.

According to Semper's speculative art history, the tapestry and the loincloth may in fact have a very deep connection, since both are coverings, one for walls and the other for the human body. Semper believes there to be linguistic evidence for their connection: "In all Germanic languages the word *Wand* [wall] (of the same root and the same basic meaning as *Gewand* [garment]) directly recalls the old origin and type of the *visible* spatial enclosure," Semper wrote in 1851[2]; and each depends for its properties on the special attributes of textile itself. "All operations in the textile arts seek to transform raw materials with the appropriate properties into products, whose common features are great pliancy and considerable absolute strength . . . to cover, to hold, to dress, to enclose, and so forth."[3] Semper claims that "the *pen*, bound together from sticks and branches, and the interwoven *fence* [is] the earliest vertical spatial enclosure that man invented, whose construction required a technique that nature, as it were, put into the hands of man."[4] Plaiting led to weaving, in Semper's scheme, and thence to pattern. And in a statement of singular boldness, he writes:

> *Woven fabrics almost everywhere and especially in the southern and warm countries carry out their ancient, or original function as conspicuous spatial dividers: even where solid walls become necessary they remain only the inner and unseen structure for the true and legitimate representatives for the spatial idea: namely, the more or less artificially woven and seamed-together, textile walls.*[5]

Hence the tapestry, as a woven hanging, implies the enclosing wall as the loincloth implies the sexed human body through what it conceals. Tapestry and loincloth together connote not just shelter and warmth, but privacy, property, and decorum. As artifacts they are realizations of the elements of moral distinction that define the shapes of social life. And, if Semper is right, they provide the material conditions for the fine arts through which society conveys its system of meanings. Weaving and the materials of weaving constitute the primordial technique which "must have had and retained the most lasting influence on the stylistic development of architecture."[6] Semper is fertile in proposing reciprocal influence in early civilization between costume, sculpture, and architecture, and hence the overall influence of textile in the artistic

1   Gottfried Semper, "The Textile Art," in *The Elements of Architecture and Other Writings.* RES Monographs in Anthropology and Aesthetics (Cambridge and New York: Cambridge University Press, 1989), 245.

2   Semper, 254.

3   Semper, 215.

4   Semper, 254.

5   Semper, 255.

6   Semper, 227.

expressions of those civilizations. But this gives me a further and more immediate reason for juxtaposing the tapestry and the loincloth at the outset of an essay on fabric.

The *Acts of the Apostles* was a collaboration between one of the most esteemed artists of the sixteenth century and a workshop, that of Pieter van Aelst, of Brussels, and it marks a high point in the history of collaborations between artists and specialists in fiber—a history to which the later collaboration between Francois Boucher and the tapestry workshop of the Gobelins belongs. Tapestry, for reasons I will sketch, has very largely disappeared from what is today spoken of as "fabric art," but the *spirit* of the Raphael-Van Aelst collaboration lives on in an institution like The Fabric Workshop and Museum in Philadelphia, insofar as it has sought to commission artists, of considerable reputation as well as achievement but often with no special prior involvement with fiber, to collaborate with their staff of craft-artists to produce works conceived of in terms of fabric. Fabric, however, is not merely a medium, as it was in Raphael's tapestries. It is in its own right a *source* of meaning, often of very powerful meanings, such as the loincloth was perceived symbolically to possess in India's struggle for political independence and economic autonomy. Fabric carries such meanings because of the way it fits into forms of life that are lived by very ordinary people in contexts typically remote from those of high or fine art, to which the tapestry now belongs. I refer, among other things, to articles of clothing, the materials of shelter, the vestments of ceremony, and accessories of decoration and domestic embellishment, not to speak of explicitly symbolic objects such as flags. Clothing does not simply cover our nakedness—it communicates a dense array of information, which individuals who share a form of life are able to read and to integrate into differential sets of actions and attitudes toward its wearers. And much the same may be said of the countless other modes in which fabric has a practical and symbolic use.

Transformations in the practice of art in recent decades has made these meanings available to artists in realizing works that draw on the meanings fabric possesses in vernacular forms of life. This has become possible because artistic meaning has been liberated from the pictorial criteria that had defined the visual arts in the West until well into the twentieth century, making it out of the question that something as unpictorial as a loincloth could have been a work of art when it became part of the language of political discourse during the breakup of the British Empire. That something of as little visual interest as it *could* be a work of art today—an imagined work, say, consisting of a loincloth exhibited under the title *Portrait of Gandhi*—is testimony to a revolution in the criteria of visual art to which I refer. By bringing into their works objects and materials with often powerful meanings in lived forms of life, artists have been able to appropriate those meanings for their art, and even to communicate with audiences in ways considerably beyond what pictorial representation would allow. It is such appropriations that I have in mind by the concept of *realization*. It is realization, one may say perhaps too simply, when one uses rather than represents something, and where the use within art carries the meaning which that use would carry outside of art, in real life itself. And the immense transformation from representation to realization has made available to visual artists entire languages that were denied them when art was construed in pictorial terms alone.

The tapestry, then, was a woven picture. By contrast with non-pictorial artworks made of fabric, tapestry has a relatively circumscribed share of present artistic production. This marks a profound change from the time when the woven picture had only painted pictures, carved pictures, drawn pictures, marquetry pictures *(tapissiers en bois)*, and sculpture in various materials as its peers and rivals. Today it has, in the domain of "fiber art"—art that is made of or that makes use of fabric— a multitude of non-pictorial peers hardly imaginable in earlier times, where objects made of cloth (including of course clothing) carried meanings unavailable to art except indirectly, when they were pictured.

In his fascinating study of the formation and dispersal of the great art collections of the seventeenth century, Jonathan Brown writes *en passant* about tapestry:

> *Nowadays, no artistic medium is less appreciated than the tapestry, which seems to enjoy about the same esteem as second hand clothing. In the Renaissance and Baroque, however, tapestry was the art of kings, prized for its scale and intricate craftsmanship as well as its insulating properties. Tapestries were expensive because they required considerable expenditure of labor and materials. Give a painter a few yards of linen, a pot of glue, some cheap home-made pigments and a brush or two, and in a few hours or days you could have a picture. To produce a tapestry required miles of thread, a team of skilled workers, a large site for production and months if not years of labor.[7]*

And this was reflected in, if it did not entirely explain, the value once set on tapestries. Brown compares the price of the most expensive tapestry in the collection of Charles I as against that of the most expensive painting: "The tapestry was a nine-panel set of Raphael's *The Acts of the Apostles*: it was valued at nearly 7000 pounds."[8] The most expensive painting, also by Raphael, went for 2000 pounds, but it was, Brown

7   Jonathan Brown, *Kings & Connoisseurs: Collecting Art in Seventeenth Century Europe* (New Haven: Yale University Press, 1995), 228-229.

8   Brown, 229.

adds, "a rare picture that was worth more than a few hundred."

We live today with the precise reverse of this situation, aesthetically and economically. Raphael's *cartoons*—his drawings for *The Acts of the Apostles*—are among the artistic treasures of Great Britain, and not only would their value, were they offered at auction, vastly exceed that of the tapestries they generated, but it would be regarded as a national calamity if they were allowed to leave the nation. Aesthetic pilgrims to England, moreover, will make a point of seeing the cartoons far sooner than any set of tapestries held in that country, even if, as drawings, they are not especially pleasing to look at as such. They were working drawings, after all, and Raphael conceived of them as instrumental to a finished product as different from them as a print is from a block or plate. The size of the looms specified what the size of the drawings had to be (or vice versa when the artist was as great as Raphael), and since sheets of paper in the required dimensions were not made, Raphael's cartoons—executed in a coarse medium of pigment mixed with glue (since they really only were working drawings)—are on sheets of paper composed of a patchwork of smaller sheets pasted together. It is difficult to imagine that Raphael's contemporaries, who after all lacked our passion for master drawings, assigned anything like the high valuation on them, which the tapestries themselves aroused when they were executed. The latter were appreciated by Vasari as "so well-done that they do not look like a mere texture woven in the loom, but like paintings executed with the brush."[9] This is a high tribute not so much to Raphael himself, as to the Flemish weavers to whom the cartoons had been sent. We can see in Vasari's compliment the beginning of a critical agenda for tapestries: the best tapestries would be those that looked most like paintings, and that disguised the fact that they were woven. In point of beauty, the tapestries for which Raphael's cartoons were instruments are perhaps not to be compared with the latter. But such is the grip upon us of the idea that the drawings came directly from the master's hands, whereas the tapestries themselves were the collaborative achievement of nameless skilled handworkers who translated drawing into woven images. This, combined with the fact that the drawings are unique whereas there could be as many sets of tapestries as there were patrons prepared to buy them, leads us today to attach a greater artistic value to the cartoons than to the tapestries. And this disproportion is heightened by the fact that the precious materials woven into tapestries seem to us irrelevant to their artistic value, even if preciousness was integral to the meaning of the tapestries as they were initially conceived, as objects of maximal sumptuousness. In the seventeenth century, as Brown observes, "Not illogically, collectors tended to equate price with material value,"[10] and

this equation explains in part why tapestries were considered so much more valuable than paintings: paintings typically lacked gold and silver. Nevertheless, in the course of that century "significant steps were taken in the long process by which the symbolic value of an art work was uncoupled from its material value,"[11] and this was correlative with the high value set on the artist and whatever issued directly from the artist's hands—like the cartoons of Raphael, however aesthetically short those drawings fall by comparison with the tapestries they enabled to come into being.

It is important to recognize that tapestries were associated with forms of life very distant from those in which we today experience these works, seeing them as representing episodes from narratives we often know little about, woven into heavy fabric, and hanging glumly along museum corridors. Part of what makes tapestry so remote from us, by comparison with stained glass, is that while the glass is installed in the architectural frame for which it was intended, interacting with light to produce its great effects, we often have no sense for how tapestry was to be installed in living contexts, which brought features out that are simply invisible in the heavy hangings we see in museums, to whose walls the great works have been consigned. Imagine, instead, experiencing the entire sequence of nine tapestries hung along the middle register of the Sistine Chapel when some high ritual was in process of being celebrated. The surfaces of the images would form a kind of shimmering, undulating veil, through which one could view the figures performing the miraculous acts the text describes: the tapestries would have a life not to be found in paintings, just because of the way they would stir in the rising heat and reflect the dazzle of taper light. The effect would be illusory in a way that painting was not capable of, and the silk, gold, and silver would contribute to an effect available only by means of hanging heavy cloth, shot through with metallic threads. With all this surface excitement, the figures, seen as it were in a medium that changed moment by moment, had to be strongly modeled or they would lose focus and integrity, like the outlines of objects seen submerged in water. So the style of drawing as well as the specification of the kinds of threads to be used were dictated by an effect in which both would be transcended. Vasari thought the tapestries looked like painting because he saw them *displayed*, and because they really were more like paintings than tapestries had ever been. But in what I assume was the intended effect, the tapestries would not have been displayed as such. They would have *brought the acts of the Apostles to life*, as in a collective vision that materialized just above the heads of those who took part in the high rituals. It would have been something altogether extraordinary. And the integrated contributions of artist and weaver would have been,

9 Giorgio Vasari, *Lives of the Most Eminent Painters, Sculptors, and Architects*. Translated by Mrs. Jonathan Foster (London: Bohns Library, 1868), III, 60.

10 Brown, 229.

11 Ibid.

as I have wanted to illustrate, transcended.

I have introduced considerations that bear on the uniqueness of cloth in the achievement of visual effects. Wood and plaster, the usual supports of painted images in the Renaissance, are in their nature rigid. But cloth is flexible and supple, and is capable of moment to moment interaction with drafts and lights—just think of how gowns interact with the bodies that wear them!—giving a motility to images woven into it that would have been unavailable before the advent of the moving picture. My sense is that we overlook precisely those features of cloth an artist like Raphael would have prized for the facilitation of dazzling effects now lost to us. Raphael's innovations set the standard for the next 150 years, but it was very much as though the vectors of tapestry's history were to underwrite Vasari's praise of *The Acts of the Apostles* by making painting the model for the execution of tapestry well into the eighteenth century. When the painter Boucher took over the ateliers of Beauvais, the weaving became increasingly refined, to the point where, as one writer put it, the weaver

> had to learn to paint with a bobbin, and to this end hundreds of new dyes were perfected for both wool and silk, until about 10,000 hues were available, to effect almost imperceptible tonal modulations; and interlocking of the wefts was introduced to render the transitions practically invisible, while the finest textures practical were used, from 20 to occasionally as many as 40 warps to the inch.[12]

With Boucher, in brief, tapestry was put under pressure to become indiscernible from painting, and had it not been for historical upheavals in 1789, we could imagine tapestries that used the works of the Impressionists or the Pointillists as cartoons, in the production of works of astonishing effect. But of course the history of tapestry was not allowed to develop in this way precisely because of those historical upheavals, mainly because that art was associated with the aristocracy, from which it received its chief patronage, and the values of the aristocracy were something one kept at a distance after the French Revolution. And with the industrialization of weaving, tapestry became what we find it today, a largely marginalized art, subject to fitful efforts at revitalization, but typified by the projects in which the paintings of modern artists—Picasso, Matisse, Miró—are translated into fabric for the luxury trade. And so the tapestry as a form of expression has lost contact with the realities of lived life, and it has suffered aesthetically since the contexts in which it could have a use and meaning other than the reduced aesthetic it shares with paintings have vanished from modern life. As matters stand, they are

12 "Tapestry," *Encyclopaedia Britannica* (1965), Vol. 21, 802B.

appreciated only as paintings in an alien medium, viewed primarily in museums of fine art.

I want now to turn to my other paradigm, the loincloth, which gained its symbolic weight against the very sorts of economic and political upheavals that marginalized tapestry, and turned it into a largely underappreciated art. I refer to the Industrial Revolution and its paradigm, the industrialization of textile manufacture, which, in transforming cloth-making from a handcraft to a mechanical process, turned society as irrevocably upside down as a cataclysmic political revolution could have done. Ironically, the great technical inventions of the industry were made at just the same time that the doomed art of tapestry was brought to its highest levels of refinement. The flying shuttle, the spinning jenny, the power loom—and of course the cotton gin—were all in place by the time of the French Revolution. But they required for their full utilization an integration into a total productive structure, which in turn depended upon a mass demand for textiles and the economic wherewithal to pay for them. So it may be argued that British imperialism was the political face of Britain's textile economy through the nineteenth century. It is instructive in this respect to consider how the insatiable appetite for fine muslin on the part of Jane Austen's female contemporaries entailed a total reorganization of society, collecting workers into British factories and under the discipline of the machine, while at the same time promoting the growth of slavery in the United States in order to provide sufficient cotton to accommodate the increased capacity of the factories. Industrial muslin challenged through its fineness what the nimblest fingers of Indian weavers could produce, and by time the fashion for muslin passed, an entire complex was in place that made hand-weaving less and less profitable. Its practice became more and more a form of craft associated with the handwork of peoples who would, in India and elsewhere, themselves come to prefer manufactured cloth when they could obtain it, creating export markets for the British cotton mills, where, before this transformation, Britain had been an export market for India's handmade cloth. These immense social transformations were almost made to order for the theories of capitalist enterprise and social revolution formulated by Karl Marx and Friedrich Engels. The Industrial Revolution really was a revolution, transforming society in a total and irreversible way, and though there have been responses to its more dehumanizing consequences through labor organizations and various environmentalist initiatives, the overall structure of life it generated defines the form of life in advanced industrial nations, as well as that to which developing nations aspire. Still, the original industrial product was the *bolt* of cloth, hence manufactured as against hand-loomed textiles, which came to stand in symbolic opposition to one another, far more, for example, than the automobile and the horse-drawn carriage.

As a corollary to this history, then, hand weaving became one among a number of symbolic expressions of an anti-industrial attitude as the nineteenth century wore on, and acquired in consequence a political meaning it could not have had before the Industrial Revolution took place. The *meaning* of such cloth came to be read as a critique of industrial society, as indeed it was understood in the various arts and crafts movements of the latter part of the century. The artist and social activist, Tim Rollins (pp. 240–243), puts this succinctly:

> The textile and wallpaper designs of William Morris and his workshop from the late Nineteenth century in England pointed to a way to reconsider the languages possible for a new political art—an art political not so much in its form or content, but political in the very way it is made. (I still find it amazing that the greatest indictment of capitalism can be found in but a yard of Morris's perfect, beautiful materials.) [13]

The primary antonym of "craft," at the end of the nineteenth century, was accordingly not "art" but "industry": to eschew the industrially produced textile and to affirm the qualities of hand-loomed cloth, was to endorse a profound political and economic alternative to the form of life industrialization at once caused and represented. That very gesture could take on a revolutionary significance, as it did in the textile movement that Gandhi invented and led in India, where the hand-spun garment became a badge of independence not only from modern industrial methods, but from British domination. The spinning wheel became the symbol of the *Hind Swaraj*—or Indian Home Rule movement—as well as an emblem against everything for which the machine (and not merely the power loom) had come to stand. And the homespun hand-woven garment became, as well, an economic weapon in the theater of India's political autonomy. Indeed, Gandhi took to the loincloth in 1921, declaring that "Millions are too poor to buy enough khadi to replace their discarded cloth. Let them be satisfied with a mere loincloth."[14] Everything about the loincloth—its size, its use, its material, its mode of manufacture, and its contrast with European costume and cloth—became part of its meaning. It was pure defiance disguised as a minimal traditional garment made by hand. It was the product of political genius, and the wearing of the loincloth by Gandhi became part of a political performance: the sight of the lean spectacled leader, dark in contrast with the whiteness of the cloth, squatting barefoot at the loom, enacted Indian separatism at a symbolic level as well as in the form of real resistance.

It would be conceptually awkward to regard the loincloth as a *work of art*, however, if we think of it with the tapestries of Raphael and the kinds of criteria the latter satisfies. But that is because of the striking visual interest of the tapestries, especially if my imagined scenario is valid, when they introduced, on the occasions for which they were designed, an experience verging on hallucinatory in the Sistine Chapel during enactments of high ritual. By contrast, the loincloth was an object so laden with symbolic power in the context in which it was used to repudiate an entire form of life and affirm a different one, that to think of it as a work of art would detract from "the meaning of the cloth." It had a power works of art rarely possessed, and while it was historically closed to artists to pre-empt that sort of power for their works at that time, it is certainly a possibility for them today, which is one of the reasons, it seems to me, that the appropriation of fabric to non-pictorial artistic uses has become so attractive an artistic possibility. Clothing itself is so richly symbolic, so dense with meaning, so woven into the fabric of meanings—of gender, class, authority, status; of hope, humiliation, and dream—that defines our form of life that artists must welcome some way of making all that symbolic energy their own, and appropriate for their art the tremendous human meanings garments can possess and transmit.

I offer a few examples. In a site-specific work entitled *Indigo Blue* in Charleston, South Carolina, Ann Hamilton (pp. 122–127) made use of an immense table on which she piled up a mountain of neatly folded working clothes—shirts and pants. The shirts were uniformly a faded blue cotton, and distinguished by their ordinariness. These were the kinds of shirts workers would wear to work at specifically blue-collar jobs. The blue was perhaps a local allusion to the indigo history of Charleston's past, but the larger implication of the shirts, in a place so filled with historical references—to the firing on Fort Sumter, to episodes in the American Civil war, and to the rich, the famous, and the fashionable men and women of the Confederate South—lies elsewhere. The reference here was to the anonymous army of working persons—those whose names did not figure in the history books, whose mode of existence was outside the story of great events, at the level of productivity and labor upon which the economy of the place depended. Hamilton placed, next to the tableful of working clothes, someone erasing the text from what were identified as "history books," as if, by rubbing out the descriptions of battles and speeches, one arrived at the plain uninflected pages of real lived life—the life lived by the wearers of the blue shirts. Of course the meaning of her work was underdetermined. It could have had a different meaning altogether. The working clothes could have been neatly piled up as their wearers put on battle-

13 Tim Rollins, "Notes on *Amerika I*," in *Amerika: Tim Rollins + K.O.S.* Ed. Gary Garrels. (New York: Dia Art Foundation, 1989), 69.

14 "Gandhi," *Encyclopaedia Britannica* (1965), Vol. 9, 1129.

clothing and went off to war. The table of working clothes could then have had the meaning of peace, and the erased history books the meaning of memory decaying. The work is capable of many interpretations, and though it is thinkable that a painting of piled shirts could have those meanings, it would lack the power of the shirts' actual presence. Hamilton found a way of using that presence to release that power.

A second example is a work by Christian Boltansky, which consists of a great many pieces of cheap, colorful children's clothing—dresses and shirts, jackets and pants of the kind one buys at discount stores in shopping malls—the most ordinary kinds of clothing for the most ordinary kinds of children: the clothes they play in, or in which they go to school. I forget whether the clothing was hung on the wall or simply piled on the floor, but the effect was one of moral desolation, as if their wearers had been stripped and sent off to their death— as if (since the title of the piece was *Purim*) the wearers had been Jewish boys and girls, though the clothing was not of a kind which marked its wearers as any different from children anywhere: there was nothing Jewish about the garments. For a real-life correlative to Boltansky's work, think of the drawers and closets, filled with just such permanent-press overalls and skirts, which stunned parents dumbly showed the viewing audience on CNN after the Oklahoma bombing. Boltansky's work seemed to have the symbolic weight of a massacre of the innocent. The gay colors and cheap fabrics conveyed an almost unendurable sense of vulnerability.

One of the great emblems of contemporary art is Joseph Beuys' multiple, consisting of a shapeless suit, made of heavy grey flannel, as blank and basic as a garment can be. It expresses, as so much of Beuys' work does, life lived at the level of subsistence, and it implies, the way his blankets and his lumps of fat do, the most fundamental human needs met in the most basic way—the need for warmth, for sustenance, for covering, and for care. The suit looks like the product of a clothing industry which has patched together its devastated productive capacity in order to meet a terrible demand for clothing. There is no room for ornament or color, or for the slightest concession to fashion or to tailoring. It is subsistence suiting, and though it could be seen as the platonic essence of the suit—not this or that kind of suit, but "suitness" embodied— it comes, since part of Beuys' oeuvre, with the implicit smell of cold and dark and loss. It is like the first bit of green to appear at the bomb-site, a sign of life and recovery, even if but a weed. As a garment, it has a real-life kin in the jumpsuit worn by Winston Churchill in the war, in its own right as precise a symbol of austerity and engagement as Gandhi's loincloth had been, but of course in another vocabulary of conflict altogether.

These are imaginative appropriations of garments, which derive their meanings from the meanings of the garments themselves, but which go on to make further statements about society, history, vulnerability, peace, war, urban reality, and, as the advertisements say, "much much more." In part the power of the work derives from the numbers of garments—the absolute mountain of shirts, the indeterminate plenitude of childwear. Beuys' suits, being multiples, are intended, like prints, to be sold to individual collections. And they are exceedingly moving when seen one at a time, hanging shapelessly and heavily on a wall. But they imply having been issued in large numbers for a needful population, and one can imagine them stacked, like general issue army apparel in the quartermaster's room, to be handed out one by one. In my view, at least, the works have a power, conferred by the reality of the means used, which paintings bent on achieving the same impact could not have.

Because of the close association of fabric with the concept of craft in contemporary consciousness, it is worth stressing that only in the case of the loincloths among the items I have mentioned is it important that the cloth had been hand-loomed, and its made-by-handedness is important less for aesthetic than for political reasons, symbolically expressing resistance to the domination of the industrialized colonial power. As such, the garment had two modes of symbolic meaning, one provided by its mode of manufacture, and the other through the difference from European clothing it marked in the language of garment. Gandhi was especially sensitive to this language, and he describes in some detail the stiff formal suit and top hat he wore in England as a young man, anxious to exhibit his intended Englishness. *That* part of the loincloth's meaning would, independent of the meaning contributed by its hand-madedness, enable wearers to proclaim their cultural difference through loincloths which happened to be machine-loomed, in much the way the colorful *dashiki* proclaims the Africanness of its wearer even if the garment should be mass-produced in Mississippi. And so with garments in general.

Works of art are embodiments of meaning, and the meaning of hand-woven cloth would be irrelevant to the actual works of art I cited. One imagines Ann Hamilton's workshirts were purchased rather than fabricated to her specification, just because the uniformity of the manufactured process carries a meaning which goes with the concept of the industrial working-class her shirts seem to imply. The blue-collar shirt (but why a collar at all?) is the uniform of the masses, which contrasts with the individuals of standard history—the generals, the politicians, the personages whose names are known and mentioned in recounting the stories of wars and elections. It would, one feels, be irrelevant or even contradictory to have had the shirts made by hand of hand-loomed materials. On the other hand, it would be altogether consistent, and add a meaning of its own, were the shirts bought secondhand, bearing the marks of wear—stains, frayings, missing buttons, and torn pockets.

Beuys' suits, finally, could be run up by individuals or manufactured, both meanings being consistent with their effect. But it seems to me the material itself, the heavy, durable basic felt, should not have been hand-made. It should feel like the product of a textile mill that had begun to run again, after the devastations, and that the pants and jackets are cut and shaped as minimally as possible, so that there is as little room for style (for lapels, say, or cuffs, or linings) as in the heavy undistinguished housing projects that went up under socialism: an architectural message of basic no-frills shelter was projected and continued to be projected, reminding their dwellers that society's needs were peremptory, and that neither time nor money was available for amenities.

This is a good place to pick up the thread of the distinction, as it has come to be drawn, between art and craft. However one defines the philosophical difference between them, the twentieth century has demonstrated that it is consistent with being an artist that one can use industrial products for the meanings they carry. Craft essentially involves a rejection of the industrial production of the same kinds of products the craftsperson makes by hand: cloth, vessels, furniture. The presence of the hand is of diminishing significance in the visual arts today, as they become increasingly conceptual. I cannot see it disappearing from the concept of craft, however. Craftspersons have sometimes hoped to close the gap between craft and art by shunning the idea of functionality. But it is hard to see how they can repudiate the presence of the hand. Because of the hand, craft has often carried a political message in its implication of a form of life contrary to that implied by the flawless, uniform products of mechanical manufacture. The lumpy cloth, the bumpy clay, the heavy wood bearing the marks of having been hewn—the standard marks of craft-fair ware— are but one form the rejection takes, though, as with the Arts and Crafts Movement of William Morris, the concept of craft is consistent with the most refined aesthetic virtues. In the Arts and Crafts movement, the craft personality was essentially not at home in industrial society, finding its true spiritual habitat in pre-industrial forms of life—in peasant life, in the life of the medieval guild, or in the life of societies in which the making of cloth, for clothing and for shelter, was associated with one or another ritual. My sense is that the idea of the functional object cuts across the distinction between art and craft. The great first generation of Soviet artists worked under the slogan "art into life." They rejected art as emblematized by the easel painting, but because machinery was so central to the new socialist society they envisioned, craft was not an appealing

concept, though function was. Liubov Popova claimed to have found greater satisfaction in seeing an ordinary woman walking along in a dress, the fabric of which she, Popova, designed, than in any oil painting she had achieved in her career as a painter. But the fabric was industrially produced. Rosemarie Trockel, working today in a period of complete artistic pluralism within which painting has a place—within which painting has to compete with photography, with film, with video, with installation, with appropriation, and with "objects"—has found reason to knit hangings, the dimension of large tapestries, fabricated by the machinery of knitting mills. She has appropriated to her own expressive ends the knit balaclavas that have become an item in the costume of terrorists, familiar from newspaper photographs and clips on the evening news—but she does not knit them herself! Whatever the original use and function of the balaclava, it has become a symbolically charged piece of headgear—as much so as the silk hat, the derby, the stetson, or the baseball cap worn backwards—and Trockel's contemporaneity as an artist is emphasized by her fertile use of such potent and universal symbols in making her at times sardonic, at times satirical, at times urgent messages. What makes a knit dress by Rosemarie Trockel a work of art and a knit dress by a dressmaker merely a dress, is the kind of question in the ontology of art that has preoccupied much of my philosophical life, but it is quite general, and has nothing particular to do with garments. I have been talking about garments because of the rich vocabulary they make available to artists, but this is true of functional objects in general because of the deep meanings they derive from human life as lived: vessels, articles of furniture, rugs and throws and pillows. They refer to the human body and to the human soul as embodied. Non-functional fiber objects can have meaning—and if they are art they must have meaning—but often what they mean is simply the craft of fiberwork. Given the role that fabric has played in every culture, that is by no means contemptible, and can even be metaphorical.

Leonardo Drew

About the artist

American, born 1961, lives in New York City

Leonardo Drew was born in Tallahassee, Florida, and moved to Bridgeport, Connecticut, when he was six years old. He began making art at a very young age, and pursued formal art training at Parsons School of Design, New York (1981–1982), and The Cooper Union for the Advancement of Science and Art (BFA, 1985). Drew is best known for his abstract, monumental sculptural assemblages. His works are never titled because the artist does not want to impose an interpretation on the viewer; instead they are assigned numbers. Drew has had many one-person exhibitions in national and international museums, including the Royal Hibernian Academy in Dublin, Ireland (2001), the Hirshhorn Museum and Sculpture Garden in Washington, DC (2000), and The Bronx Museum of the Arts in Bronx, New York (2000).

About the work

Number 80 represents a transition in Leonardo Drew's work. A significant portion of his previous work is assembled, piece by piece, from the debris of contemporary life, which he transforms and presents back to us. Often, early works were painted over in one color or covered by rust, which gave a uniform patina to the disparate parts of the whole, and emphasized the decay of the discarded objects. More recently, in works such as *Number 77*, the artist chose to leave the objects unchanged, adding to the tension between the chaos of the vast number of interacting objects and the grid-like pattern in which they are carefully arranged. In his collaboration with the FW+M, Drew continued his investigation of collected objects, but instead of presenting the objects themselves, he made paper casts—thin shells or ghost forms of the original objects.

To create the installation, Drew collected over four hundred common objects— toys, furniture, appliances, and household wares—from thrift stores, junkyards, and off the street. With a large group of interns and staff, he cast each object in paper, removing the original object once the paper cast was created. They are hollow, nearly weightless forms that echo the original objects from which they were made more than they replicate them.

Drew's work has been described as "somber and full of memory" (Patrick Murphy, Royal Hibernian Academy, Dublin, 2001) and though *Number 80* is a departure from the darker tones of much of the artist's previous work, a contemplative mood still prevails. Instead of presenting the ongoing and transformed life of discarded objects, the installation takes us beyond the life of the object itself and portrays the ethereal essence of things that once existed.

Number 80, 2002 (detail). Paper. Dimensions vary with installation. Collection of the artist.

Number 80, 2002. Paper. Dimensions vary with installation. Collection of the artist.

Tom Friedman

American, born 1965, lives in Northampton, Massachusetts

About the artist

Tom Friedman lives in rural Western Massachusetts. He completed a BFA in graphic illustration at Washington University in St. Louis (1988), before going on to earn an MFA in sculpture from the University of Illinois at Chicago (1990). Since 1995, when the Museum of Modern Art, New York, featured Friedman's work in their *Projects* series, he has been the focus of many solo exhibitions, including a major show organized by the Southeastern Center for Contemporary Arts in Winston-Salem, NC (2000), which traveled to the Museum of Contemporary Art in Chicago, the Yerba Buena Center for the Arts in San Francisco, and the New Museum of Contemporary Art in New York, among other venues. In 1993 he was awarded The Louis Comfort Tiffany Foundation Award.

About the work

Tom Friedman's *Untitled* project, created with the FW+M, is the most recent of his self-portraits. Earlier endeavors have included a carving of his face on an aspirin pill and a full-body sculpture measuring five inches and carved from a block of Styrofoam.

Taken from a passport-size photograph, Friedman's FW+M collaboration is based on a mathematical formula by which 256 copies of this image were duplicated, dissected and re-configured to create an abstracted photographic self-portrait. Friedman used a similar technique to create two previous projects—a U.S. one-dollar bill and a cereal box. The images for *Untitled* were cut into 1/4-inch squares—33,072 pieces in all—based on a series of nearly imperceptible 1/64-inch deviations. One by one, they were then assembled to create a magnified, out-of-focus mosaic of the original self-portrait.

Friedman has said of the complexity involved in fabricating his work that it arises partly from his "inability to process everything that I'm confronted with and the idea of the whole . . . What unifies what I do is the phenomenon of taking something that is crystal clear to me, something I seem to know, and finding that the closer I get and the more carefully I inspect it, the less clear it becomes" (*Tom Friedman*, Phaidon Press Limited, London, 2001).

Untitled, 2001 (detail). Photographs, museum board, and adhesive. 60 x 40 inches (152.4 x 101.6 cm). Private collection.

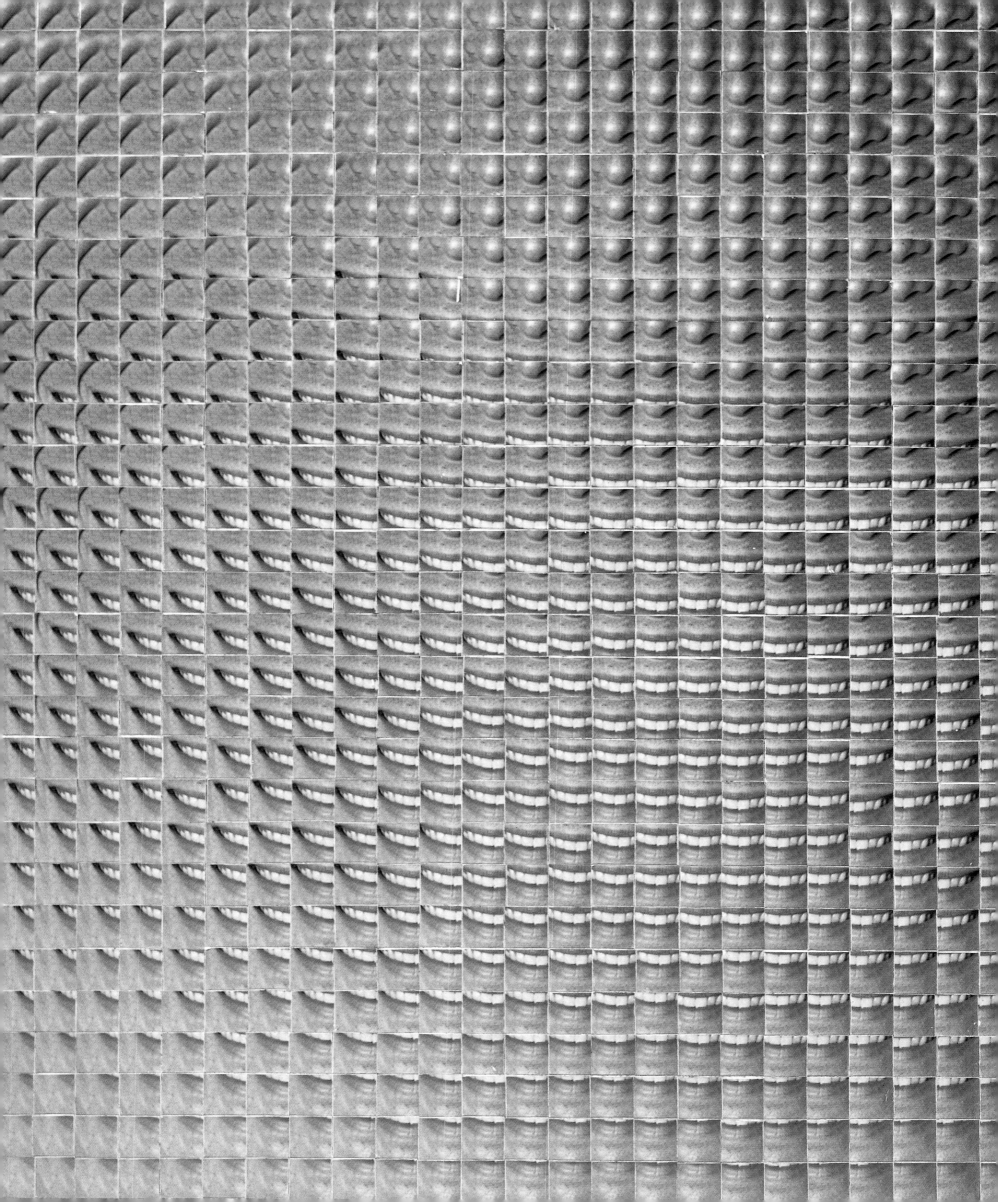

Passport photograph used to create *Untitled*, 2001 (above). 2 x 3 inches (5.08 x 7.62 cm).

Untitled, 2001 (right). Photographs, museum board, and adhesive. 60 x 40 inches (152.4 x 101.6 cm). Private collection.

Thelma Golden

About the author

American, lives in New York City

Thelma Golden is the Deputy Director for Exhibitions and Programs at The Studio Museum in Harlem. In 2001, she curated *Freestyle*, an exhibition she has described as a showcase of "postblack art" by a new generation of African American artists. Other curatorial projects at The Studio Museum include one-person exhibitions such as *Gary Simmons* (2002; organized with the Museum of Contemporary Art, Chicago); *Yinka Shonibare* (2002); and *Martin Puryear: The Cane Project* (2000). From 1988 until 1998, Golden held curatorial positions at the Whitney Museum of American Art in New York, organizing exhibitions such as *Black Male: Representations of Masculinity in Contemporary Art* (1994–1995); the 1993 Biennial (directed by Elizabeth Sussman); and numerous solo exhibitions at the Whitney Museum at Philip Morris, including site-specific commissions by Alison Saar, Romare Bearden, Lorna Simpson, and Jacob Lawrence. Ms. Golden earned her BA in art history and African American Studies at Smith College in Northampton, MA. She is a member of the Graduate Committee of the Center for Curatorial Studies at Bard College. Ms. Golden serves on the Artist Advisory Committee for The Fabric Workshop and Museum, and, in 1998, she curated *Cut on the Bias: Social Projects of the 90s from the Permanent Collection*.

Thelma Golden in Conversation with Glenn Ligon and Gary Simmons

I came to understand and even, perhaps, appreciate boxing late in life. My father was neither a boxing fan, nor a sports fan for that matter. He was an insurance broker by profession. He viewed any sort of knowledge in the area of sports as insurance for the inevitable black male bonding conversations that would come his way in the barber shop or wherever: "How about those Knicks?" or "Did you catch the fight?" and the like would allow him to participate without having any specific knowledge except, perhaps, that the basketball team that played in New York was called the Knicks, and, when he was home on Saturday night listening to his *Phantom of the Opera* soundtrack, that there may have been a boxing match. He, I think, was very conflicted about sports. He didn't like the fact that black progress was linked to physical achievement, or that the spectacle confirmed many myths about black men that he personally worked against. He had exceptions—Joe Louis, Arthur Ashe, Michael Jordan, and now Tiger Woods—but generally sports worship had no place in my home. For that reason, boxing did not inform my thinking about black manhood in America until much later.

Glenn Ligon (pp. 170–173) and Gary Simmons (pp. 260–263) arrived at the subject of boxing from two starkly different vantage points. Ligon is a text-based painter, Simmons a sculptor. Ligon is fascinated by the iconographic power of boxing within black American culture, while Simmons approaches it with the exuberance of a fan. Their work on boxing, however, participates in a shared history. In 1993, when Ligon and Simmons were offered the opportunity to work at The Fabric Workshop and Museum, both artists chose boxing as their subject independently of each other. Two years later, Paula Marincola organized an exhibition of their projects at The Fabric Workshop and Museum and the Beaver College Art Gallery, where she was then curator. Their pairing was so obvious it was almost irresistible. Here, after all, were two African American men reflecting on a sport inextricably bound to the idea of black masculinity in the American imagination.

One cannot come to these works and not explore the inherent clichés. The boxer personifies a vivid combination from the ongoing (and ever-expanding) catalogue of stereotypes of black men: violent, brutish, hyper-aggressive, savage. Boxing is the most brutal of sports. It's also one of the most spectacle-driven, presenting a kind of modern-day gladiatorial arena wherein poor, desperate men fight for the pleasure of mass audiences. The fact that most of the boxers are black and brown—and most live fight fans white—makes the sport even more profoundly problematized. The first thing we notice about these pieces is how savvy Ligon and Simmons are with respect to their subject. Both artists approach this situation knowingly, with an acute detachment and a sense that beyond the ring lies something bigger and wider than the clichés about machismo and bravery allow.

I am often drawn to images of boxing in art. They are among the most visceral representations of race we have in American culture, stripping away all the euphemisms that often veil the problem of the color line. Consider, for instance, George Bellows' 1909 painting, *Both Members of This Club*. It's an archetypal depiction of a black boxer and a white boxer in furious battle. The black boxer is fast overtaking his opponent, and Bellows vividly captures the blood and anguish of the match with his brush. According to the art critic Robert Hughes, Bellows originally intended to title the painting *A Nigger and a White*, a title eerily reminiscent of the grotesque street chant "fight, fight, fight, a nigger and a white." The painting was inspired by Jack Johnson's victory over Tommy Burns in 1908, which terrified white America while bringing hope to black Americans. Since Johnson's triumph, boxing has come to symbolize racial conflict, racial warfare, with uncommon bluntness and force.

These days, fights between black boxers and "great white hopes" are far less common than fights between black and brown men. The fights are shorter and shorter, and the monetary stakes are higher than ever, with astronomical prizes for the winners. Yet there remains a bleak, private side to this public spectacle of desperate black men brawling with one another in stadiums. As writer and cultural critic Hilton Als observed, boxing is "the public acknowledgment of the private drama, becoming a symbol before you've become a person, which is what being a black man in America can mean, knowing what you might mean for other people before you know yourself."

Simmons' *Step in the Arena (The Essentialist Trap)* is not his first work about

Reprint of select pages from
Glenn Ligon and Gary Simmons,
published by The Fabric Workshop
and Museum, 2000.

boxing. His 1993 piece, *Everforward* . . . features a pair of sumptuously produced white leather boxing gloves. It's an ironic and somewhat grim appropriation of the ubiquitous Everlast™ (i.e., "made to last forever") logo. Using the Everlast™ typeface, Simmons embroidered "Everforward" on one glove and "Neverback" on the other— signs of the prodigious hopes, all too often dashed, that young black men invest in their gloves. The logo is embroidered in white; it can hardly be seen on the white leather. Once discerned, it's all the more cutting.

Ligon's first depiction of boxing was a 1993 sculpture made in collaboration with the painter Byron Kim, *Rumble, Young Man, Rumble*. In the work, Ligon and Kim took a punching bag and stenciled it with a quotation from *The Greatest*, William Klein's documentary about Muhammad Ali. The title of the piece was coach Bundini Brown's exhortation to the practicing Ali in the film. Ligon and Kim were interested in the way Ali talked himself up (and his opponents down), the way he made himself into a legend by his verbal extravagance, and his florid and seductive self-flattery. Stenciled around the bag in Ligon's signature style, sure enough, was a dizzying spiral of Ali's sayings that left you off balance if you tried to follow it.

Ligon and Simmons share a similar passion for boxing which inspired their respective Fabric Workshop and Museum projects. When these works were originally shown together, it was clear how similarly and, at the same time, how differently this passion manifests itself. Both artists examined the sport through the complexities of race and identity, and created works that also expanded their individual working processes. For Ligon this project was a headlong move into three-dimensional work, a direction he still pursues in the context of his painting practice. *Step in the Arena* saw Simmons meld his sculpture and his drawing into a seamless whole. Viewed together, these two highly personal works open a very vital public dialogue about the difficult and ambiguous place that exists between race, professional sport, and identity.

(The following interviews were conducted in 1999 in New York City.)

Interview with Glenn Ligon

Thelma Golden: When did your interest in boxing begin?

Glenn Ligon: I don't really remember when I became interested in boxing. I don't think I became interested in boxing outside of any other sport spectacle until I was a teenager. I wasn't at all interested in sports, though I knew of the famous fighters and certainly knew and admired Muhammad Ali.

TG: When did boxing enter your artwork?

GL: It came into my work at the time I made the Mapplethorpe piece, in 1991, titled *Notes on the Margin of the Black Book.* I was making a series of works dealing with masculinity. This seemed to be another arena in which I could continue this investigation. Actually, I was most interested in Ali as a persona and a public figure and this role he had in his prime of being a spokesperson for the black community, than I was interested in him as an athlete. The sport also entered my work because boxing encompassed so many issues. Boxing is the space of hyper-masculinity. It engages notions of sexuality and relies on the mythology of the brutish black man. Prowess in boxing generates respect despite coming primarily from the physical use of the body. It shows the ambivalent relationship white Americans have to black bodies. All of that is in there. I am attracted to the complicated fact that, on one level, black people were brought here and subjugated for the physical labor of their bodies. On another level, Ali becomes a public persona who is respected, listened to, and admired based on his achievement as a fighter, which is based on this same physicality. This admiration allowed him to transcend the stereotypes. This was rather unique. Mike Tyson, for example, does not have that same effect.

TG: Why?

GL: Because Tyson fits too much into the cultural stereotype of what a black man is. Tyson is a thug. And he always presents himself that way. Ali had the same kind of physical skill but he presented himself as a highly principled man. Tyson does not.

TG: Is this why you chose to conflate hip-hop culture and boxing in your installation *Skin Tight*?

GL: Yes. I was interested in rappers who were using hip-hop as a means of social critique, which, to me, was very related to what Ali had done. Some of the old-school rappers, Public Enemy and KRS-1 especially, were using their platform to speak in a similar way. The thought process of certain rappers seemed to be: "I'm in this position, so how do I use this position? Do I reproduce the cultural stereotypes? How do I use this space I've created as platform to speak about other political agendas?"

TG: Are you interested in any other sports in relation to these issues?

GL: No.

TG: Football? Basketball?

GL: No, though basketball is another way you could tackle some of these issues. Basketball would allow a discussion of race and class, but with boxing you also have sexuality. The erotic is so much more heightened or hyped in boxing.

TG: It seems that this is the subtext for you, this interest in the erotic.

GL: Eroticism is ever-present. There is a quote from George Plimpton in his writing about Ali where he says Ali glowed. He meant it, perhaps, in an asexualized way, but the subtext is sexual. This speaks to the kind of desire around boxers, the sense of the physical strength also being a kind of hyper-attractiveness.

TG: What does it mean then, talking about boxing in the contemporary moment? Talking about black boxers?

GL: Boxing is a safe space. It is a controlled spectacle. People can satisfy their desire in a controlled environment. It is why, perhaps, Ralph Ellison chooses the boxing match as one of the opening sequences of *Invisible Man* as a way to explore the safety of what would otherwise be socially unacceptable. There are always spaces in the cultural arena where otherwise unacceptable behavior is sanctioned—behaviors and speech. Richard Pryor could say the things that he said because he was on stage doing comedy.

TG: He is not sitting in a boardroom with his colleagues.

GL: The culture creates these spaces where certain behaviors are acceptable for black men, where these primal contests can be watched and enjoyed by a white public without the threat of all of this ugly anger and aggression being aimed at them. Ali became truly dangerous after he converted to Islam and began to encourage other black people, through his words and his actions, to join Islam and to resist the Vietnam War. That's when Ali was truly dangerous.

TG: More dangerous than when he was a champion in the ring . . .

GL: That was when his actual power was apparent.

TG: How did you come up with the idea for *Skin Tight*?

GL: When I was offered the opportunity to work at The Fabric Workshop and Museum, I had already made a work about Ali with the painter, my friend, Byron Kim. That work was an actual punching bag with stenciled text. It was made from a real bag, and I thought that I could have my own bags made at the Workshop and silkscreen images and text onto them. So we began by buying a bag, taking it apart, and studying it in order to figure out how to make one. Then we experimented with different fabrics for the bags and figured out what to print on them and how to print it. There was a fair amount of experimentation, which is what was so amazing about working there.

TG: And its installation?

GL: After collecting all the raw material, I began to work on constructing the individual bags. The bag with the rapper Ice

Cube's eyes, for example, began with the image. I got the image from a St. Ides malt liquor advertisement. The format of the ad had the company logo above Ice Cube's eyes, incorporating this image of his eyes into their logo. I then appropriated the image and substituted it for the place where a logo would go on the bag. Each of the bags developed in this way. I kept playing with different ways of getting images and text onto the bags until I came up with the seven that made an interesting installation. I was interested in how they would fill a space and I think that also determined the format.

TG: All of the bags hang from the ceiling, as in life, except one, which is propped against the wall. Why?

GL: Because in boxing the bag is supposed to be your opponent's body. I thought some of the bags should reflect this in their design. Not only what was on them, but also how they sat in the room. That bag reflected the idea of the opponent punched out, sitting on the floor. That idea of the opponent also informed the black bag with the vinyl see-through pockets.

TG: I thought that one was S&M inspired.

GL: No. When you go to athletic stores some of the commercially produced bags actually have faces printed on them, literalizing this idea of an opponent. I felt that these bags were so overdetermined, so easily read that you could stick any image onto them. In a way you don't need an image but the idea that any image can go there and serve the same role—that bag provides a slot for that.

TG: In some ways you didn't venture very far from the complicated conventions already at work with these bags.

GL: No, I just heightened them. I didn't change very much about the bags from their real sources. I just strategically exchanged or replaced certain things. There was also heightened sensitivity to the issues of race and masculinity because the works exist in an art context and within the context of my body of work. They were within the realm of what people knew my work to be about.

TG: We read them through what we knew to be the intellectual and conceptual lineage of your work, and your replacements make the viewer more conscious. You're a painter and had been known, up to this point, for working two-dimensionally. Was this your first sculptural work?

GL: Almost. The collaborative piece with Byron Kim was the very first, but this was my first major sculptural work.

TG: What prompted this move into sculpture?

GL: There had always been a deep anthropomorphic aspect to my work. My early paintings, those based on Zora Neale Hurston's text *I Feel Most Colored*, were made on door panels, which were scaled to the human body. The Mapplethorpe piece was about the depiction of the black male body. There had always been the presence of the body in my work, though almost never literally represented. If the body was represented,

it was someone else's representation that I was commenting on. So when I made that first punching bag work with Byron, which was a sculpture, it came about in a very incidental yet important way: Byron had a punching bag in his studio.

TG: A real one?

GL: Yes, he used it. Byron boxed. He and Leonardo Drew (pp. 90–93) boxed together and Leonardo often knocked him out.

TG: So Byron is a technically proficient fan?

GL: Yes, very much so.

TG: And you never had a desire to go with them and spar and experience a bit of what you were making work about?

GL: No! [emphatically]

TG: So this bag was in Byron's studio?

GL: Yes, and whenever I was there I would see it. And when we began to make work for a project we were doing together for the AC Project Room, we began by thinking of things we had in common as the basis for the collaborative works we would make. Muhammad Ali was one thing we had in common. I mentioned to Byron how much of an Ali fan I was and Byron mentioned that he was too. Until then, this was something we did not know about each other. He was a fan as a point of rebellion. His parents told him Ali, the outspoken conscientious objector, was an example of what you were not supposed to be as an American. We shared an interest, but our approach to him was different. I came to Ali through text, through his words, whereas Byron came to Ali through boxing, through his actions. For the piece, I went back to the William Klein film *The Greatest* and stenciled a portion of the text on the bag. Essentially I didn't think of it as sculptural, I was just making a painting on this surface which was literally right in front on us.

TG: And that surface happened to be canvas.

GL: So the transition to sculpture came through the collaboration with Byron.

TG: What does the title of the project refer to?

GL: *Skin Tight*?

TG: Isn't that an Ohio Players song?

GL: Yes. [He sings] "You're a baad baad misuss wearing those skintight britches." I used that title because I thought it insinuated bodies and blackness and the conflation of bodies and those bags.

TG: For me it signals something grotesque and violent along those lines.

GL: Well, the action is grotesque and violent, normalized by existing in the realm of sport. And then at the same time, the physical spectacle can be utterly and amazingly transcendent.

TG: Have you made another work about boxing, or do you plan to?

GL: No, I don't plan to make any more work specifically about boxing. In the end, this work was really about a bigger investigation of masculinity, race, and sexuality, and that investigation continues in my work.

Interview with Gary Simmons

Thelma Golden: What was the first boxing match you remember seeing?

Gary Simmons: It was probably an Ali–Foreman match. I was probably 2 or 3 years old. I am sure it was on *Wide World of Sports*.

TG: With Howard Cossell?

GS: Yes.

TG: Is that how you became such a fan?

GS: Completely. Boxing, all sports, really, were a big part of my childhood. Also my father was an amateur boxer. He had what they called a "glass jaw," so he had to give it up.

TG: What is a "glass jaw"?

GS: It was like his Achilles heel. When someone punched him in the jaw that was it, he was down for the count.

TG: Did your father teach you how to box?

GS: No he didn't. He said you shouldn't make a hobby or a living out of someone beating you up.

TG: That was probably very good advice.

GS: But I was an athlete.

TG: And you remain a fan of many sports.

GS: Huge fan.

TG: When did boxing enter your work?

GS: As a student I made several works with indirect references to boxing. But the first work that directly referred to the sport was a sculpture titled *Fuck Hollywood* that I made in 1991. Boxing was something I had been thinking about for a long time. It had the ignition points for me to start dealing with issues that I wanted to examine in my work. The place boxing holds within African American culture is huge. That was an influence. It also contains many subtexts about class, race, masculinity, and prowess that I wanted to explore. I have also been deeply interested in the role that boxing plays as an exit from poverty and crime for young black men. There is a very interesting contradiction there.

TG: It is an exit, but one can enter something completely different.

GS: I am also interested in the historic, somewhat controversial aspects of the sport, the way in which black boxers have innovated the sport and the way the sport and the sports establishment have had to respond. Jack Johnson was such a phenomenal boxer that the rules had to be changed to acknowledge his skills. Like so many other black athletes, he redefined the sport. He has always been a big hero of mine. He and also, of course, Joe Louis.

TG: Jack Johnson's image appears in *Fuck Hollywood*. Was that piece all about heroes?

GS: No it wasn't. That piece was made from a group of shoeshine props and shoes like one would find in an old shoeshine parlor. Over each shoe is a shine towel and on each towel I embroidered an image of a character or person who com-

plicates the notion of black stereotypes either by defying them, like Johnson, or promoting them, like racialized Disney cartoon characters, or by using them, like Elvis Presley or Al Jolson.

TG: That work also was one of your earlier uses of shoes, which appear later in The Fabric Workshop and Museum piece.

GS: Shoes have always been a big part of my work, from the early sneaker pieces I made, to the incorporation of tap shoes later on. I am interested in shoes and sneakers as markers of identity. The use of tap shoes comes from my interest in tap dance, which has always been related to my interest in boxing.

TG: After *Fuck Hollywood* you made a multiple of a pair of boxing gloves that you subtly redesigned.

GS: That piece was created from real, custom-made white boxing gloves. I replaced the Everlast™ logo with, on one glove, "EverFoward" and, on the other, "NeverBack." That statement was both a conscious wordplay on the Everlast™ logo and an appropriation of a West Indian slogan I grew up with. It's a common saying: "Ever forward, never back." It means you should always look forward to the future and never back to the past. I also thought there was an interesting connection with the sentiment of that statement and the idea of boxing as this vehicle of social mobility.

TG: I know your sculpture *Us/Them*—two terry cloth bathrobes, one embroidered with "us," the other "them"—does not have an intentional reference to boxing, but I think there is an interesting reference in the way the text insinuates an opposition of some sort—us vs. them. When one thinks about the opposition between the races that this "us/them" could indicate, it brings to mind the racialized opposition in boxing movies, most of which present a battle between a black and a white fighter. Also, the way in which the piece is shown, with both robes on hangers and hung on the wall, is reminiscent of how boxing robes are displayed as souvenirs or mementos after the match.

GS: That's true. Those various connections were all there. Also I am very interested in boxing memorabilia. I have always wanted to get one of those "enter the ring" robes. The best of them are fabulous objects!

TG: When The Fabric Workshop and Museum approached you, how did you decide to make the boxing ring?

GS: The Workshop invited me to come down and visit their facility and to view their collection of past projects. After seeing the wide range of projects artists had done there, I was immediately interested in using fabric as a component of a larger project. I knew I didn't want to make yardage, because the possibilities there indicated that so much more was possible. I wanted to work on some ideas that, in the past, I hadn't figured out how I wanted to realize. I had thought of making a boxing ring before. When I got there I realized that a ring was essentially a fabric construction, so I began to develop this idea for the project.

TG: Your work has always involved a lot of complex fabrication.

GS: It has, but in this case, given the particular skills of the Workshop, I was actually able to realize what I had been thinking. I worked with Pam VanderZwan at the Workshop and she was completely focused on figuring out a way to get the piece made. The original drawing for the piece was made on a napkin at a coffee shop in the West Village. I knew the overall structure from the start. We discussed ideas and processes back and forth and she would take my ideas and propose ways to fabricate them. I would go down there with drawings and sketches for various aspects of the project and we would work them out.

TG: It sounds as if the research and development process was very collaborative.

GS: It was.

TG: The resulting piece, which you titled *Step Into the Arena (The Essentialist Trap)*, was a less-than-life-size boxing ring.

GS: It is quarter scale.

TG: Over the ring ropes there are tap shoes, and the ring floor is a silkscreen of one of your erasure drawings of a dance instruction pattern. This is a very interesting mix of elements. How do all of these elements relate to each other?

GS: All of these elements are related to boxing. It was my framework. The floor references dancing and the relationship between these two forms of entertainment. The boxers I most admire all have dancer-like styles. Like Louis and Ali, they would literally dance around the ring. That dancing was a method of avoiding the punch, but done very beautifully, very gracefully. A match with a boxer like that is like a partnered dance. When you see footage of Ali sparring he often had someone there "dancing" with him. The dance instruction pattern I used in that piece is for a waltz, and I was interested in this clash of two class-based or class-defined activities. I was also interested in the conventions of partnered social dancing—one person leads and the other follows. Using the chalkboard element allowed me to create the sense of movement and the flurry of the feet.

TG: Which is the effect you create with your drawings.

GS: My use of the tap shoes was also a way to talk about another form of entertainment, tap dancing mostly. Watching Savion Glover tap dance has had a profound effect on my thinking about tap and the visual qualities of movement. His style is so unique that when I watch him dance, it is almost impossible to see the exact movement. Again, it is this flurry. I placed the tap shoes across the ropes to mimic the way gloves are casually thrown across the ropes after a fighter finishes a match. I found that casual placement very striking. It also is reminiscent of the way in urban neighborhoods kids throw their old sneakers over the telephone wires.

TG: Why?

GS: There are different reasons. When I was growing up this was done as a way to mark getting a new pair or as a way to taunt another kid by throwing his shoes up there out of his reach. In Los Angeles it is a way to mark the beginning and the end of various gang or drug territory. It is a culturally specific act.

TG: You have said that your practice has been inspired by minimalism. How does that play out in this work?

GS: I was influenced by both conceptually driven and formally driven art practices. I was interested in the structures of minimalism and wanted to infect the coolness of the discipline with the heat of my content. I was also interested in the shape of the ring and the resonance with a cube.

TG: It is also like a stage.

GS: A boxing ring is a stage. I am very interested in the entertainment aspects of boxing. Boxing used to be entertainment because of the skill of the boxers and the drama of the matches. Now boxing, unfortunately, is entertainment in the mode of the World Wrestling Federation.

TG: The title of this piece, *Step Into the Arena*, is a song by the rap group Gangstarr. Many of your works are titled after hip-hop songs.

GS: Most, and most after Gangstarr songs. The title of the song is a challenge. It refers to the kind of provocation that happens in break dancing and rap when one challenges someone to a battle.

TG: The title also has a subtitle, *The Essentialist Trap*.

GS: That was a reference to how I knew some people would read the piece.

TG: Misread?

GS: Yes! Misread.

TG: Were you making a statement about the way in which you knew, as a black man making work about the issues and symbols of boxing, how this would be narrowly read.

GS: Yes. I knew I would be essentialized.

TG: But you worked with the ideas anyway?

GS: Because I want to re-empower these symbols, these ideas. I want to move beyond the stereotypes that condition the reading of me and my work. I want to make viewers question and examine their reactions to the piece.

TG: So you are challenging your critics to a fight, in a way. And you think you are going to win?

GS: I always win.

TG: Do you think you will make other work about boxing?

GS: Yes, because the sport is a passion for me. My interest is not entirely conceptual. It is because the sport is part of my life and because of this it will appear and reappear in my work.

Felix Gonzalez-Torres

About the artist

American, born Cuba 1957, died 1997

Felix Gonzalez-Torres was born in Cuba and grew up in Puerto Rico. In 1979, he moved to New York City, which became his home. He attended the Whitney Museum's Independent Study Program in 1981, before completing his BFA at Pratt Institute in Brooklyn, NY (1983), and a MFA at the International Center for Photography at New York University (1987). For many years, Gonzalez-Torres was a leading member of the political art collective Group Material (1987–1992). With the sensibility of a poet, Gonzalez-Torres built his career on making works of art from benign materials—stacks of paper, strings of lightbulbs, plastic beads, candy, and photographs of clouds—that he transformed into delicate artistic interventions into contemporary culture. His work has been the subject of numerous solo exhibitions, including a major show at The Solomon R. Guggenheim Museum in New York (1995), and a traveling show organized by the Museum of Contemporary Art, Los Angeles (1994), with additional stops at the Hirshhorn Museum and Sculpture Garden in Washington, DC, and the Renaissance Society in Chicago.

About the work

In late 1993, Felix Gonzalez-Torres agreed to inaugurate the FW+M's then-new space at 1315 Cherry Street with an exhibition of new and selected works, chosen by the artist and placed in both prominent and discrete locations throughout the largely unfinished offices, studios, and exhibition spaces. To mark the occasion, Gonzalez-Torres extended his series of sheer blue curtains (*"Untitled" (Loverboy)*, first made in 1989) and created a text portrait of the FW+M, which poetically chronicled significant milestones in the FW+M's history as well as major cultural or world events with connection to the museum. The resulting exhibition—which also included pieces such as *"Untitled" (Orpheus Twice)*, *"Untitled" (Last Light)*, *"Untitled" (A Corner of Baci),* and *"Untitled" (Perfect Lovers)*—was not only a significant showing of Gonzalez-Torres' work, it was also a sensitive introduction to the FW+M's new home for the museum's public.

The materials of Felix Gonzalez-Torres' work are minimal, and often involve repetition—*"Untitled" (A Corner of Baci)* (see p. 46), for example, is a pile of chocolate, available to visitors to eat and enjoy, and the installation instructions give specific directions to maintain the pile at 42 pounds. While the pile shrinks on a daily basis with the appetite of each passing visitor, it is later restored to its full size. This piece, like many of Gonzalez-Torres' sculptures, is reconstructed with each installation; that is, the candy is purchased and the piece reconstituted each time the piece is shown. In 1993, Gonzalez-Torres said that " . . . all these pieces are indestructible because they can be endlessly duplicated" *(Felix Gonzalez-Torres,* A.R.T. Press, Los Angeles and New York*,* 1993*).* Inherent in his enigmatic and poetic works of art are questions about context and meaning, the nature of authority and power, and ideas of beauty and loss.

Text for *"Untitled" (Portrait of The Fabric Workshop, a gift to Kippy)*, 1994. Private collection.

"I have a dream..." 1963 Nylon 1939 washing machine 1907 "E.T." 1982 horse hair 1993 T.V. 1926 vacuum cleaner 1901 Watergate 1972 Dirt 1988 Operation Desert Storm 1991 no kitchen 1994 CNN 1980 Will Stokes Jr. 1974 K.O.S. 1989 Civil Rights Act 1964 WPA 1935 a loss 1994 NEA 1963 Louise came, and stayed 1992 MTV 1981 Peace Corps 1961 telephone 1876 Donald's Flag 1991 the sewing machine 1829 Salsa 1991 Bob's birthday 1993 moving 1988 moving again 1993 Fabric Workshop founded by Kippy 1977 moonwalk 1969 streakers 1974 VCR 1978 Poland 1939 x-rays 1895 Black Monday 1987 Great Society 1965 Rosa Parks 1955 Moon Balls 1989 Apprentices 1977-1994 Collaboration 1977 The New Deal 1933 N.O.W. 1966 "Jaws" 1975 marshmallow sofa 1994 Mandela 1990 Reagan Empire 1980-88 "Dallas" 1980 Einstein 1916 blue curtains 1994 Cement 1989 first birds 1987 Mylar collection inventory 1992 Scott Burton 1979 the Berlin Wall 1961-1989 DNA 1953 photography 1839 Spirits 1992 camera obscura 1267 Oscar Wilde 1990 Kippy's dream 1977 Gandhi 1948 Vietnam 1973 I.Q. test 1917 Woodstock 1969-94 JFK 1963 4' x 8' 1992 Barbie Doll 1960 Electric Light 1879

"I have a dre

am…." 1963

"Untitled" (Portrait of The Fabric Workshop, a gift to Kippy), 1994 (detail, preceding pages). Paint on wall. Dimensions vary with installation. Private collection.

"Untitled" (Orpheus Twice), 1991 (above). Installation at The Fabric Workshop and Museum. Mirror. 75 x 55 inches (190.5 x 139.7 cm) overall. Each part: 75 x 25 ½ inches (190.5 x 64.77 cm). Private collection.

"Untitled" (Loverboy), 1989 (right). Installation at The Fabric Workshop and Museum. Blue fabric and curtain rod. Dimensions vary with installation. Private collection.

Installation at The Fabric Workshop and Museum, 1994 (left). Foreground: *"Untitled" (Last Light)*. 1993. 10 watt lightbulbs, plastic light sockets, extension cord, and dimmer switch. Dimensions vary with installation. Edition of 24. Private Collection. Background: *"Untitled" (Loverboy)*, 1989. Blue fabric and curtain rod. Dimensions vary with installation. Private collection.

"Untitled" (Perfect Lovers), 1987–1990 (above). Installation at The Fabric Workshop and Museum. Wall clocks. 13 $\frac{1}{2}$ x 27 x 1 $\frac{1}{4}$ inches (34.29 x 68.58 x 3.18 cm) overall. Each: 13 $\frac{1}{2}$ inches (34.29 cm) diameter. Edition of 3. Private collection.

© The Estate of Felix Gonzalez-Torres (all images)

Renée Green

About the artist

American, born 1959, lives in New York City

Renée Green was born in Cleveland, Ohio. She studied for a year at the School of Visual Arts in New York (1979–1980), before attending Wesleyan University and earning a BA in 1981. In 1990, she participated in the Whitney Museum's Independent Study Program in New York. Green's work has been the subject of numerous one-person exhibitions, organized by museums such as the Centre d'Art Contemporain-Kunsthalle, Fribourg (1996); The Museum of Contemporary Art, Los Angeles (1993); and the Institute of Contemporary Art, Boston (1990). Her work as a visual artist is enhanced by her equally important endeavors as a writer, social critic, and theorist.

About the work

In creating *Mise-en-Scène: Commemorative Toile* with the FW+M, Renée Green deftly utilized fabric and the silkscreen printing process to make a highly-charged yet surprisingly subtle commentary on social class, race, and aestheticism. Starting with a familiar historic, narrative fabric design—toile, an upholstery fabric first popularized in France in the 17th century—Green made small yet significant changes to the usual figural vignettes that characterize toile's highly decorative patterning. Specifically, Green replaced some of the original vignettes with images she discovered in the groundbreaking book *The Image of the Black in Western Art* (Harvard University, 1989). The benign and bucolic scenes from the original fabric are now side by side with scenes from antebellum America and colonial Europe.

The manipulated toile was then used to upholster chairs, settees, and chaise lounges, and to make wallpaper and drapes. Arranged as a stylized parlor, the installation is reminiscent of the period rooms found in museums. Alluding to domestic comfort more than actually attaining it, the installation's true nature is revealed in the images of the toile. Green has stated that the aim of her work is to "help people think about themselves in relation to different histories and alternative ways of seeing." In this case, her mise-en-scène, or stage setting, is a reminder of the simultaneous realities that comprised an historic period in our collective past—one that was passed down prominently in history books and through cultural artifacts, and another that was silenced.

Mise-en-Scène: Commemorative Toile, 1992 (detail). Pigment on cotton sateen. Width: 57 inches (144.78 cm).

Mise-en-Scène: Commemorative Toile, 1992. Pigment on cotton sateen upholstered furniture, and pigment on paper-backed cotton sateen wallpaper. Dimensions vary with installation.

Marie-Ange Guilleminot

French, born 1960, lives in Paris

About the artist

After studying at the Villa Arson in Nice (1980), Marie-Ange Guilleminot moved to Paris, where she continues to live and work. Her artwork has been exhibited throughout the world, with recent exhibitions in the United States at the Santa Monica Museum of Art (1999) and the San Francisco Art Institute (1999), and international exhibitions at the Hiroshima Peace Memorial (2000) and the Israel Museum (1995). Marie-Ange Guilleminot combines performance and object-making in her artistic practice, and her demonstrations of well-known forms such as *Life Hat* have taken place in venues as diverse as the rooftops of Jerusalem to the streets of Venice.

About the work

In collaboration with the FW+M, Marie-Ange Guilleminot created *Sea Urchin*, a sculptural object that, like many of her previous works, derives its meaning from its potential to be transformed. In this case, the simple materials of Tyvek® and rope are ingeniously designed to create a cape, pillow, skirt, parachute, and tent—the object can be transformed from one incarnation to the next by using the system of rope pulls, which are made functional by a series of sliding and end knots. The potential forms of *Sea Urchin* range from garment to shelter to mode of transportation, and *un geste*—a gesture—connects them to one another. Guilleminot's final touch was to apply a shimmering silver-blue metallic paint to the closed form of each *Sea Urchin*; in its virgin state the form glows discretely, yet once it is opened and transformed, it can never again return to this same pattern.

In 2000, Guilleminot exhibited *Sea Urchin*—in two sizes (120 cm in diameter and 400 cm in diameter)—at the FW+M as part of a larger show entitled *Nevers Hiroshima*. The exhibition brought *Sea Urchin* together with other works for which Guilleminot has become known. The first, *Transformation Parlor*, was originally shown at the 1997 Venice Biennale and involves a circular space of 4 meters in diameter in which visitors learn origami techniques. Specifically, participants are taught how to make the Tsuru bird, a Japanese symbol of hope and longevity which has become a symbol used to commemorate those who perished in the 1945 bombing of Hiroshima. The second project is *Hiroshima Collection* (1998), in which the artist remakes garments worn by victims on the day of the World War II bombing as a gesture of care and restoration. Guilleminot linked these works after one of her experimentations with *Sea Urchin* led her to float the parachute form to the floor; she watched as it opened and took on the shape of the mushroom cloud of Hiroshima.

Guilleminot's FW+M residency was undertaken in conjunction with the San Francisco Art Institute, where the artist experimented with the transformation of *Sea Urchin* with students, and created two videos of these performance dialogues, entitled *Dialogues– Sea Urchin, Ø120* and *Test–Sunday 31 October 1999* (1999). Guilleminot wrote about the videos: "These experiments with *Sea Urchin* exist as demonstrations against the use of atomic testing."

Marie-Ange Guilleminot with *Sea Urchin, Ø120cm*, 1999. Tyvek, rope, and pigment. 3 x 7 inches in diameter (closed) (7.62 x 17.78 cm). Unlimited edition.

Marie-Ange Guilleminot with *Sea Urchin, Ø120cm*, 1999 (left). Tyvek, rope, and pigment. 3 x 7 inches in diameter (closed) (7.62 x 17.78 cm).

Installation at The Fabric Workshop and Museum with *Sea Urchin, Ø400cm* in foreground, *Fold–Sunday 31 October 1999* (video projection) in background, 1999 (above).

Ann Hamilton

American, born 1956, lives in Columbus, Ohio

About the artist

Ann Hamilton studied textile arts at the University of Kansas, where she completed her BFA in 1979. She went on to earn an MFA from Yale University in sculpture in 1985. Her varied background in the visual arts informs her artistic practice, which takes the form of installations, videos, objects, and performance. Hamilton's work has been the subject of numerous solo exhibitions, including the Irish Museum of Modern Art (2002), Musèe d'Art Contemporain in Lyon, France (1997), and the Museum of Modern Art, New York (1994). In 1999, Hamilton was selected to represent the United States at the Venice Biennale. Her honors include a John D. and Catherine T. MacArthur Fellowship (1993), The Louis Comfort Tiffany Foundation Award (1990), and a Guggenheim Memorial Fellowship (1989).

About the work

The installation *tropos*, like all of Ann Hamilton's works, is a sensory experience. Created as a site-specific installation for Dia Center for the Arts in New York City, *tropos* refers to the idea of tropism, meaning a natural tendency, or a living being's proclivity to respond to stimuli in a specific way, such as a plant that grows towards light.

The installation is made primarily from horse hair—a vast landscape of varying shades of hair from the tails of horses covers the entire floor of the 5,000-square foot space. Hamilton altered the floor beneath the hair with poured concrete, the effects of which are subtle shifts in the floor's topography beneath the hair, which becomes clear only when a visitor walks across the room. Further on into the interior of the space, Hamilton has placed a small metal table, at which a seated attendant works diligently to burn the printed words from a book as smoke rises from the seared text. Muted, but audible, is a distant voice struggling to articulate words, which remain unintelligible for the most part. A final, subtle aspect of *tropos* is the sealed unity of the room, an effect created by Hamilton's use of translucent glass in the windows; light beams in, yet sight to the outside is precluded.

Like many of Hamilton's large-scale works, *tropos* was created by hand through the collaborative efforts of many individuals, both at the FW+M and Dia Center for the Arts. The community that evolves from labor-intensive production is an important component of Hamilton's methodology and artistic practice.

In 1994, after the completion of *tropos*, Hamilton created a second project with the FW+M. A limited edition multiple encased in a glass and wood vitrine, her *Untitled* project is a collar fabricated from linen and horse hair. Strands of horse hair were used to embroider a 16th century-style alphabet on the inside of the collar. The unfinished ends of the embroidered hair pass through to the exterior of the collar, forming a swirling, circular mass of hair. The object recalls historic relics—an Elizabethan ruff, for example—yet remains connected to sensory experience through its assumed placement around a person's throat with the letters of the alphabet resting near the voice box. *Untitled* references a relationship between the rapid growth of literacy and a gradual devaluation of non-verbal knowledge, such as that learned and experienced in the body.

Untitled, 1993 (published in 1994) (detail). Horse hair, linen, and antique buttons. 4 x 20 inches in diameter (10.16 x 50.8 cm). Edition of 12. Collection of The Fabric Workshop and Museum; Philadelphia Museum of Art; Whitney Museum of American Art, New York; Museum of Fine Arts, Boston.

tropos, installation at Dia Center for the Arts, New York, 7 October 1993–19 June 1994 (preceding pages, above, and facing page). Translucent industrial glass windows, gravel topped with concrete, horsehair, table, chair, electric buren, books, recorded voice: audiotapes, and audiotape player and speakers. Overall dimension: 180 x 1,128 x 1,080 inches (457.2 x 2,865.12 x 2,743.2 cm).

Mona Hatoum

About the artist

Palestinian, born Lebanon 1952, lives in London

Born in Beirut, Mona Hatoum was visiting London in 1975 when civil war broke out in Lebanon. Unable to return home, Hatoum remained in London to study and begin her artistic practice. She attended The Byam Shaw School of Art (1975–1979) followed by The Slade School of Art (1979–1981). Hatoum first became known for her highly personal performance pieces begun while she was a student, but her work has evolved to include video, installation, and sculpture. In 2000, Hatoum's work was featured in a one-person exhibition at the Tate Britain. In 1997, a mid-career retrospective, organized by the Museum of Contemporary Art in Chicago (1997), toured widely to venues throughout the world including The New Museum of Contemporary Art, New York; Museum of Modern Art, Oxford; and the Scottish National Gallery of Modern Art, Edinburgh. She was also included in the influential exhibition *Sense and Sensibility: Women Artists and Minimalism in the 90s* (Museum of Modern Art, New York, 1994).

About the work

Mona Hatoum used the opportunity of a residency at the FW+M to challenge a traditional form of textile production—the carpet—by creating two sculptures made from non-traditional carpet materials: stainless steel straight pins and silicone rubber.

Pin Carpet was made by pushing 750,000 pins through a needlepoint canvas—one pin for every other opening in the 4 x 8-foot canvas. Created face-side down, the final effect of the sculpture was not known until it was finished and then turned and placed on the floor. Its visual effect changes with the movement of light across its surface—at times it is a rich, dark abyss, at others, a reflective bed of shimmering white. *Pin Carpet* evokes a functional carpet, a prayer rug, and a fakir's bed of nails, suggesting the possibility of standing, kneeling, or lying down on this inhospitable surface.

Entrails relates to Hatoum's longtime interest in the human body, this time with a never-ending maze of intestine-like coils. Cast from silicone rubber (the same material used by Dow Corning Corporation to make breast implants), the glistening sculpture has the confounding ability to both attract and repel. Its elegant surface and mesmerizing pattern are visually and tactilely seductive, but equally apt to deter or even repulse once the identity of what is depicted becomes clear.

Entrails, 1995 (detail). Silicone rubber. 1 $\frac{1}{2}$ x 116 x 77 $\frac{1}{2}$ inches (3.81 x 294.64 x 196.85 cm). Edition of 3.

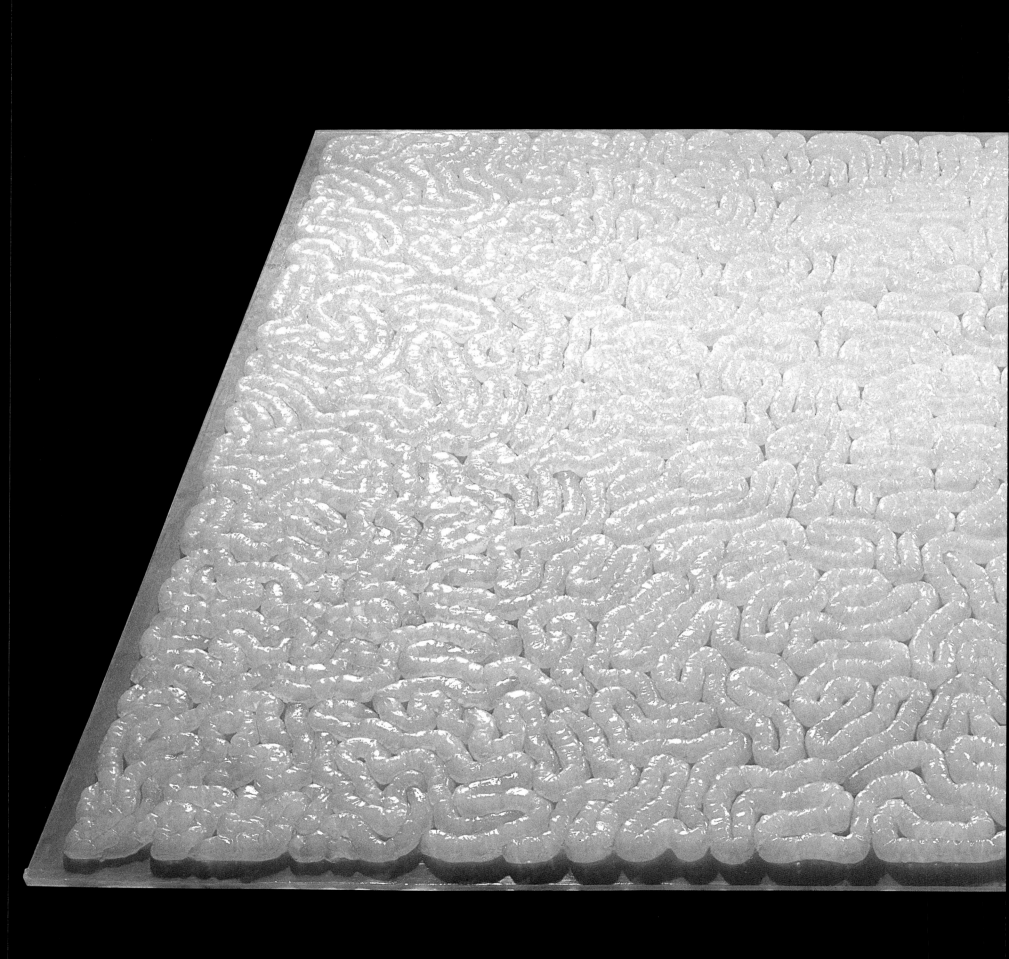

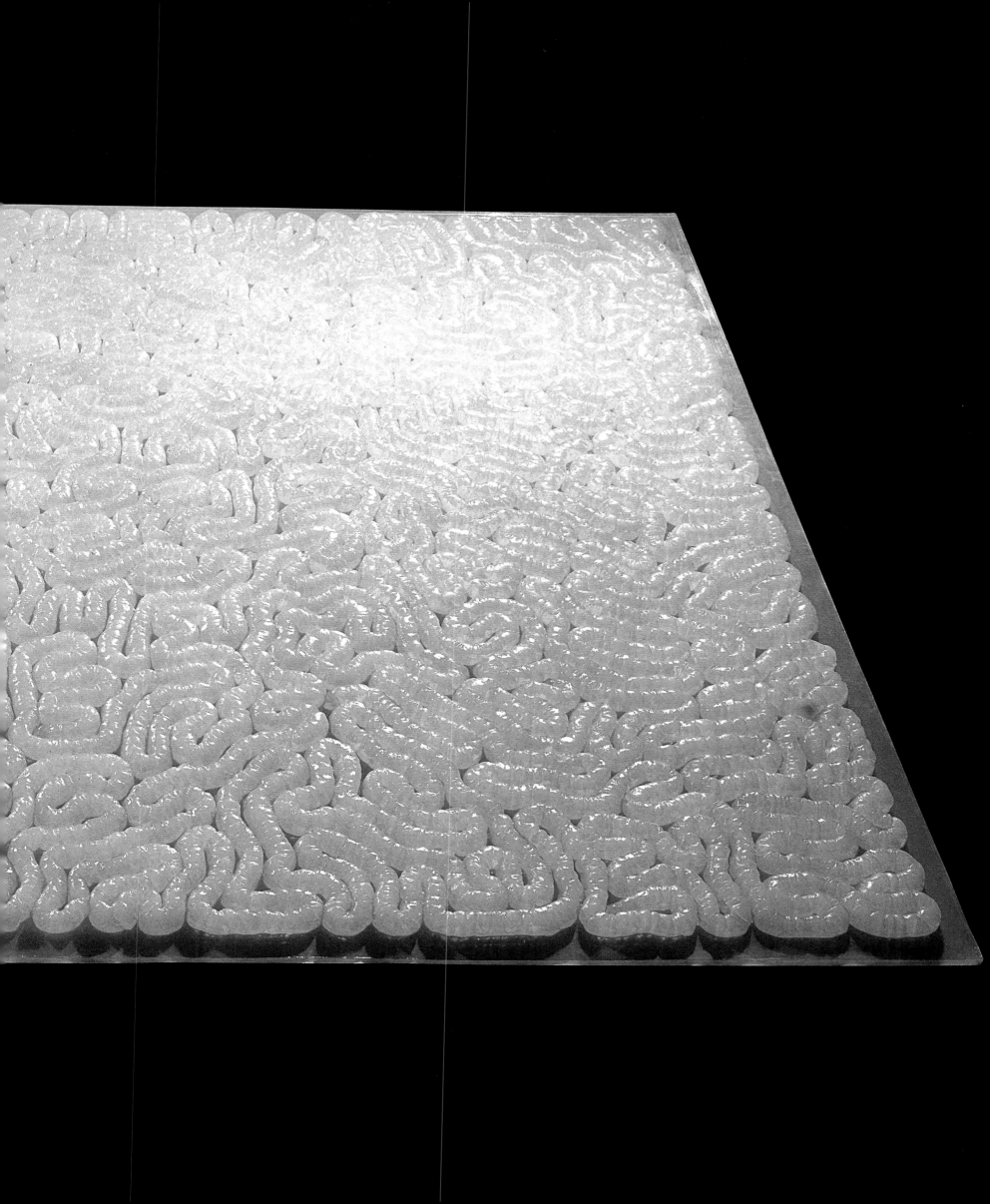

Entrails, 1995 (preceding pages). Silicone rubber. 1 ¹⁄₂ x 116 x 77 ¹⁄₂ inches (3.81 x 294.64 x 196.85 cm). Edition of 3.

Pin Carpet, 1995 (above). Stainless steel pins, cotton needlepoint fabric, and adhesive. 1 x 98 x 48 inches (2.54 x 248.92 x 121.92 cm).

Pin Carpet, 1995 (detail, right).

Jim Hodges

American, born 1957, lives in New York City

About the artist

Jim Hodges was born and raised in Spokane, Washington, where he also completed an undergraduate degree (BFA, Fort Wright College, 1980) before going on to earn an MFA from the Pratt Institute in Brooklyn, New York (1986). Hodges was trained as a painter, but soon after graduating from school, he began experimenting with ordinary materials (stemming partly from his lack of money at the time), such as paper clips, tarpaper, and dirt, believing that "the materials of art are all around us." He has become known for his sculptural work, sometimes monumental in scale, made from silver chain, broken mirrors or flower petals—ephemeral materials that offer symbolic associations in addition to their aesthetic attributes. Hodges' work has been exhibited widely throughout the United States and internationally, including solo exhibitions at the Miami Art Museum (1999), the Museum of Contemporary Art in Chicago (1999), the Institute of Contemporary Art in Boston (1999), and SITE Santa Fe (1997).

About the work

Introduced to the FW+M in 1994 by his friend and colleague Felix Gonzalez-Torres, Hodges completed *Every Touch* in 1995. This piece marks the first in his now well-known series of large, sculptural floral veils. The creative process involved selecting silk flowers, which were then deconstructed, ironed flat, and pinned to paper backing before being stitched together at the edge, where one petal touched the next. After the backing was removed, a lace-like cascade of petals and leaves remained, fragile yet powerfully seductive in its simplicity and beauty.

The bright and multi-colored *Every Touch* is a meditation on the many lives that brought the sculpture into being. Its title suggests the artist's acknowledgment of the numerous people who literally touched this piece during the course of its making—from the workers who fabricated the flowers, to the artist and his collaborative team of staff and students at The Fabric Workshop and Museum who made the richly-textured finished cloth through their careful handwork.

Hodge's returned to the FW+M in 1997 to create a second piece, entitled *You*. It differs from *Every Touch* in its striking, monochromatic color scheme—it is nearly all white with just a few splashes of color—and its conceptual intention. While *Every Touch* references the makers, *You* is made for everyone who views this piece.

You, 1997 (detail). Silk flowers and thread. 216 x 192 inches (548.64 x 487.68 cm).

Every Touch, 1995. Silk flowers and thread. 192 x 192 inches (487.68 x 487.68 cm). Collection of Philadelphia Museum of Art.

Howard Hodgkin

About the artist

British, born 1932, lives in London and Wiltshire

Howard Hodgkin attended the Camberwell School of Art, London, from 1949 to 1950, and the Bath Academy of Art, Corsham, from 1950 to 1954. One of the most prominent British artists of the postwar era, Hodgkin's paintings and prints have been exhibited steadily in England and around the world since his first one-person show in 1962 at Arthur Tooth and Sons in London. In 1995, a major exhibition of Hodgkin's painting was organized by the Museum of Modern Art of Fort Worth, Texas, and the tour extended to the Metropolitan Museum of Art in New York, and the Kunstverein für die Reinlande und Westfalen in Dusseldorf. A major exhibition of his prints was organized and shown at the Tate Gallery in London in 1985. Hodgkin was invited to represent his country at the 1984 Venice Biennale, and the selection of forty paintings eventually toured to venues in the United States and Europe, including the Phillips Collection in Washington, DC, and Yale Center for British Art in New Haven, Connecticut. Among Hodgkin's honors is his 1992 Knighthood, and the Turner Prize, awarded by the Tate Gallery, London, in 1985.

138

About the work

Howard Hodgkin participated in a residency at the FW+M in 1991. He painted a brightly-colored watercolor on rag paper, which served as the basis for a silkscreen printed scarf, made with acid dyes on silk. Hodgkin's abstract design involves distinct swatches of saturated blue and gold, covered with a web of overlapping and clustering lines of bright red. The plane of the red also covers and extends beyond a painted black border, reminiscent of Hodgkin's style of painting over frames, which gives a sense of protection to the interior of the piece. There is ambiguity in the surface and depth of the watercolor, as in the final silkscreen print. Each color of the artist's original watercolor was separated and made into its own silkscreen, coming together only in the final print when all colors were layered to recreate the original design. As a scarf, the dramatic gesture of Hodgkin's watercolor is further accentuated by the printed version's soft fold and drape when worn on the body.

While Hodgkin is often labeled an abstract painter, he has countered this idea, saying: "I am a representational painter, but not a painter of appearances. I paint representational pictures of emotional situations" (*Howard Hodgkin*, Thames and Hudson, London, and Harry N. Abrams, New York, 1994). The specific references in Hodgkin's work are left to the imagination of the viewer to determine, and paintings are often based on the artist's memory or experience of a place or a person. He describes the process of painting:

> *I start out with the subject and naturally I have to remember first of all what it looked like, but it would also perhaps contain a great deal of feeling and sentiment. All of that has got to be somehow transmuted, transformed, or made into a physical object and when that happens, when that's finally been done, when the last physical marks have been put on and the subject comes back—then the picture's finished and there is no question of doing anything more to it. (Howard Hodgkin: Forty Paintings: 1973–84*, George Braziller, Inc., New York, in association with the Whitechapel Art Gallery, 1984*)*

Untitled, 1991 (detail). Acid dyes on silk. 50 x 50 inches (127 x 127 cm). Edition of 50.

Untitled, 1991. Acid dyes on silk. 50 x 50 inches (127 x 127 cm). Edition of 50.

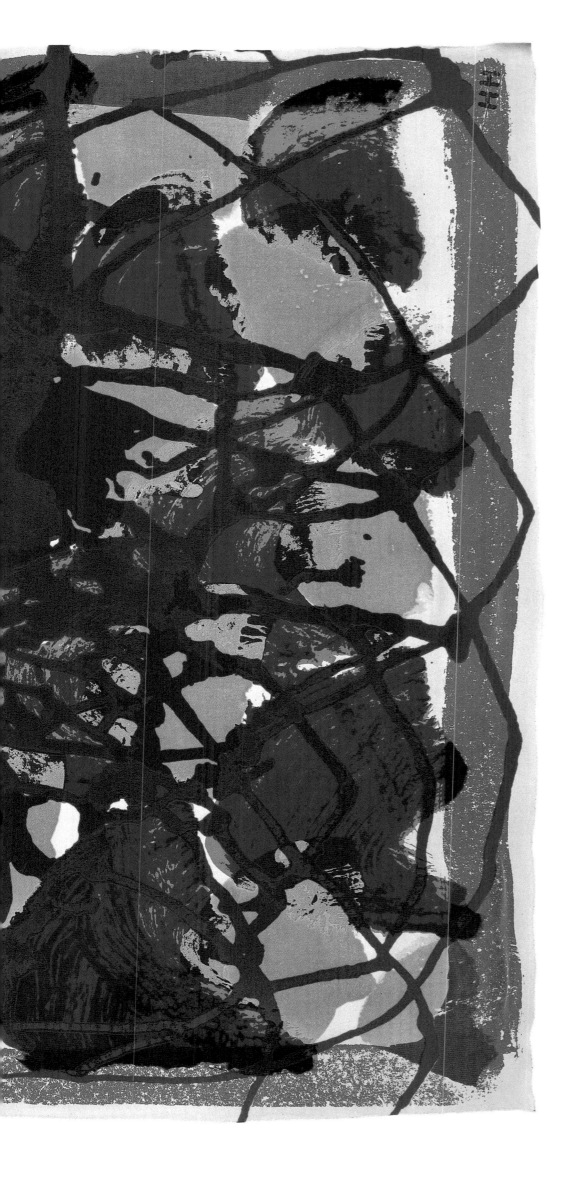

David Ireland

American, born 1930, lives in San Francisco

About the artist

David Ireland was born in Bellingham, WA, and began his undergraduate studies at Western Washington State University (1948–1950) before moving to San Francisco to complete his degree at the California College of Arts and Crafts (BA, 1953). He traveled extensively and ran a gallery for African art before returning to graduate school, first at Laney College in Oakland, CA (1972–1974), and then at the San Francisco Art Institute, where he earned an MFA in 1974. Ireland's philosophy can be summed up by an early poster he printed with the text, "You can't make art by making art." It is the concept and intention behind artmaking that has interested Ireland, and he has made the most unremarkable and humble materials (dirt, concrete, tar, bits of paper) his media of choice. He is best known for transforming a dilapidated house in San Francisco into an ongoing "social sculpture," working for nearly three years to clean and then preserve the abstract patternings of glue-stained walls, making sculpture from debris, and generally performing everyday actions with the intention of an artist and performer. Ireland's work has been the subject of many one-person exhibitions, including shows organized by the Center for the Arts at Yerba Buena Garden in San Francisco (1996), the Walker Art Center in Minneapolis (with Ann Hamilton, 1992), the Hirshhorn Museum and Sculpture Garden in Washington, DC (1990), and the Museum of Modern Art in New York (1988).

142

About the work

During the month of February 1989, David Ireland was "in residence" in the galleries of the FW+M. Titled *In Studio*, the project was part installation and part performance as the artist and the FW+M constructed a large muslin tent in the gallery for Ireland's use as a working studio. Windows were made so viewers could witness Ireland's creative process.

Ireland gathered materials from the refuse of an out-of-business textile manufacturing company located in the same building as the FW+M—materials seemingly lacking in aesthetic content such as metal tables, old lockers, pieces of wood, and metal rods. Surrounded by bags of opened gravel mix and makeshift tables, Ireland cast and molded concrete into sculptural forms, creating assemblage sculptures from this combination of found objects and concrete.

Table of Chunks, for example, is a metal table on top of which sits a careful arrangement of concrete "chunks," the casts of corners, stairs, and other architectural spaces in the building. *Cascade* combines a small table and a metal pitcher, which are dramatically lit by a single metal floor lamp. This still-life arrangement has a humorous undercurrent: concrete appears to pour out of the pitcher, though placed upright as it is, this gesture defies gravity.

During the course of his residency, Ireland also fabricated a series of *Dumb Balls*, made by tossing a handful of wet concrete back and forth from hand to hand over many hours until it hardened. For the FW+M's exhibition brochure (1989), Ireland said about his work:

> I call myself a non-media installation artist. I prefer to explore without any end or purpose in sight, an active inquiry on an architectural scale. I just live my life and my art occurs in the process.

Dumb Ball, 1989. Concrete. Dimensions vary (approximately 4 inches (10.16 cm) in diameter). Unlimited edition.

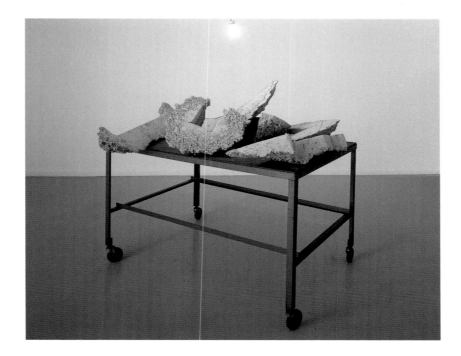

Cascade, 1989 (left). Metal, concrete, wood, and light. 77 x 45 x 26 inches (195.58 x 114.3 x 66.04 cm). Collection of the artist.

Table of Chunks, 1989 (above). Cement, masonite, and metal. 48 x 60 $\frac{1}{4}$ x 36 inches (121.92 x 153.04 x 91.44 cm). Collection of the artist.

Anish Kapoor

British, born India 1954, lives in London

About the artist

Anish Kapoor was born in Bombay, India, into a family of mixed cultural heritage—his mother is Jewish, his father Hindu. He moved to London in 1973 to study at the Hornsey College of Art and the Chelsea School of Art, from which he graduated in 1978. He has made London his home since that time. One of the leading sculptors to emerge on the British art scene in the 1980s and 1990s, Kapoor is known for his enigmatic forms that engage philosophical opposites—darkness and light, presence and absence, male and female—to evoke a physical and emotional response from the viewer. He deftly responds to his chosen materials, drawing forth essential qualities that heighten the physical presence of his sculpture; Kapoor has been equally at home working with marble, fiberglass, and stainless steel. In 1991, Kapoor won the prestigious Turner Prize, awarded by the Tate Gallery, London, and in 1990, he was selected to represent Great Britian at the Venice Biennale and was honored with the Due Mille Prize. His work has been exhibited internationally at the Hayward Gallery in London (1998), Musée d'art Contemporain de Bordeaux (1998), Tel Aviv Museum of Art (1993), and the Tate Gallery, London (1990).

About the work

Anish Kapoor collaborated with the FW+M to explore the possibilities of felted and woven wool—both handmade and industrially-produced. Although the medium was entirely new to the artist, the resulting series of sculptures shares its overall aesthetic sensibility with the whole of Kapoor's oeuvre. Color and form are paramount, playing an allegorical role in communicating the sculptures' meaning. The color red, for example, is primary in Kapoor's work; through non-verbal cues, it denotes the intimacy of the body through associations with blood, sexuality, birth, and death. As three-dimensional objects, Kapoor's forms often use illusion to heighten the sense of depth or lend mystery to the piece. Curving, organic, sensuous shapes, the sculptures often evoke the human body, particularly wombs, navels, and phalluses.

Body to Body is formed by the artist's careful manipulation of layers of woven felt, supported in part by a fiberglass structure, which allows the hanging, bulbous form in the sculpture's center to hold its shape. The long, sensual drape of deep red felt spills onto the floor, pooled in rippled valleys of cloth. In *Untitled*, Kapoor transforms a large white square of industrial felt by simple twists, folds and turns, and then imbeds a red wool sphere in this undulating field of white.

The essence of Kapoor's artistic practice is to evoke a sense of mystery, or the experience of the sublime. In a 2000 interview on BBC radio, Kapoor explained of his work: "As an artist, I suppose that one of the things I'm working with is mystery. I sense also that we all have a deep need to believe. I think that process of wishing to believe is mysterious. It's one of the things I'm feeling my way towards" (*Belief*, BBC Radio 3, December 28, 2000).

Body to Body, 1997 (detail). Wool and fiberglass. 115 x 58 x 9 ½ inches (292.1 x 147.32 x 24.13 cm).

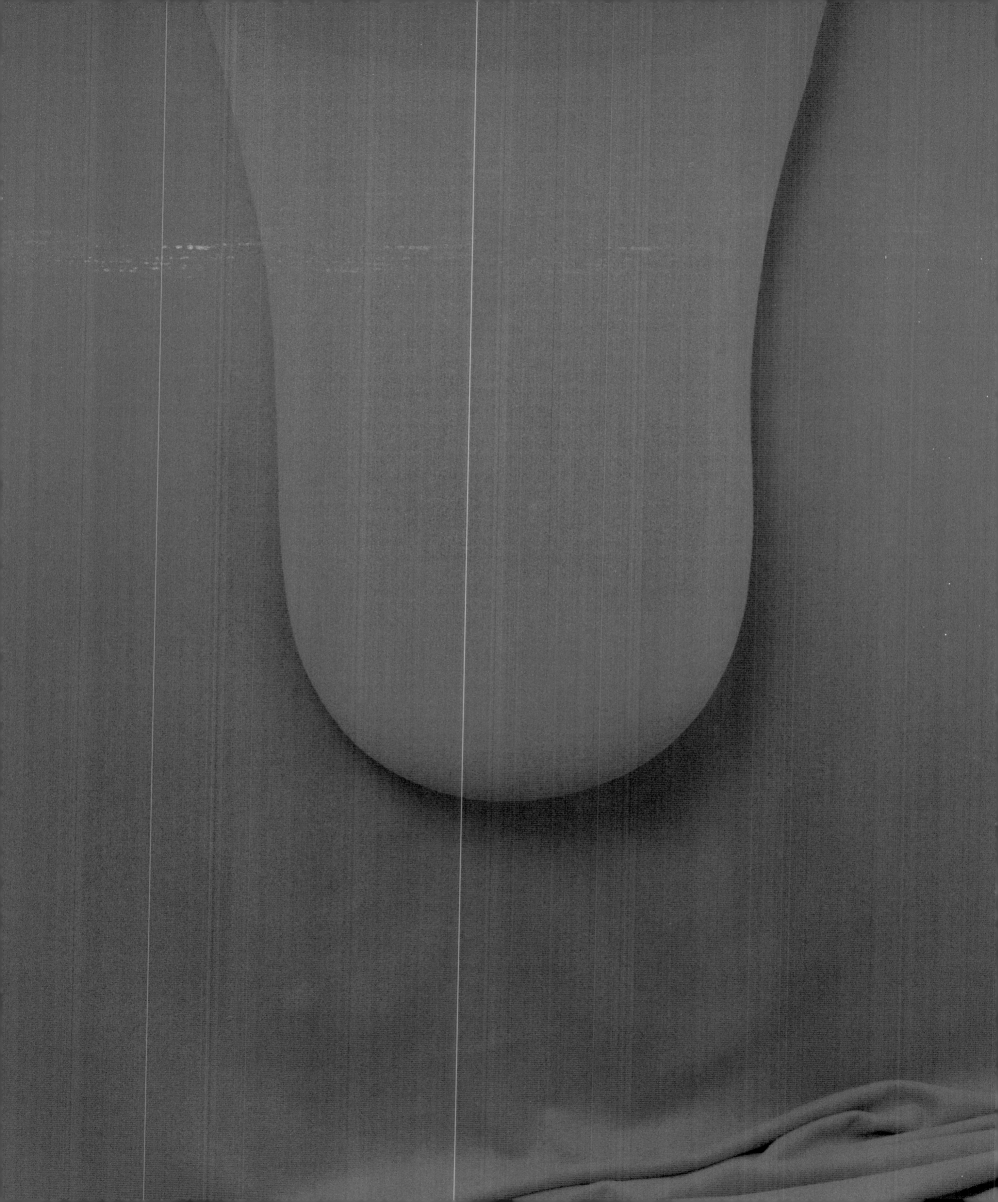

Body to Body, 1997 (left). Wool and fiberglass. 115 x 58 x 9 ½ inches (292.1 x 147.32 x 24.13 cm).

Untitled, 1997 (above). Felt, wool, and fiberglass. 54 x 114 x 29 inches (137.16 x 289.56 x 73.66 cm). Collection of the artist.

Mike Kelley

American, born 1954, lives in Los Angeles

About the artist

Mike Kelley was born and raised in Detroit, Michigan, and attended the University of Michigan where he earned a BFA in 1976. He moved to California to pursue graduate school, studying at the California Institute of the Arts in Valencia (MFA, 1978). While still a graduate student, Kelley developed a performance style that would dominate his work until 1986 (when he stopped performing) in which he incorporated sculptural objects as props and demonstration pieces. The style of Kelley's performances and his subsequent sculptural works have been described as perverse and adolescent, and he himself has stated that the adolescent period interests him: ". . . an adolescent attitude is the attitude of the humorist, like somebody who knows the rules but doesn't see any reason to be involved with them." Kelley's work has been exhibited in major museum exhibitions, including shows at the Whitney Museum of American Art in New York (1993), the Los Angeles County Museum of Art (1993), Basel Kunsthalle in Basel, Switzerland (1992), and the Hirshhorn Museum and Sculpture Garden in Washington, DC (1991).

About the work

While in residence at the FW+M, Kelley created two large-scale knitted afghan installations, projects in keeping with his interest in craft materials during the 1980s and early 1990s. Entitled *Lumpenprole* and *Riddle of the Sphinx,* they employ a similar technique in their fabrication. The FW+M identified a studio at the Philadelphia College of Textiles and Science (now Philadelphia University) where artists are trained to operate computerized knitting machines, and Kelley's pattern for the room-size afghans was translated into panels of appropriate size for the machines to accommodate. The panels were then hand sewn together to form the finished pieces. For *Riddle of the Sphinx*, Kelley chose the gradation of hues based on color names that suggested the evolution of a day—"purple dawn" and "midnight" are two examples.

Like many of Kelley's previous works that incorporate worn toys and domestic objects, these two installations introduce the aesthetics of the artist's lower-middle class background through their association to handmade, knitted afghans. Kelley has said that this choice was intentional, though he doesn't want them to be interpreted as "exotic," but rather he wants "to present these 'poor' materials as text themselves" (*Mike Kelley,* Kunsthalle Basel, Basel, 1992).

Hidden beneath each afghan are objects, the outlines of which can be seen protruding through the knitted yarn—in *Lumpenprole*, stuffed animals are the covered forms, while in *Riddle of the Sphinx*, metal bowls are concealed. The bowls in *Riddle of the Sphinx* refer to the stages of man, as posed in a riddle to Oedipus: What walks on four legs in the morning, two at noon, and three in the evening?

Riddle of the Sphinx, 1991 (detail). Yarn and found objects. 360 x 156 inches (914.4 x 396.24 cm). Collection of Solomon R. Guggenheim Museum, New York.

Riddle of the Sphinx, 1991. Yarn and found objects. 360 x 156 inches (914.4 x 396.24 cm). Collection of Solomon R. Guggenheim Museum, New York.

Riddle of the Sphinx, 1991. Yarn and found objects. 360 x 156 inches (914.4 x 396.24 cm). Collection of Solomon R. Guggenheim Museum, New York.

Lumpenprole, 1991. Acrylic yarn and found objects. 240 x 384 inches (609.6 x 957.36 cm). Collection of Vienna Museum.

Lee Bul

About the artist

Korean, born 1964, lives in Seoul

Lee Bul earned her BFA in sculpture from Hong Ik University in Seoul (1987). She has become known for her sculptural and multi-media installations that explore trends in popular culture, themes of feminine identity, and science fiction fantasies such as her series of female cyborgs, which were included in the 1998 Hugo Boss Prize Exhibition at the Guggenheim Museum SoHo, New York. Organized by the FW+M and the San Francisco Art Institute, her one-person exhibition *Live Forever* traveled to numerous North American venues in 2002 including the Orange County Museum of Art in Newport Beach, CA and the New Museum of Contemporary Art, New York City. In 1999, Lee was selected to represent her country in the Korean Pavilion at the Venice Biennale. Other solo shows have been organized by Fukuoka Asian Art Museum in Japan (2000), Kunsthalle Bern in Switzerland (*Projektraum*, 1999), and the Museum of Modern Art, New York (*Projects* series, 1997).

About the work

Live Forever is a multi-media installation consisting of three karaoke pods in the form of futuristic race cars, and three original videos. This ambitious project continues Lee's investigation of karaoke, a form of entertainment that has been wildly popular in Asian urban centers for over a decade. Her earlier project exploring the subject was *Gravity Greater Than Velocity*, an installation first exhibited at the Venice Biennale in 1999.

Each karaoke pod in *Live Forever* was first carved in Styrofoam, which was then used to cast the forms in fiberglass. The interiors are upholstered in leather, and equipped with sound systems and a small video monitor that plays one of three videos—*Amateurs*, *Anthem,* or *Live Forever*—while the words of the chosen song scroll by. The enclosed pods are comfortable and private, allowing individual participants to sing their favorite song at full volume should they desire to do so. While the audio is not played outside the karaoke booths, the video and lyrics are projected onto the wall opposite each pod, a gesture that heightens the ambivalence between public and private that characterizes each participant's performance.

The exhibition of *Live Forever* was produced collaboratively with the FW+M and the San Francisco Art Institute. While the FW+M worked with Lee to produce the karaoke pods, the San Francisco Art Institute assisted the artist with the production of the video by the same name, filmed in the Tonga Room of the historic Fairmount Hotel.

Live Forever I, 2001 (detail). Fiberglass with acoustic foam, black leather upholstery, plexiglass, and electronic equipment. 100 x 60 x 38 inches (254 x 152.4 x 96.52 cm). Collection of the artist.

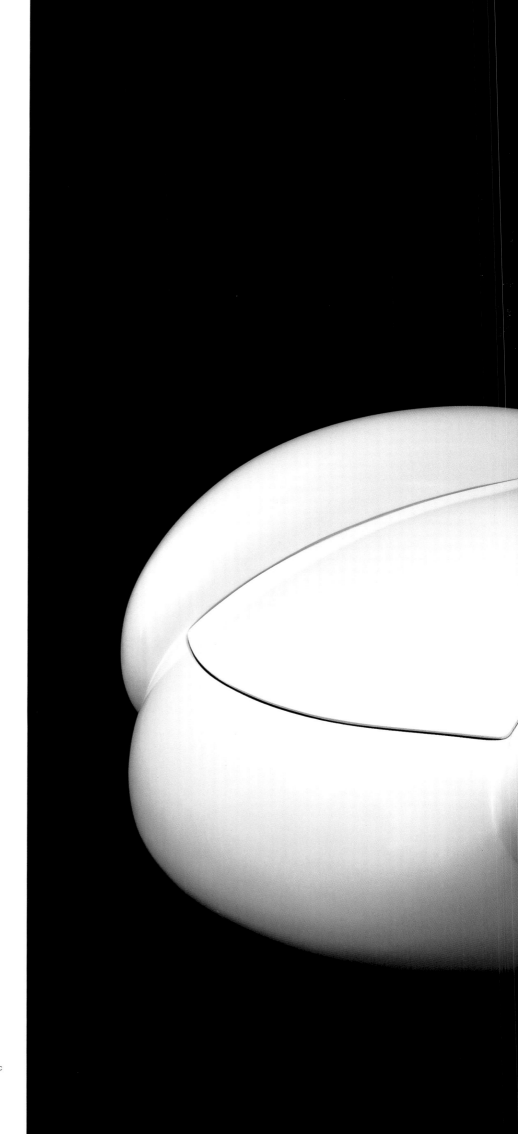

Live Forever I, 2001. Fiberglass with acoustic foam, black leather upholstery, plexiglass, and electronic equipment. 100 x 60 x 38 inches (254 x 152.4 x 96.52 cm). Collection of the artist.

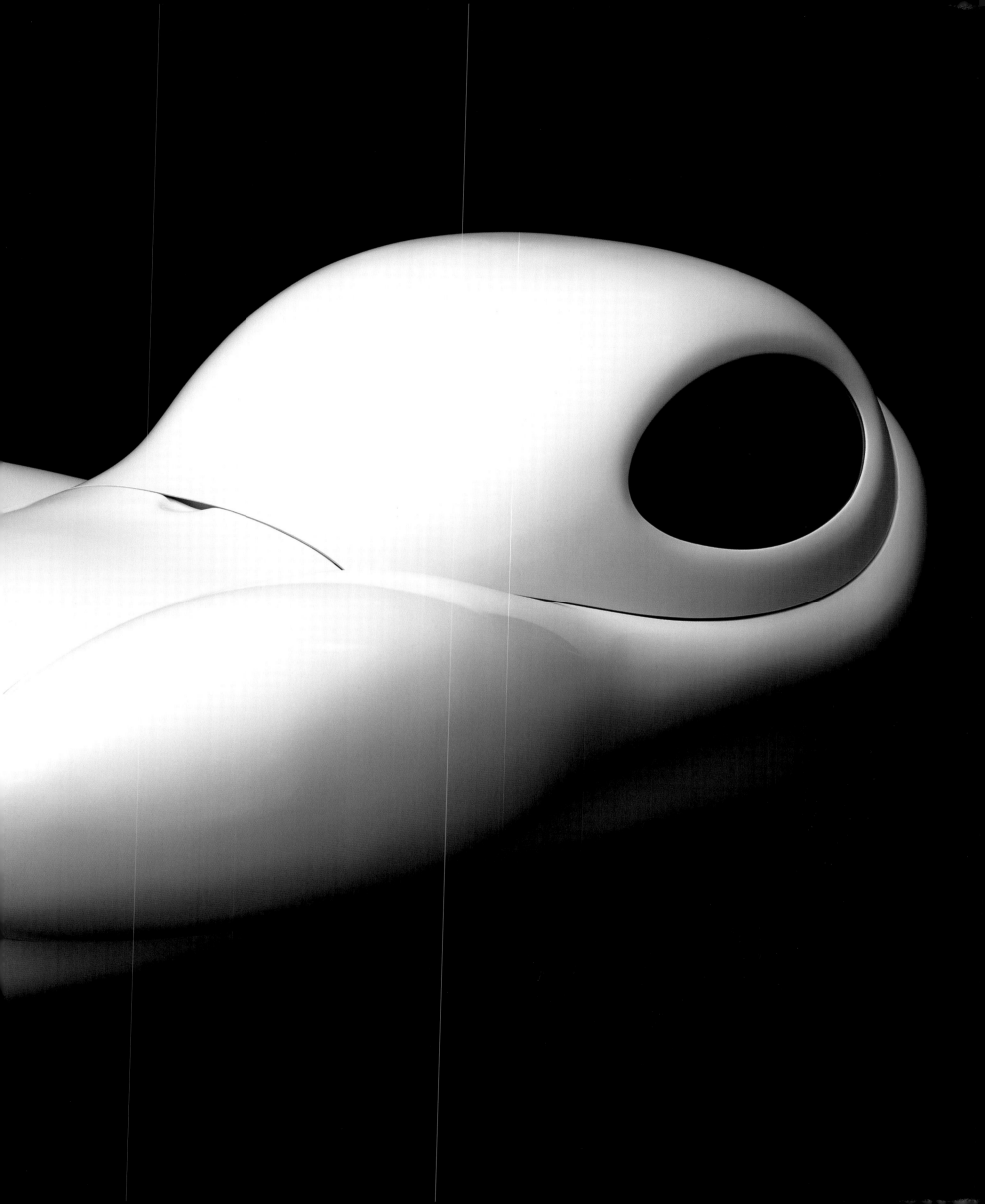

Live Forever installation at The Fabric Workshop and Museum, 2001.

Lee Mingwei

About the artist

Taiwanese, born 1964, lives and works in New York City
and San Francisco

Born and raised in Taipei, Lee Mingwei attended high school in
the United States before going on to earn a BFA from the California
College of Arts and Crafts in San Francisco in 1993, and a MFA
from Yale University in 1997. Lee was exposed from an early age to
Buddhism and to Catholicism, and both traditions find resonance in
his work. First known for his performance projects inviting strangers
to his home for dinner, Lee continues to focus on work that engages
members of the public in simple yet ritualistic acts, such as
conversing, eating, and writing letters. His first interactive project
was *Money for Art* (1994), in which he made nine small sculptures
from folded ten-dollar bills and gave them to strangers who agreed
to let him know the fate of the sculpture over the course of a year;
some kept the sculptures, one was stolen, and others used the
sculpture as cash to make a purchase. Lee has had one-person
exhibitions at museums such as the Museum of Contemporary Art
in Taipei (2001), the Isabella Stewart Gardner Museum in Boston
(2000), the Museum of Contemporary Art in Tokyo (2000), and the
Whitney Museum of American Art in New York (1998).

About the work

The Letter-Writing Project consists of three booths fabricated from wood and translucent glass. Subtly lit from within, a warm and inviting light emanates from the chambers. Inside each booth, the artist has designed a place for the viewer to stand, sit, or kneel—the three positions of meditation in Ch'an Buddhism. Viewers are invited to enter the booth of their choice and compose a letter to a person, either living or dead, reflecting on events that have inspired feelings of gratitude, insight or forgiveness— themes that correspond to the meditation positions. Completed letters are placed inside the booth for others to read, or they can be sealed in an envelope for privacy. During the exhibition, letters with addresses were mailed weekly, while all others were gathered together and kept by the artist. Lee currently has approximately 15,000 unsent letters, a number that continues to grow as the project is exhibited around the world. As most of these letters are written to the deceased, he plans to ritualistically release them from this world; at an appropriate time, Lee will place the letters on a series of paper lanterns, which will be set on fire as they float down a river.

In keeping with the tradition of Lee's work, *The Letter-Writing Project* finds its meaning in the interrelationship between art and spirituality. Lee creates an offering for those who come into contact with his work, including the opportunity for meditation, self-reflection, and re-awakening.

The Letter-Writing Project was first exhibited as two booths at the Whitney Museum of Art in New York as part of their "Contemporary Series" in 1998. The third booth was completed at The Fabric Workshop and Museum and exhibited there later in 1998.

The Letter-Writing Project, 1998 (detail). Wood and glass. Three booths: 114 x 67 x 91 inches (289.56 x 170.18 x 231.14 cm) each. Collection of Whitney Museum of American Art, New York, and the YAGEO Art Foundation, Taipei.

The Letter-Writing Project, 1998. Wood and glass. Three booths: 114 x 67 x 91 inches (289.56 x 170.18 x 231.14 cm) each. Collection of Whitney Museum of American Art, New York, and the YAGEO Art Foundation, Taipei.

Roy Lichtenstein

About the artist

American, born 1923, died 1997

Roy Lichtenstein was born in Manhattan, and grew up on the Upper West Side. He began his undergraduate studies in 1940 at Ohio State University, but was drafted into the U.S. Army in 1943. Sent to Europe in 1945, Lichtenstein returned home in 1946 and completed his BFA at Ohio State under the G.I. Bill. He continued his studies at Ohio State University, earning a MFA in 1949. From the time of his first one-person show in New York—organized by the Carlebach Gallery in 1951—Lichtenstein's work has been the subject of hundreds of exhibitions throughout the world. By the 1960s, Lichtenstein was actively involved in the Pop Art movement, and had developed his signature style, introducing comic-strip figures, followed by Benday dots, speech balloons, and lettering into his work. Inspired by everyday objects and consumerized American culture, his paintings and prints depict product packaging, stylized portraits and landscapes, and satirical renderings of other artistic styles and other artists' work. The Solomon R. Guggenheim Museum organized one major retrospective of Lichtenstein's work in 1969, and another in 1993, both of which traveled to many venues throughout the United States and, in the case of the second, Europe. His drawings were the subject of a major exhibition at the Museum of Modern Art in New York in 1987.

About the work

Roy Lichtenstein fashioned his 1979 *Untitled* shirt in collaboration with the FW+M and to benefit Artists Space, a not-for-profit visual arts organization in New York City. Produced as an edition of 100, the shirt was silkscreen printed with pigment on silk sateen and sewn into a basic shirt design, based on the artist's specifications.

A non-representational print, the design of the shirt is unmistakably Lichtenstein. His signature Benday dots, stripes, and palette of primary colors comprise the abstract composition of diagonal bands of red, blue, yellow, black, and white. Lichtenstein was sensitive to the functionality of a shirt, as the stripes of color wrap around the body, alluding to the three-dimensional, curving form of its potential wearer. Made from silk, the drape of the shirt, too, emphasizes the dynamic play of the diagonal bands of color, which ripple and flow at the slightest movement.

Untitled, 1979 (detail). Pigment on silk sateen. 30 x 36 inches (76.2 x 91.44 cm). Edition of 100. Commissioned by Artists Space, New York. Collection of The Fabric Workshop and Museum and the Philadelphia Museum of Art.

Untitled, 1979. Pigment on silk sateen. 30 x 36 inches (76.2 x 91.44 cm). Edition of 100. Commissioned by Artists Space, New York. Collection of The Fabric Workshop and Museum and the Philadelphia Museum of Art.

Glenn Ligon

American, born 1960, lives in New York City

Raised in the South Bronx, Glenn Ligon earned his BA in 1982 from Wesleyan University and later studied in the Whitney Museum Independent Study Program (1985). He is most known for his paintings of literary text, usually borrowed from pivotal African American writers such as James Baldwin and Ralph Ellison. His work has been exhibited widely throughout the United States, including one-person exhibitions at the Walker Arts Center, Minneapolis (2000); the Institute of Contemporary Art, Philadelphia (1998); and the San Francisco Museum of Modern Art (1996). Curator Thelma Golden included Ligon in her acclaimed 1994 group exhibition entitled *Black Male: Representations of Masculinity in Contemporary American Art*, organized for the Whitney Museum of American Art. For that exhibition, Ligon created a collaborative project with Byron Kim—a punching bag with stenciled text.

Skin Tight is Glenn Ligon's first major sculptural work. Building on his Whitney Museum project—a single standard-issue punching bag with stencilled text borrowed from *The Greatest*, a film about Muhammad Ali—*Skin Tight* is an investigation into the form and symbolism of the punching bag and its connection to American societal ideas of black men, boxing, and rap music.

Though Ligon wanted this series of eight punching bags to look and feel like authentic bags, he also wanted to individualize each bag and create a strong statement formed by a series of distinct "voices." A standard Everlast™ bag was disassembled and used as a pattern for making the series in a range of fabrics, including canvas, vinyl, and satin. Ligon then designed patterns for silkscreen printing—one bag depicts an image of Muhammad Ali, another the rapper Ice Cube's glaring eyes. A black vinyl bag is printed with the altered logo "Thuglife," which alludes not only to the Everlast™ logo but also to the slogan tattooed on the late rap artist Tupac Shakur. One bag is covered with clear plastic pockets, a reference to the idea that the image of any opponent could be inserted and used to rouse the anger of the punching bag's user.

Collectively, the punching bags of *Skin Tight* convey a physical presence, as if each bag represents a body, and specifically a black male body. One is glorified and heightened with the sheen of satin fabric; another, made from black vinyl, is slumped on the floor, a defeated and limp form.

Skin Tight, 1995 (detail). Cotton canvas, leather, vinyl, pigment, and metal chain. Eight bags: each from 45 to 51 inches x 13 inches (114.3 to 129.54 x 33.02 cm) in diameter. Edition of 7.

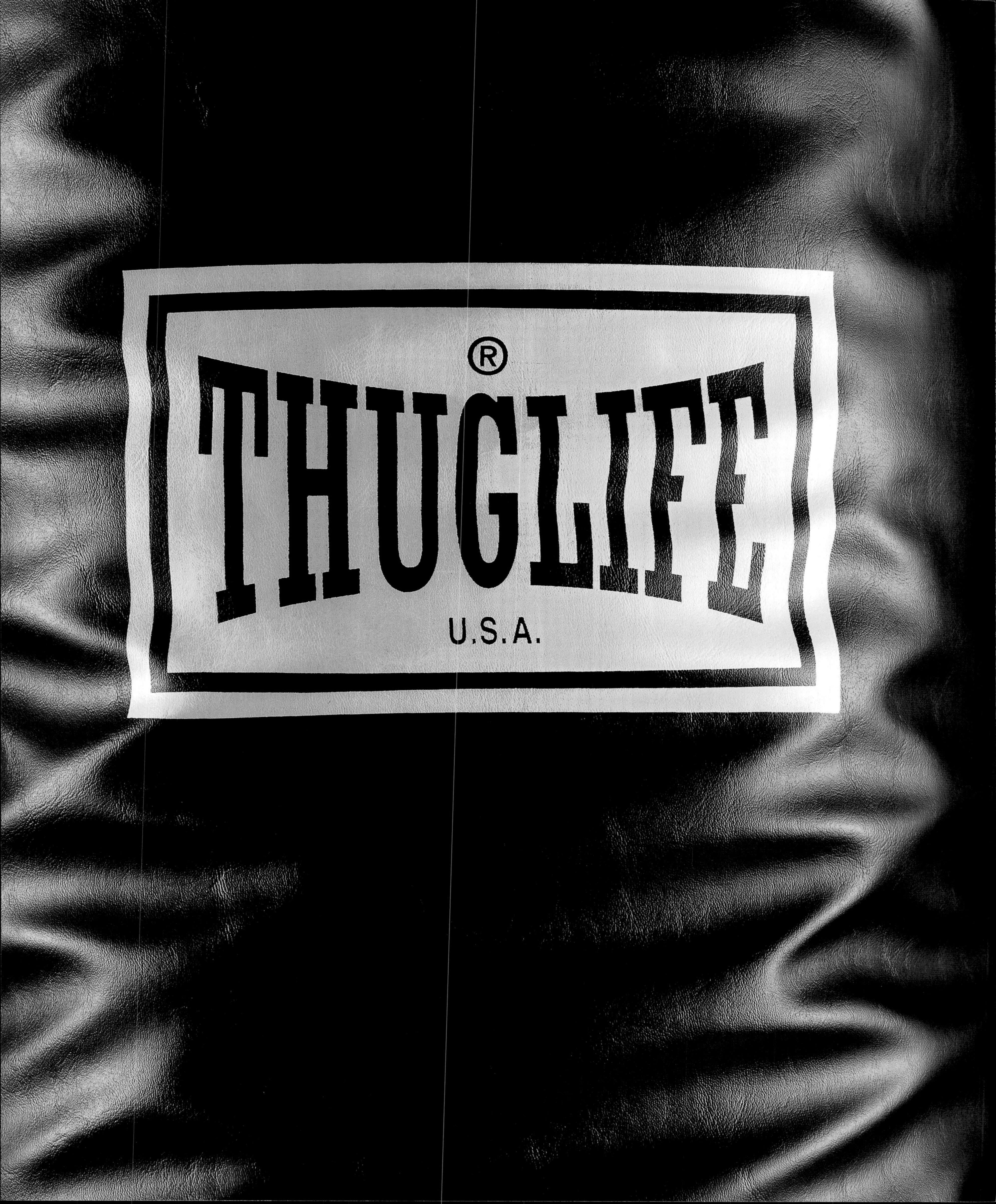
®
THUGLIFE
U.S.A.

he greatest has been p...

e. Santa Claus is white. America is white. Miss ...en you go to Heaven yo... to Heaven you washed ...ay. They teach us in T.V... White Swan Soap, King ...hite Rain Hair Rinse, Wh... ...o be white: I'm dreamin...

Skin Tight, 1995 (detail, left).

Skin Tight, 1995 (above). Cotton canvas, leather, vinyl, pigment, and metal chain. Eight bags: each from 45 to 51 inches x 13 inches (114.3 to 129.54 x 33.02 cm) in diameter. Edition of 7.

Donald Lipski

About the artist

American, born 1947, lives in New York City

Donald Lipski attended the University of Wisconsin, receiving his BA in 1970, before moving to Michigan to pursue graduate study at Cranbrook Academy of Art, where he earned his MFA in 1973. Lipski believes that art can be made from anything, and his range and combination of materials attests to this conviction—match books, carrots, paintbrushes, and Christmas trees are just a small sampling of objects transformed by the artist in his alchemical artistic practice. One-person exhibitions have been organized by the Miami Art Museum (2000), Capp Street Project in San Francisco (1993), and P.S. 1 Contemporary Art Center in Long Island City (1992). Lipski's 1990 exhibition at the FW+M was organized jointly with Beaver College Art Gallery (now Arcadia University) and the University of the Arts. Public commissions include works for Grand Central Station (2000) and the entrance to Central Park (1997), both in New York City. Among his many awards are a Prix de Rome from the American Academy in Rome (1990), and a fellowship from the Guggenheim Memorial Foundation (1988).

About the work

In *Who's Afraid of Red, White & Blue*, Donald Lipski used the American flag as his starting point to make a prolific series of sculptural projects. Using techniques of assemblage common to his oeuvre—such as wrapping, twisting, tying, and knotting—the artist worked with the FW+M to transform a shovel, a pair of scissors, a tree, and saw blades by wrapping them in American flags. Other projects included woven flags, flags made from various primary colors, a puzzle flag, and impressively, two large-scale flag installations. One, *Who's Afraid of Red, White & Blue #31*, was created from translucent nylon and measured four-stories high; it was installed in the glass ceiling atrium of the Haviland Building of Philadelphia's University of the Arts. Another, *Black by Popular Demand*, comprised two 40-foot flags made from silk organza and installed as intersecting diagonals at the Corcoran Gallery of Art in Washington, DC. Another series of sculptures, made in conjunction with students at Beaver College (now Arcadia University), involved wrapping and rolling cut bands of flags to make flag balls; one outdoor flag ball measured eight feet in diameter, while the Beaver College gallery was filled with thirteen balls, each measuring 2-1/2 feet in diameter.

By 1990, when Lipski's project with the FW+M was completed and exhibited, a national debate raged about the sanctity of the American flag. A strong supporter of artistic expression, Donald Lipski wrote about this project in 1991:

> When The Fabric Workshop approached me to do a project, I already had flags on my mind. With the federal court's overthrowing of a Texas statute that outlawed flag "desecration," there was overwhelming sentiment for a federal law or even a constitutional amendment to "protect" the flag. I have long felt that anything in the world can be used to make art. The prospect that the flag be put out of bounds to me seemed foolish and un-American. So, I filled my studio with flags and went to work using them as I would any other material. Whatever statement is made by this work issues from the complexity of my often contradictory feelings for my country and my government. (*Donald Lipski,* The Fabric Workshop, Philadelphia, 1991)

Who's Afraid of Red, White & Blue? # 31, 1990. Nylon. 840 x 288 inches (2,133.6 x 731.52 cm). Installation at the University of the Arts, Philadelphia. Collection of the artist.

Black by Popular Demand, 1990 (left). Silk organza. 360 x 360 x 252 inches (914.4 x 914.4 x 640.08 cm). Collection of the Corcoran Gallery of Art, Washington, DC.

Who's Afraid of Red, White & Blue? American Flag Ball #2, 1990 (above). Muslin. 32 inch (81.28 cm) diameter.

Tristin Lowe

American, born 1966, lives in Philadelphia

About the artist

Tristin Lowe studied art at the Parsons School of Design in New York from 1984 until 1986, before moving to Boston to complete his BFA in sculpture at the Massachusetts College of Art. Lowe's choice of materials has always been low-tech and low-brow; he has intentionally focused on crude materials and often crass ideas—a bed that continually wets itself or a foam figure that throws up on itself, as examples. Identifying with the clown, Lowe sees the archetype as having license to make a fool of himself, an association that, in turn, allowed Lowe as an artist to explore unorthodox new directions and materials in his work. It also relates to his interest in the risk-taking of authors allied with the Theater of the Absurd. One-person exhibitions of Lowe's work have been organized by the Rosenbach Museum and Library in Philadelphia (1999), New Langton Arts in San Francisco (1998), and the Samuel S. Fleisher Art Memorial in Philadelphia (1996). He was awarded a Pew Fellowship in the Arts Award in 1994.

About the work

Tristin Lowe's *Alice* is inspired by Lewis Carroll's *Alice in Wonderland*, as well as more general ideas about the role of fairytales as stories that inspire curiosity and wonder. He began to develop the idea for *Alice* after reading Carroll's book, and further expanded his ideas after subsequent visits to the Rosenbach Museum and Library in Philadelphia, where Lowe studied the first draft of *Alice in Wonderland*, along with many of the author's letters, paintings, and early photographs. Lowe learned of Carroll's background as a mathematician at Oxford University who began accompanying an Oxford dean and his children—one of whom was named Alice—on canoe trips and picnics. Carroll made up stories to entertain the children along the way, and one of these he later published as *Alice in Wonderland*.

Lowe was intrigued by the mythology surrounding the gifted yet purportedly reclusive and deviant Carroll, who was said to be more at home with children than with adults. The feeling of curiosity and surprise that the story of Carroll's Alice evokes in its readers matched Lowe's own artistic preoccupations. A driving impulse in the artist's work is a desire to experiment with "non-art" materials (balloons, motors, kickballs filled with concrete) in part to unburden himself from the weight of art history, but also to intrigue, surprise, and challenge the viewer with the spectacle of these often awkward materials and ideas.

Lowe's *Alice* is a 23-foot inflatable, vinyl-coated fabric, bright blue girl. She is unclothed, with shoulder length hair surrounding a face defined by one large eye. The sculpture, which was made in an edition of two, is a blow-up figure, evoking Carroll's Alice who grows and shrinks depending on the food or potions she imbibes. *Alice*, like her fairytale counterpart, offers a rich metaphor for the universally fraught transition from childhood to adulthood. This blue stand-in for a child is full of ambivalent yet intriguing qualities—she is sexually undeveloped (yet in many cases Lowe installs the two Alices together in what are unmistakably sexualized poses), larger than life in scale, at once naïve and terrifying. Her single eye—reminiscent of the rabbit's hole that begins Alice's journey of self-discovery—references an Eastern spiritual concept of the mind's eye, or the unconscious, unexplored territory within every individual.

Alice, 1998 (detail). Vinyl coated fabric, paint, internal fan, cotton terry cloth, acrylic "fur," and thread. 280 x 96 x 84 inches (711.2 x 243.84 x 213.36 cm). Edition of 2.

Alice, 1998. Vinyl coated fabric, paint, internal fan, cotton terry cloth, acrylic "fur," and thread.
280 x 96 x 84 inches (711.2 x 243.84 x 213.36 cm). Edition of 2.

James Luna

About the artist

American, born 1950, lives on the La Jolla Reservation in Valley Center, California

James Luna was born in Orange, California, to a Luiseño mother and a Mexican father. He studied art as an undergraduate student at the University of California in Irvine (BFA, 1976) and as a graduate student pursued a master's degree in counseling at San Diego State University (1983). Luna has gained a national reputation as a performance, conceptual, and installation artist confronting and reshaping stereotypes of Native American identity. For his 1987 performance project, *Artifact Piece*, Luna situated himself inside a museum vitrine, lying on a bed of sand as an anthropological display with labels marking his scars and personal objects such as family photos surrounding him. Luna's performance and sculptural works have been showcased at the Hood Museum of Art, Dartmouth College in Hanover, New Hampshire (1995); the National Gallery of Canada in Ottawa (1992); the San Francisco Museum of Modern Art (1991); and at the Whitney Museum of American Art in New York (1991).

182

During his residency at the FW+M, Luna created a series of related works, centering on two costumes, made to fit the artist and for use in a performance or as elements of larger installations.

High-Tech War Shirt is fabricated from smoked hide and adorned with a range of symbolic, decorative elements: beaded medallions commissioned by Luna on the La Jolla Reservation; long filaments of horse hair, which specifically reference American Indian tradition; and a necklace made from a large shell encasing a plastic Sunbeam thermometer with plastic toys dangling from the rim. The back of the shirt is made from nylon netting, referencing the trendy sports clothing worn by athletes. The combination of traditional Indian objects and contemporary trinkets highlights the humor and irony that play a part in all Luna's work.

Indian Lounge Suit is a flashy, tailored man's suit made from wine-colored, sharkskin silk, the surface of which is smooth and iridescent. Luna wanted to recreate an ostentatious suit that might be worn by a shyster, something slick yet debonair like Jerry Lewis' attire in *The Nutty Professor*. The FW+M worked with a professional embroiderer to stitch a rendition of James Earle Fraser's famous image, *End of the Trail* (c. 1894), on the reverse of the jacket. Fraser's bronze sculpture depicts an American Indian slumped forward on a weary horse, a strong visual rendering that introduced the stereotype of the noble, yet defeated Indian.

These costumes have been used in various installations, but have also been incorporated into the sequel to Luna's well-known performance, *Shameman*. Each costume represents an opposite persona: the entertainer or con man of white popular culture, and the authentic spiritual man of American Indian culture. Taking on these personas and writing scripts with a great deal of humor, Luna address the complex nature of the contemporary Native American man.

High-Tech War Shirt, 1997–1998 (detail). Smoked hide, silk, horse hair, metal buttons, beads, and watches. 45 x 53 x 8 inches (114.3 x 134.62 x 20.32 cm). Edition of 2.

High-Tech War Shirt, 1997–1998 (above). Smoked hide, silk, horse hair, metal buttons, beads, and watches. 45 x 53 x 8 inches (114.3 x 134.62 x 20.32 cm). Edition of 2.

Indian Lounge Suit, 1997 (right). Silk with rayon embroidery. 62 x 22 x 9 inches (157.48 x 55.88 x 22.86 cm). Edition of 2.

Maisin Artists of
Papua New Guinea

The Maisin community of Collingwood Bay, Papua New Guinea, has consciously begun the arduous and ongoing task of simultaneously preserving their traditional culture, protecting their environment, and becoming citizens of the global village. They have undertaken this process, nonetheless, with optimism, dedication, and an understanding that their pioneering work is an inspiring example for other communities throughout the world who are attempting to maintain their traditional way of life while participating in the global economy of the new century.

Long before this larger goal of culture and land preservation became a focus for the entire community, the Maisin—for centuries—have been dedicated artists of a type of bark cloth painting called tapa. There are two distinct varieties of tapa cloth—those used for ceremonial roles and those used for everyday purposes. The ceremonial, or sacred, tapa are embellished with designs that have been passed down from generation to generation in each clan. These sacred designs are never exhibited or sold, but rather reserved for ceremonial use by the members of each clan. The everyday tapa is generally created from the imagination of each artist and is non-pictorial. It was and continues to be used as everyday clothing and as a commodity for bartering with neighboring tribes; nowadays, it is also available for sale to outsiders for commercial markets.

The tapa cloth created by the Maisin was brought to the attention of the FW+M by Larry Rinder, currently the Anne & Joel Ehrenkranz Curator of Contemporary Art at the Whitney Museum of American Art, New York. In early 1997, Rinder was invited to curate an exhibition at the FW+M; this invitation resulted in a long-term collaboration with the Maisin, including an ambitious program of international exchanges, a residency, and an exhibition.

In response to an offer by the FW+M of a residency in Philadelphia for tapa artists, the Maisin women and elders held community meetings and selected three women representing various clans and villages. In September of 1997, Natalie Rarama, Kate Sivana, and Monica Taniova came to the FW+M's studios in Philadelphia where they were introduced to silkscreen printing techniques and a variety of materials, pigments, and dyes.

While in residence at the FW+M, the Maisin artists experimented with translating their designs into prints on silk, repeat cotton yardage, and even a woven wool carpet. The range of colors available for printing created both interest and dismay for the artists; no longer limited to the natural dyes available to them at home, they were drawn to bright colors reminiscent of birds and plants of the rain forest. Ultimately, however, they were most drawn to the traditional Maisin palette of red and black.

Lonnie Graham, *Welcoming Ceremony, Ganjiga Village*, 1997. Gelatin silver print. 20 x 24 inches (50.8 x 60.96 cm).

188

Lonnie Graham, *Young Women from Ganjiga Village*, 1997–1998 (left). Gelatin silver print. 48 x 60 inches (121.92 x 152.4 cm).

Lonnie Graham, *Monica Taniova*, 1997–1998 (right). Gelatin silver print. 20 x 24 inches (50.8 x 60.96 cm).

Lonnie Graham, *Women from Ganjiga Village*, 1997–1998 (left). Gelatin silver print. 48 x 60 inches (121.92 x 152.4 cm).

Lonnie Graham, *John Taniova*, 1997–1998 (right). Gelatin silver print. 48 x 60 inches (121.92 x 152.4 cm).

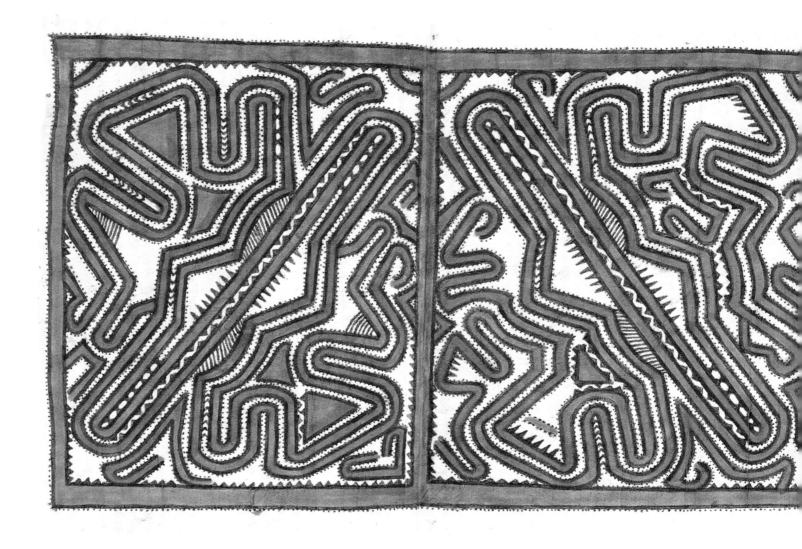

Constance Godima, *Untitled (Traditional Maisin Tapa),* 1997. Pounded mulberry bark cloth, and natural pigments. 22 x 65 inches (55.88 x 165.1 cm).

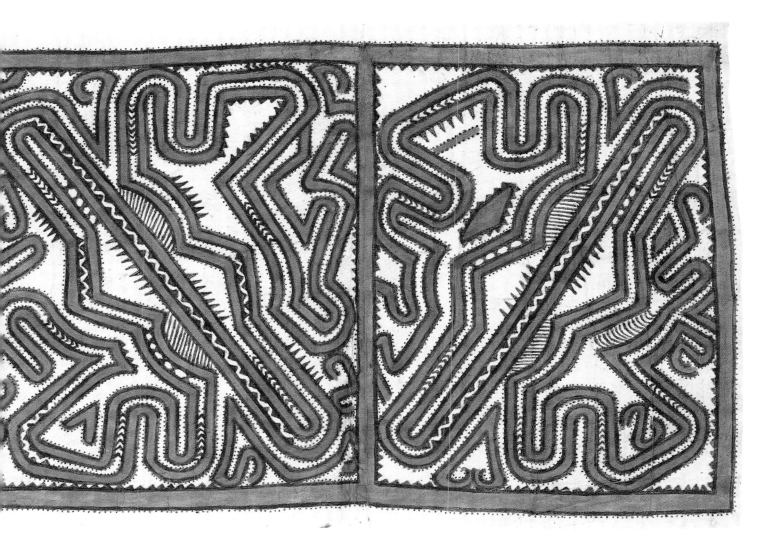

Kate Sivana, *Untitled*. 1997 (detail, following pages, left). Pigment on Thai silk. 80 $\frac{1}{2}$ x 43 $\frac{1}{2}$ inches (204.47 x 110.49 cm).

Natalie Rarama, *Untitled*, 1997 (detail, following pages, right). Pigment on Thai silk. 80 $\frac{1}{2}$ x 43 $\frac{1}{2}$ inches (204.47 x 110.49 cm).

Virgil Marti

About the artist

American, born 1962, lives in Philadelphia

Raised in Missouri, Virgil Marti attended Washington University in St. Louis, where he completed a BFA in 1984, prior to earning a MFA from Tyler School of Art at Temple University in Philadelphia (1990). His awards include a Pew Fellowship in the Arts (1995) and The Louis Comfort Tiffany Foundation Award (1997). An emerging talent of increasing national reputation, Marti has had solo exhibitions at the Pennsylvania Academy of the Fine Arts in Philadelphia (2001), Thread Waxing Space in New York (1998), and White Columns in New York (1996), and his work has been acquired by major museums such as the Philadelphia Museum of Art and the Victoria and Albert Museum, London.

About the work

Virgil Marti created *For Oscar Wilde* as a site-specific installation in and around a prison cell in Philadelphia's now-abandoned Eastern State Penitentiary (*Prison Sentences: The Prison as Site/The Prison As Subject*, organized by Julie Courtney and Todd Gilens). Taking Oscar Wilde's imprisonment in 19th century England as his cue, Marti borrowed from the William Morris-inspired design of Wilde's day and fashioned an aesthetically pleasing cell, one that the playwright himself might have found bearable during his own confinement.

The piece progresses from the natural to the artificial, with beauty as one of its central themes—an idea with heightened poignancy considering the decay and desolation of the once-formidable stone prison. An outdoor garden bed of radiant sunflowers marks the entry into the prison itself, while a meandering path made from a border of silk lilies in full bloom leads to the doorway of the cell. Once inside, the cell itself contains a single bed—a ribbed iron frame made slightly more enticing by its pure white velveteen slipcover—and the walls are covered with silkscreen printed wallpaper of the artist's design, sunflowers above, lilies below. A band of scripted text of Wilde's writings divides the Arts and Crafts floral patterns.

For Oscar Wilde is an homage to Wilde, but it also offers commentary on the terrible irony of his life as a champion of art and beauty over conventional morality. During his final years, Wilde found himself imprisoned for what was deemed a lack of morality, as his homosexuality was viewed at that time.

For Oscar Wilde, 1995 (detail). Installation at Eastern State Penitentiary, Philadelphia. Live sunflowers, ceramic plaque, silk lilies, silkscreen printed wallpaper (pigment on paper-backed cotton sateen), cotton velveteen, and iron bed. Dimensions vary with installation.

For Oscar Wilde, 1995. Installation at Eastern State Penitentiary, Philadelphia. Live sunflowers, ceramic plaque, silk lilies, silkscreen printed wallpaper (pigment on paper-backed cotton sateen),
cotton velveteen, and iron bed. Dimensions vary with installation.

Robert Morris

American, born 1931, lives and works in New York City

Robert Morris played a pivotal role in the early development of Minimalism during the 1960s by creating simple sculptural forms, which were often used as props for dance performances. He was also one of the first artists to use a textile form—felt—as the medium for ambitious sculpture, and his early works in felt played with the pliability and sensuousness of the material. Morris had his first one-person exhibition at the Dilexi Gallery in San Francisco in 1957, and since then he has earned a place among the most influential American artists of the late 20th century. Other exhibitions have included major retrospectives at the Centre George Pompidou, Paris (1995), and the Solomon R. Guggenheim Museum, New York (1994), as well as one-person exhibitions at the Museum of Contemporary Art in Chicago (1986), the Stedelijk Museum in Amsterdam (1977), The Tate Gallery in London (1971), and the Whitney Museum of American Art in New York (1970).

Restless Sleepers/Atomic Shroud belongs to an unofficial series of works exploring the dark themes of nuclear destruction and death that Robert Morris began in the early 1980s. A bed comprised of sheets and pillowcases, this project presents a literal and ominous vision of world events gone terribly astray. To create the bottom sheet, Morris painted a human skeleton with ink and rolled it on fabric to give the effect of a moving, turning, restless corpse. This print was then used to make a silkscreen, from which the finished linen sheets were printed. The top sheet is laden with images of mushroom clouds from a nuclear explosion, also silkscreen printed on linen. The pillowcases offer printed text (taken from the writings of physicist Ted Taylor) reviewing the practical potential of nuclear destruction, which heightens the nightmarish terror implied by the tousled sheets. One paragraph states that "it would be difficult to achieve erasure with a single thermonuclear device . . ." while the other gives a more pragmatic prediction of destruction: " . . . more practical and more certain would be the utilization of several dirty, fairly high megaton yield devices . . ."

Created during the beginning years of the Reagan era when the Cold War still dominated world politics, *Restless Sleepers/Atomic Shroud* holds new relevance today with the fear of nuclear terrorism.

Restless Sleepers/Atomic Shroud, 1981 (detail). Pigment on linen. Two sheets: 114 x 90 inches (289.56 x 228.6 cm) each. Two pillow cases: 20 x 36 inches (50.8 x 91.44 cm) each. Edition of 8 related works (5 on linen, 3 on satin). Collection of The Fabric Workshop and Museum and the Philadelphia Museum of Art.

Restless Sleepers/Atomic Shroud, 1981. Pigment on linen. Two sheets: 114 x 90 inches (289.56 x 228.6 cm) each. Two pillow cases: 20 x 36 inches (50.8 x 91.44 cm) each. Edition of 8 related works (5 on linen, 3 on satin). Collection of The Fabric Workshop and Museum and the Philadelphia Museum of Art.

Louise Nevelson

About the artist

American, born Russia 1899, died 1988

Louise Nevelson immigrated to the United States in 1905 with her family, settling in Rockland, Maine. She moved to New York City in 1920 after her marriage to Charles Nevelson, and began studying at the Art Students League of New York in 1928. By the 1940s, Nevelson had begun to create assemblage sculptures, for which she used pieces of wood, broken glass, and nails; by the late 1950s, she created her first wall sculpture. In 1967, the Whitney Museum of American Art in New York presented Nevelson's first major museum retrospective. Other one-person exhibitions were organized by the Walker Art Center in Minneapolis (1973), the Seattle Art Museum (1980), and the Solomon R. Guggenheim Museum in New York (1986). Nevelson created many large-scale public sculptures, including commissions for the Massachusetts Institute of Technology in Cambridge (1975) and The Port Authority of New York and New Jersey, which was installed in the World Trade Center and destroyed in the terrorist attacks of 2001. She was honored with three honorary doctoral degrees, and her work has been collected by over 100 public institutions.

About the work

Louise Nevelson's early artistic training included study in the performing as well as visual arts. During her residency at the FW+M, Nevelson turned her attention to the design of opera costumes, a project commissioned by the Opera Theatre of Saint Louis for the 1984 production of *Orfeo ed Euridice*. Nevelson's commission also involved the creation of the set design, and marked her first time designing for the stage. She described the set in 1984:

> *The columns are independent, symbols of male and female, one different from the other. They will be onstage the whole time and the dancing will be around them. We are bordering on surrealism with some of this; instead of Orfeo holding a lyre symbolically I decided we'd just have a thin wire and fly it. It's not played—nothing touches it.*

To create the edition of forty costumes, Nevelson utilized the silkscreen printing process, drawing on motifs from earlier prints and drawings. The background is printed with marbled grey tones—randomized so that no two costumes are alike—with abstracted black patterning on top. The costumes are bold and sculptural in their form, and graphically draw on the same muted tones and dark color that define her well-known three-dimensional work. The element of shadow, which Nevelson called the "fourth-dimension," is clear in the patterning of the costumes.

Opera Costume, 1985 (detail). Pigment on cotton twill. 67 x 69 inches (170.18 x 175.26 cm). Edition of 40. Commissioned by the Opera Theatre of Saint Louis.

Opera Costume, 1985. Pigment on cotton twill. 67 x 69 inches (170.18 x 175.26 cm). Edition of 40. Commissioned by the Opera Theatre of Saint Louis.

Claes Oldenburg

About the artist

American, born Sweden 1929, lives in New York City

Claes Oldenburg was born in Stockholm, Sweden, the son of a diplomat. After moving to different cities in Norway and the United States, his family settled in Chicago in 1936. Oldenburg completed his undergraduate degree at Yale University in 1950 before returning to Chicago, where he took classes at the Art Institute. He became an American citizen in 1953. Often considered the quintessential American artist, Oldenburg championed issues of "high" versus "low" in his art, blurring the line completely with The Store, a shop he opened in 1961 and filled with plaster and muslin sculptures of consumer goods—clothing, food, and domestic objects. His large-scale public sculptural works are known throughout the world, including *Clothespin*, a 45-foot stainless steel sculpture erected in Philadelphia's Centre Square Plaza in 1976. Oldenburg's work has been the subject of numerous one-person exhibitions, including major retrospectives at the Museum of Modern Art, New York (1969), the National Gallery of Art, Washington, DC (1995), and the Solomon R. Guggenheim Museum, New York (1995).

About the work

Created in 1997, *Calico Bunny* is reminiscent of Claes Oldenburg's seminal soft sculpture work and "happenings" of the 1960s. For these experimental theatrical performances, Oldenburg created large objects made of fabric and filled with foam. Often mundane and familiar objects (light switches or toilets, for example), these fabric objects were exaggerated in some way to accentuate their ordinariness and their place in our consumer culture.

Calico Bunny looks like a benign child's toy, with the subtle exception of the protruding black wooden eye, intentionally oversized compared to the scale of the bunny. The eye, which flops uneasily forward, and the slightly understuffed body, contribute to the image of this bunny as tossed aside or abandoned. The bunnies are made from a classic calico pattern, silkscreen printed on canvas, and designed based on a simple bunny cookie cutter. They are meant to be viewed individually, in small groups, or as one large mass of proliferating bunnies.

Oldenburg created *Calico Bunny* as a limited edition multiple of 99 bunnies in red, yellow, and blue—33 of each colorway. They were originally made to benefit Doctors of the World/Médecins du Monde, an international not-for-profit organization that provides medical support to developing nations or countries in crisis.

Calico Bunny, 1997 (detail). Pigment on canvas, polyester, painted wood, and metal. 13 x 10 x 6 inches (33.02 x 25.4 x 15.24 cm) each. Edition of 99.

Calico Bunny, 1997. Pigment on canvas, polyester, painted wood, and metal. 13 x 10 x 6 inches (33.02 x 25.4 x 15.24 cm) each. Edition of 99.

Dennis Oppenheim

American, born 1938, lives in New York City

About the artist

Dennis Oppenheim earned his BFA from the California College of Arts and Crafts in Oakland (1965). In 1966, he moved to New York City, where, in 1968, he was given his first one-person show (John Gibson Gallery) and included in the *Sculpture Annual* at the Whitney Museum of American Art. Oppenheim has not been wed to one medium over his career, but rather has moved freely between media to convey his ideas, employing conceptual art, earth works, performance, sculpture, and video. His work has been the subject of many exhibitions, both national and international, including one-person shows at the XXIV Bienal São Paulo in Brazil (1998), the 2nd Johannesburg Biennale in South Africa (1997), Los Angeles County Museum of Art (1997), and the University Art Museum at the University of California at Berkeley (1993).

210

About the work

Blue Tattoo is a complex installation of mechanical and physical parts. The centerpiece is a small mechanized bull engraved with a heart on its shoulder. A blue light illuminates the heart, while the bull paws the ground with its leg. The bull is connected to a series of three teapots on hotplates, which are filled with water and attached to rubber tubing that shoots steam into the bull's nostrils.

The "blue tattoo" of the pulsing, animated bull is projected—via video camera focused on the bull's shoulder—onto an oversized man's work glove, which was fabricated in collaboration with the FW+M. Suspended at a distance from the bull and close to a bank of red lights, the glove is altered from its coarse suede and heavy canvas prototype, and made instead from a combination of soft suede and delicate dotted Swiss fabric. The text, "Mo-mo-mo-mother" and "Si-sis-siss-sister," is printed on the glove, a reference to dialogue from the film *Chinatown*.

This playful and enigmatic installation is characteristic of Oppenheim's history as an inventor of his own artistic tableaux. There is a relentless quality to the beating of the bull's heart—and Oppenheim is clearly interested in the symbols of the heart beyond mere biology.

Blue Tattoo, 1993 (detail). Silkscreen printed pigment on suede and dotted Swiss fabric, border light, projector, spotlight, motorized bull, galvanized pan, camera, and time delay relays. Dimensions vary with installation. Collection of the artist.

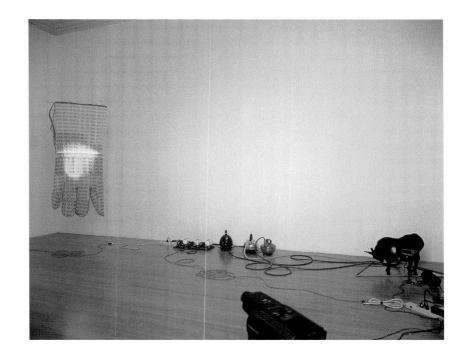

Blue Tattoo, 1993. Silkscreen printed pigment on suede and dotted Swiss fabric, border light, projector, spotlight, motorized bull, galvanized pan, camera, and time delay relays. Dimensions vary with installation. Collection of the artist.

Jorge Pardo

About the artist

American, born Cuba 1963, lives in Los Angeles and Long Island, New York

Jorge Pardo was born in Havana, Cuba, and immigrated to the United States with his family in 1969. He studied art at the Art Center College of Design in Pasadena, California (BFA, 1988). Although he had been exhibiting widely in the United States and Europe prior to 1997, his installation that year at the Skulptur Projekte in Münster, Germany, heightened international attention to his work. Entitled *Pier*, the project highlights the fine line between design and art, functional and sculptural object, that defines so much of Pardo's work. Major solo exhibitions have been organized by Dia Center for the Arts, New York (2000), the Museum of Contemporary Art, Los Angeles (1998), and the Museum of Contemporary Art, Chicago (1997). He has completed many commissions and permanent art projects, including: *Bar* at the Center for Contemporary Art, Glasgow (2001); *4166 Sea View Lane* in Los Angeles (1998); and *Reading Room* at the Boijmans Van Beuningen Museum in Rotterdam (1996).

About the work

In 1997, the FW+M commissioned Jorge Pardo to redesign the entrance to the museum, including a new reception area and a video lounge/café. Over the course of one year, Pardo radically transformed these public spaces, designing every element of the interior—from the floor to the ceiling and everything in between.

An architectural as well as an artistic undertaking, the *Untitled* project began with Pardo's design of two fabrics. Inspired by 1950s and 60s-era textile design, these fabrics were printed on linen, cotton sateen, and Swiss cotton, and were made into room dividers, wallpaper, and window curtains. He then designed the usual elements of a museum entrance space—a reception desk, light fixtures, shelving, doorways, and a table for educational pamphlets—as well as upholstered chairs and ottomans, countertops, and teacups with saucers for the café/video lounge.

Jorge Pardo's work navigates the territory between art and what is usually identified as architecture or design. The installation may appear at first as pure architecture and interior design, but its limits in this realm are revealed after stepping through one of the unmarked glass doorways leading out of the installation and into other areas of the museum: exposed 2 x 4s and hanging systems provide significant clues that the space occupies a domain beyond architecture.

Pardo returned to the FW+M in 2001 to create another 1960s-inspired textile design. Silkscreen printed pigment on sheer Swiss cotton, the fabric was used for *Curtain*, an art and architectural installation at Dia Center for the Arts.

Untitled, 1999. Silkscreen printed pigment on Swiss cotton. Dimensions vary with installation.

Untitled, 1999 (preceding pages). Entrance to The Fabric Workshop and Museum. Pressboard reception desk and video cabinet, lamps, pressboard and glass doors, cork floor, birch plywood ceiling, and silkscreen printed pigment on linen and Swiss cotton.
Untitled, 1999 (right). Video Lounge, The Fabric Workshop and Museum. Upholstered furniture, pressboard video cabinet, lamps, cork floor, birch plywood ceiling, and silkscreen printed pigment on linen and Swiss cotton.

Untitled, 1999 (above). Men's room, The Fabric Workshop and Museum. Silkscreen printed pigment on linen, pressboard and glass door, and cork floor.

Installation of *Curtain*, 2001 (right), at Dia Center for the Arts, New York, 19 September 2001–16 June 2002. Silkscreen pigment on sheer Swiss cotton, and aluminum track. 8,000 x 96 inches (20,320 x 243.84 cm).

Judy Pfaff

About the artist

American, born 1946, lives in Kingston, New York

Judy Pfaff was born in London, England, and moved to the United
States when she was thirteen. She went on to art school, earning
her BFA from Washington University in Saint Louis (1971) and
her MFA from Yale University (1973). Pfaff is known for her
sculpture, drawing, and printmaking, and in 1983 she was awarded
a Guggenheim Memorial Foundation fellowship. Her solo exhibitions
include the Bienal São Paulo (1998), where she was the United
States representative, and major shows at the National Museum of
Women in the Arts (1988) and the Denver Art Museum (1994).
Pfaff's 1991 exhibition at the FW+M was presented collaboratively
with the Pennsylvania Academy of the Fine Arts. Among her significant
public art projects is *Cirque* (1994), a permanent installation said
to be the largest suspended sculpture in the world, commissioned
by the Pennsylvania Convention Center in Philadelphia.

222

About the work

Judy Pfaff approached her residency at the FW+M as an opportunity to explore fabric's three-dimensional qualities. She reflected on its woven structure and began to investigate the fabrication methods of objects usually covered with cloth—lampshades, umbrellas, and mattresses. With the staff of the FW+M, these objects were dissected and served as inspiration for a new sculptural series.

At the FW+M, Pfaff took her work in an entirely new direction, creating porous, woven sculptures, distinct from previous works made from assembled solid objects. For the series, various metal wires (steel, copper, brass) were woven into circular shapes and tubular forms; in some places the weaving is delicate and intricate, in others coarse or more irregular. Pfaff expertly combined these woven elements with other related forms and materials (aluminum ducts and glass, for example) to make dynamic yet deliberately composed constructions. There is an uneasy balance to these works as Pfaff plays with the relationship between volume and open space.

Also new for Pfaff with this project was the absence of color. The glossy or matte surfaces of the various metals play off one another, and in one piece, shiny copper adds contrast to the rust and silver of its woven counterparts. As curator and art critic Judith Stein wrote about this series, Pfaff "exploits the unadorned surfaces of glistening industrial ductwork, or the naturally variegated coloration of tin cans and containers" (Pennsylvania Academy of the Fine Arts exhibition brochure, Philadelphia, 1991).

Untitled, 1991 (detail). Steel, copper, brass, and paint. 102 x 102 x 115 inches (259.08 x 259.08 x 292.1 cm) (approximately). Collection of the artist.

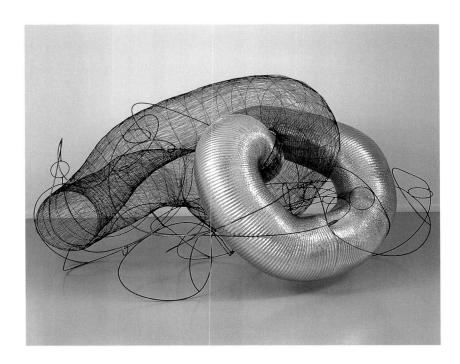

Untitled, 1991 (left). Steel, copper, brass, and paint. 102 x 102 x 115 inches (259.08 x 259.08 x 292.1 cm) (approximately). Collection of the artist.

Compulsory Figures, 1991 (above). Woven wire, painted steel, and aluminum duct. 66 x 133 x 107 inches (167.64 x 337.82 x 271.78 cm). Private collection.

Keith Piper

British, born Malta 1960, lives in London

About the artist

Keith Piper was born in Malta, and grew up in and around Birmingham, England. While attending Lanchester Polytechnic, where he took foundation classes in art and design (1979–1980), Piper joined with other young black artists to form the BLK Art Group. Their exhibitions gave rise to a new, political voice in contrast to the British art establishment. Piper continued his formal studies, earning a BA in Fine Arts from Trent Polytechnic in Nottingham (1983), and a MA in Environmental Media from the Royal College of Art in London (1986). Piper is known for his multi-media installations, which often incorporate computer technology, video, music, text, and photography. He has exhibited internationally, with a mid-career survey at the New Museum of Contemporary Art in New York (1999), and one-person shows at The Royal Observatory in Greenwich Park, London (1994), and the Camden Arts Centre in London (1991). A multi-media book project, *Relocating the Remains*, was published in 1997 by the Institute of International Visual Arts.

226

About the work

Keith Piper's work consistently interprets and reinterprets the black diaspora experience. *Western Passage*, in particular, reexamines the colonizing history of the British Empire. Comprised of twenty-four mattresses and a large-scale video projection, the installation combines text, sound, and imagery to reflect on the period of Britain's empire building, and the African and Caribbean nations whose people, resources, and political systems were exploited.

The handmade mattresses are arranged on the floor like the human cargo of a slave ship, oriented toward the sound and video projection illuminating the room from the front. The digital prints on each mattress—smaller than a standard twin bed, allowing barely enough room for a single body—are compartmentalized into squares. Each area shows an image relating to the mercenary currency of the era—coffee beans, black-eyed peas, maps of the British expansion, coins, the ocean, and bodies.

Piper is in the forefront of artists using digital media to combine and conflate multiple sources, such as ethnographic material, popular music, media clips, photography, and graphics. His video for *Western Passage* is a mesmerizing blend of images—rolling green waves, photographs of black families, a compass, and a globe—and of sounds, most striking of which is a voice that periodically states, "Beyond this, the country is unknown to Europeans."

Western Passage, 1997 (detail). Digital print on cotton sateen, and video projection. 24 mattresses: 72 x 24 x 6 inches each (182.88 x 60.96 x 15.24 cm). Dimensions vary with installation.

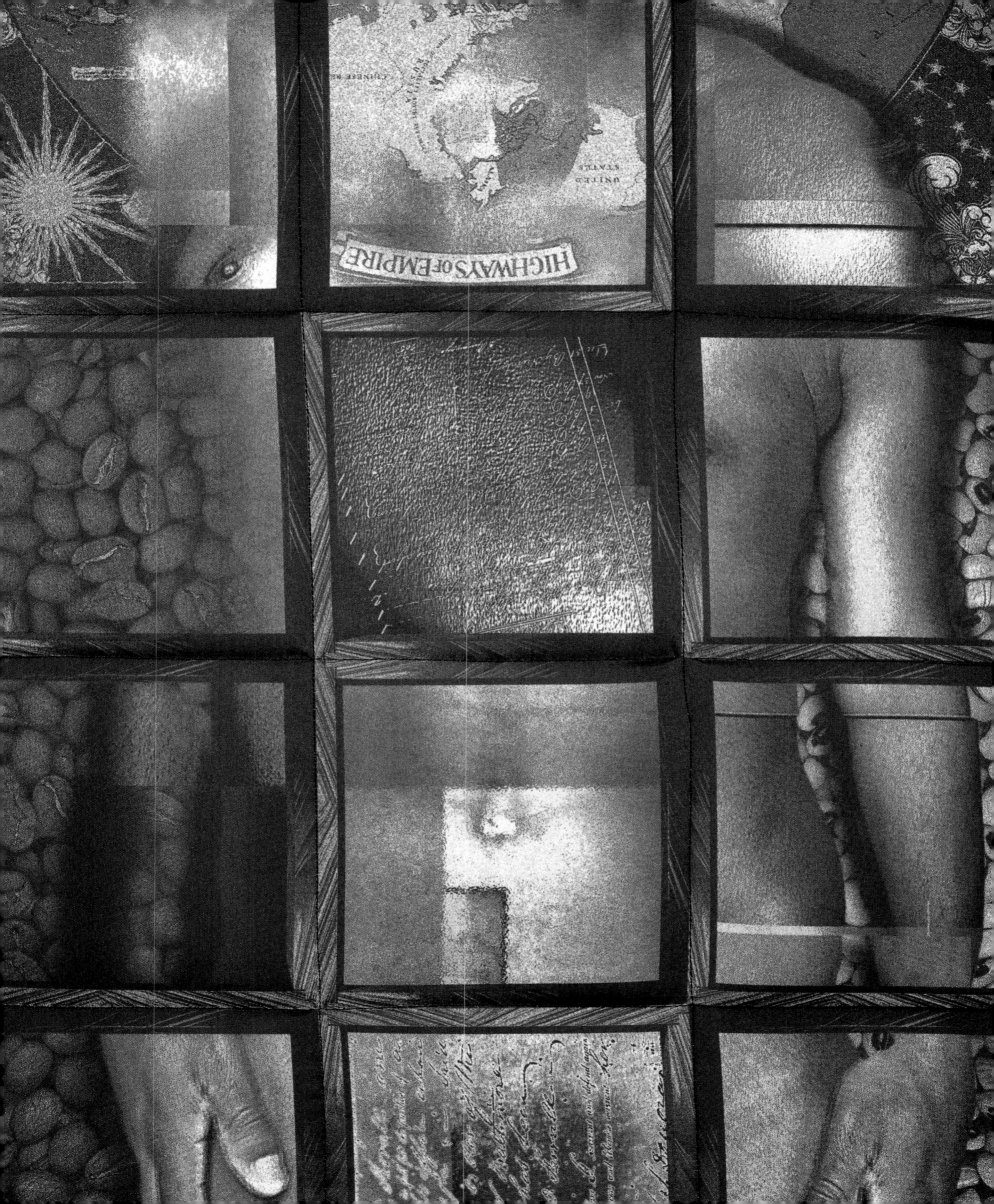

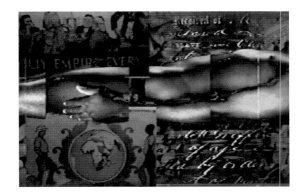

Western Passage, 1997 (left). Digital print on cotton sateen, and video projection. 24 mattresses: 72 x 24 x 6 inches each (182.88 x 60.96 x 15.24 cm). Dimensions vary with installation.

Video stills from *Western Passage*, 1997 (above).

Larry Rinder

About the author

American, born 1961, lives in New York City

Larry Rinder is the Anne & Joel Ehrenkranz Curator of Contemporary Art at the Whitney Museum of American Art, New York. In 2002, he curated the Whitney Biennial, an exhibition he also organized with five other curators in 2000. Among his other curatorial projects are *BitStreams* (co-curated with Debra Singer for the Whitney Museum of American Art, 2001), *Searchlight: Consciousness at the Millennium* (CCAC Institute at the California College of Arts and Crafts, 2000), and *In a Different Light* (Berkeley Art Museum, 1995). Mr. Rinder participated in The Fabric Workshop and Museum's visiting curator series in 1997–1998, for which he organized an ambitious international exchange with the Maisin tribe of Papua New Guinea, including a residency and exhibition entitled *Tapa Style*. A version of the following essay was first published in *Art Journal* (Vol. 57, No. 2). Mr. Rinder earned a BA in Art from Reed College and a MA in Art History from Hunter College. He is an Adjunct Professor of Art History at Columbia University.

Painting Around the Fire: Maisin Culture and Collectivity

In the autumn of 1997, three women—Natalie Rarama, Kate Sivana, and Monica Taniova, all of the Maisin tribe of Papua New Guinea (pp. 186–193)—were artists-in-residence at The Fabric Workshop and Museum. Experimenting with various materials and printing techniques, they produced several extraordinary screenprints on cotton and silk. The designs are typically Maisin patterns—twisting and jumping lines that gather together in one dynamic and complex filigree. The soft fabrics selected by Rarama, Sivana, and Taniova contrast compellingly with their traditional tapa (bark cloth) and endow the works with a soft atmosphere that enhances the delicacy of their painted designs. Their choice of colors ranges from Taniova's bronze dye printed on an emerald green silk evocative of the natural colors of the Maisin land, to Rarama's use of a refreshing pale yellow dye, known as "lemon ice," over a pale blue silk. What brought these women halfway around the world to create these innovative pieces? Certainly, they came as artists intent on exploring new aesthetic approaches to their tapa painting traditions. But they also came as emissaries of their tribe, hoping to gain insight into various modes of textile production and distribution that might further the Maisin goals of expanding markets for their tapa paintings. Thus, The Fabric Workshop and Museum residency was only one step in the Maisin's ongoing efforts to perpetuate and expand their venerable tradition of tapa painting as a response to the challenge of devising economically, ecologically, and culturally sensitive strategies for sustainable development.

Approximately three thousand Maisin live in eleven villages spread along the coast of their ancestral lands in the southeastern region of Papua New Guinea. Initially contacted by Anglican missionaries at the turn of the century, the Maisin were among the first New Guineans to learn English and to be educated in the Western mode. Today, many Maisin travel frequently between the larger cities of Papua New Guinea—where they hold prominent positions in government, medicine, and education—and their magnificently forested home on the isolated coast of Collingwood Bay. But in Maisin lands, the tribe continues to live much as their ancestors did—hunting with spears for wild pigs and cassowaries, constructing their homes almost exclusively from

1

2

1. Larry Rinder wearing Maisin
ceremonial dress in Ganjiga Village,
Papua New Guinea, 1997.

2. Maisin woman in *wuwusi* (mulberry)
tree grove, 1997.

bush materials, traveling in dugout canoes, and performing traditional dances and ceremonies. Their lands are vast—nearly half a million acres that form the watershed for at least five rivers and that stretch from outlying coral reefs to the summit of Mount Suckling, one of the highest peaks in Papua New Guinea. Because of the Maisin's particular history, especially the fact that so many traveled around their country and abroad, they possess an insightful perspective on Western society while treasuring the heritage of their ancestors, the wisdom of their customs, and the beauty, tranquillity, and abundance of their lands.

Although many changes in Maisin culture have taken place over the past hundred years—such as the adoption of Christianity and an end to intertribal and interclan violence—many traditions remain intact and are being consciously perpetuated by the Maisin, thanks to their critical awareness of the swift demise of other Papua New Guinean tribes that have lost their bearings in the modern world. The Maisin are keen on maintaining the clan structure, the authority of tribal elders, and control over their own land and natural resources. As new forms of elective government have been introduced, they have found ways of interweaving these institutions with the traditional power of clan chiefs. Highly formalized decision making in Maisin culture is carried out with thorough consultation and proper ceremonial observations. The Maisin clans and villages, which have often been at odds, are currently working actively to develop closer links. Their drive toward closer cooperation is motivated by the awareness that if they remain divided, they will become much more susceptible to the machinations of outsiders seeking to exploit their vast natural resources. Specifically, the Maisin have been repeatedly approached by representatives of industrial logging and agricultural plantation companies.

Tapa cloth painting is practiced throughout Maisin lands and is considered a defining custom of the tribe. Although tapa cloths are made and painted throughout the equatorial regions of the world, including by other tribes in Papua New Guinea, the Maisin believe—rightly, I think—that theirs are of especially high quality. In particular, they value the exceptional smoothness and whiteness of the cloth they are able to produce from the *wuwusi* (mulberry) tree that, they claim, flourishes exceptionally well on

4

5

3. Maisin women sharing a clay pot of *dun* (red) pigment to paint tapa cloth, 1997.

4. Maisin woman painting tapa on her family's *bari-bari*, 1997.

5. Maisin woman preparing *mii* (black) pigment, 1997.

their soil. Since virtually all Maisin women, and an increasing number of men, make and paint tapa cloths from an early age, the Maisin have developed a high level of skill in the preparation of pigments and in the creation of imaginative designs.

In Maisin culture, tapa cloths have traditionally played a variety of roles. Tapa paintings can be divided into two basic types: sacred and nonsacred. The sacred works are painted with so-called clan designs. These designs, repeated from generation to generation by strict convention, are the exclusive intellectual property of particular groups or clans. Many are representational, depicting images seen in dreams or other items pertinent to the history of a particular clan. One clan design, for example, depicts a medicinal plant that was discovered in a dream and retrieved from a nearby mountain to heal the clan of a persistent, widespread ailment. Clan designs are typically used—that is, worn—only on ceremonial occasions. They may not be sold, traded, or worn by someone from another clan. In recent years, this taboo has sometimes extended to photography and nonceremonial display. Despite these prohibitions, one clan's design may actually be painted, on request, by someone from another clan so long as it is not used by them.

Nonsacred tapas are also used as clothing for both ceremonial and nonceremonial purposes; today, however, most Maisin wear tapa only for dancing, feasting, or other special occasions. As clothing, tapa is divided into two general types: *embobi*, a relatively large rectangular form worn by women; and *koefi*, a long thin form worn by men. Tapa plays an important role as part of the bride price that a young man's family must pay to his bride's. For centuries, it has also been traded for clay pots made by the neighboring tribe, and since World War II it has become a cash commodity. In contemporary Maisin culture, tapa is also used as a table and wall covering, as a seat for a dignified guest, and as a covering for pots and bowls at the start of a meal.

Unlike sacred tapa, the nonsacred type is not designed with conventional images or patterns handed down over generations. On the contrary, these works are created, as they say, entirely "from the imagination," either envisioned just prior to being painted or developed during the course of creation. They are typically nonrepresentational. Different painters develop particular patterns, styles, and motifs that they may draw on repeatedly; however, virtually every painting is a unique creation. Tapa designs range from extremely spare compositions, with only a handful of lines separated by broad areas of blank tapa, to the wild jumble of the so-called *gangi-gangi* (crooked) style, to intricate, symmetrical patterns. While many artists borrow from each other, as well as from other sources, such as Western patterns seen on imported textiles, these appropriations are rarely direct. Rather, as described by Rarama in a

1997 interview, "You don't just take and copy it straight. You recall it. It comes from your memory."

Virtually all tapa are made with two pigments, *mii* (black) and *dun* (red); various other pigments, including *oman* (yellow) and *gadun* (a kind of mud used for painting mourning attire), have almost disappeared from use. First, the *mii* is applied in a linear design with a short stick. Small dots, called *sufifi*, are applied to the edge of the lines, adding visual interest. Other marks, such as short lines or cone-shaped forms, called *sisimbu*, are added as desired. After the *mii* is dry, the *dun* is painted in between areas of double black lines. Because it is impossible to erase or cover up a mark once made on the light-colored, highly absorbent tapa cloth, one of the greatest challenges of tapa painting is being able to envision a composition in advance with enough clarity to forestall the likelihood of misplacing lines. Tapas are always painted freehand with no prior sketching.

The Maisin do not have a word corresponding exactly to our word *art*. Since they began selling tapas more widely to Western and Japanese traders in the 1950s and 1960s, however, both the word and the concept have become widely absorbed. In the Maisin language a number of words cover some of the same territory as does our extremely imprecise and broadly meaningful term *art*. *Saraman* denotes design, planning, or creativity (more precisely, it signifies a conjoining of thinking and doing). But not all tapa making is considered *saraman*; sacred tapa in which the designs are repeated by convention lack the "thinking" aspect and do not qualify. *Ininimbi* is roughly equivalent to *craft* but applies to a rather specific set of practices—canoe and shield carving, or necklace and armlet making—but not, for example, to the painting of tapa, sacred or otherwise. *Diowa* is similar to *beautiful*, and it is common to hear a tapa described as *diowa tauban* (very beautiful). The Maisin have various criteria for what they consider to be a beautiful tapa design. In my experience, some of the most commonly appreciated qualities are the whiteness of the cloth, the brightness and richness of the red pigment, the darkness and sharpness of the black pigment, and perhaps, most of all, the painter's imagination. Innovation and originality are highly regarded components of the painter's skill. As Franklin Seri, a tribal elder and one of the first male tapa painters, told me in an interview conducted in Uiaku village in August 1997, an exceptionally well-designed painting extends beyond the realm of decoration or design to become a medium for the expression and transmission of aesthetic concentration, creativity, and clear-mindedness.

For the Maisin, the creation of tapa paintings has always involved a degree of collectivity. The structures of families, clans, and villages provide the network of support necessary

6

7

  6, 7. Community meetings for Maisin villagers to see and discuss FW+M collaborative projects, 1998.

to maintain a basic level of livelihood for painters. Without the support of family members and relatives, Maisin painters would not be able to clear land for the gardens where they grow the trees from which tapa cloth is derived. Without the support of others in providing food and maintaining the basic infrastructure of the community, there would be no time or energy for tapa painting. But the collective aspect of tapa art making goes well beyond such fundamental social cooperation.

Tapa cloth production and painting are in themselves highly social and, in effect, collective practices. The women, and few men, who are tapa painters typically gather their materials, make their dyes, and create their paintings together—usually in groups of two to six. The actual painting is often done in a circle around a single pot of dye kept at a low simmer to maintain the proper viscosity. While painting, they pass the time telling stories and gossiping, and they may occasionally share their artworks, passing a partially finished piece (that is, one that has been designed in *mii* but not yet painted with *dun*) to another artist for completion. Ubiquitous in the Maisin villages, tapa paintings are hung to dry from clotheslines, adorn the mats and walls of homes, and are worn by men and women. Their visual omnipresence, not to mention the common thunking sound of tapa being pounded—which allegedly was so irritating that it drove out the first missionary after only a few months in residence—creates an atmosphere in which tapa is as much a part of the Maisin environment as coconut palms and crashing waves. One even finds tapa-style designs tattooed on the faces of many of the women—a coming-of-age ritual that has become considerably less common in recent years. Finally, the skills of tapa making and painting are seen as a collective heritage handed down by the ancestors. In a profound sense, then, tapa literally and figuratively coheres the community, symbolizing a common identity that unites this string of far-flung villages on the isolated New Guinea coast.

The Maisin have participated in exhibitions of their tapa paintings in Japan, Scotland, Polynesia, and the United States. I originally approached them in 1994 to propose an exhibition at the University Art Museum, Berkeley, where I was then a curator. The Maisin community—that is, a council of the clan elders informed by the opinions of other tribal leaders, the Mother's Union, and individual artists—agreed to participate on certain conditions: that the tapa be presented in the same way as other works of art in the museum; that the exhibition be accompanied by information concerning tapa and the Maisin way of life; that Greenpeace—in collaboration with the museum—organize marketing research; and that the museum host a number of Maisin leaders at the opening.

Business contacts made during the Berkeley exhibition inspired the creation of the Maisin Tapa Business Group

(MTBG) to distribute the increased profits from tapa sales equitably). When the Maisin concluded, around 1994, that their best option for a sustainable alternative to industrial logging of their forests was to expand markets for their tapa paintings, they determined to accomplish this in such a way as not to increase divisions in the community. Indeed, at that time, there were still many tensions between the villages and clans echoing from historical antagonisms. The Maisin concluded that to withstand the blandishments of loggers, they needed to overcome these ancient divisions and unite as one voice. Thus in late 1995, the Maisin elders, along with other community leaders and tapa makers, formed the MTBG. Because this new organization set standards for pricing, quality control, and distribution of profits, the greater good and unity of the Maisin community were foremost concerns. Although the MTBG did not forbid individuals or villages from trading on their own, the group made one of its goals to offer the artists the most attractive and competitive option. About half of the profits from tapa sold through the MTBG are invested in projects that benefit the entire community: medicine, emergency fuel, a new telephone, and so on; the remainder is given to the artists.

The internationalization of the market for tapa paintings also raised numerous questions regarding potential marketing opportunities, such as the use of painted tapa cloth for items like book covers, hats, and handbags. Even more complex questions arose, such as the potential licensing of tapa designs for mass production. The continuing dialogue around these issues was enriched by the opportunity offered by The Fabric Workshop and Museum's invitation to host a residency and exhibition. In the summer of 1997, I traveled to Papua New Guinea with Christina Roberts and Kelly Mitchell from The Fabric Workshop and Museum, and Lafcadio Cortesi from Greenpeace to propose this new project. During extensive meetings we explained the parameters of the proposed project, answered questions, and noted suggestions for improvement. Among the most serious concerns raised were worries the purity of the Maisin tapa tradition might be compromised and that the United States was a long way to go simply to explore aesthetic problems that might not have any long-term application in Maisin culture (for example, silkscreen printing). After much discussion, however, the Maisin communities reached consensus and agreed to participate. Their goals were to create works of art through experimentation with new materials and techniques, to learn about various methods of fabric design that might have commercial applications for their tapa tradition, and to gain greater familiarity with the customs and culture of the West.

Three painters were selected by the Maisin women to travel to Philadelphia for a three-week residency from September to

8

9

8. Maisin woman at home, 1997.

9. Maisin artist Natalie Rarama with daughter Wilma at the FW+M in Philadelphia, with FW+M staff members Christina Roberts, Mary Anne Friel and Kelly Mitchell, 1997.

to October 1997, where they experimented with various fabrics and dyes. Faced with a bewildering array of opportunities for new applications of their creativity, they decided that whatever they made should be useful and appreciated in both Maisin and Western cultures. They spent most of their time learning basic silkscreen methods but also experimented with techniques such as silkscreened yardage and woven carpeting.

Mass production of tapa designs remains one of the most complicated issues facing the Maisin community insofar as it may conflict with their fundamental conceptual models of individuality and ownership. The commercialization of tapa paintings themselves, however, is not as profound an issue as one might think, because historically tapa have been created as objects of trade. (Some Maisin have even suggested that tapa was used for a time in certain regions of New Guinea as a form of currency.) In addition, the sale of nonsacred tapa does not pose many of the problems associated with the commercialization of many other non-Western cultural forms, whose sale can involve a compromise of their traditional meaning and function. On the contrary, the Maisin themselves report a kind of renaissance in the tapa tradition, with an increased number of women, as well as men, not only taking up the practice but creating works distinguished by a high degree of skill and imagination. Over the past ten years or so a number of formal and iconographic innovations have been introduced—such as new types of *sisimbu*, representational subjects, and an increased emphasis on the designs' borders—which may be, in part a result of commercial influences. While the Maisin community respects the innovations of individual artists, there are some who see a danger in these changes and support the preservation of more traditional forms. Questions regarding cultural continuity and change are being actively debated within the Maisin community, and it will be up to the Maisin themselves, as individuals and as a community, to determine the direction to take.

The Maisin tapa painters work collectively to create an environment conducive to tapa making, to make the tapa cloth and designs themselves, and to develop the means and opportunities to exhibit, interpret, and market their products. As such, their practice encompasses several of the functions of Western art collectives. In Western societies, art collectives usually exist for the purpose of creating collaborative art projects through the sharing of diverse skills. Members of art collectives in the West have also often been conscious of their symbolic role as progenitors of radically democratic, collaborative social practice. Whereas in most Western societies that population is large enough that a collective is formed as a subset of the general population, focusing on the special interests and needs of its members, in the Maisin society there are suf-

ficiently few people—and tapa making is pervasive enough—that virtually the entire community can be seen to constitute the "collective." This is especially true in recent years as the Maisin have joined together to support the development of their tapa tradition both to foster community unity and to generate much-needed ecologically and culturally sustainable cash income. In 1995, on their way to the United States for the opening of the Berkeley exhibition, four Maisin leaders held a press conference in Port Moresby, the capital of Papua New Guinea. "Tapa to Take on Loggers," a front-page article by Neville Togarewa published in the April 10 issue of *The Papua New Guinea Post-Courier*, announced: "Four clan leaders are to stage a tapa cloth exhibition and explain to the American people why they have declared a forest taboo, at a time when many traditional landowners are willing to sell their birthright and their heritage to foreign logging interests. The tapa paintings . . . represent a critical effort by the Maisin to improve the quality of their lives and preserve almost half a million acres of pristine and threatened rainforest, all the while maintaining the integrity of their community and culture."

Clearly, the Maisin are playing a leading role in shaping their own future, which looks much brighter than those of many of their compatriots, in large part because of their vision of the inseparability of culture, environment, and economy. Concerns about aesthetic definition, "cultural purity," and individual versus collective practice must be seen within the profoundly broad compass of this overall enterprise. The Maisin have elected to learn about the West, to study our art and our forms of institutional organization. We would do well to learn from them in return. As a model for the intersection of art and collectivity, they provide a rare and inspiring example.

Faith Ringgold

About the artist

American, born 1930, lives in La Jolla, California, and Englewood, New Jersey

Faith Ringgold grew up in Harlem, and pursued her art studies in New York, earning BS and MA degrees in visual art from City College of New York in 1955 and 1959. A strong voice within a growing community of African American artists working in New York in the 1960s, Ringgold has continued to create artwork that overtly addresses political themes as well as works inspired by her interest in traditional handcraft and folklore. She has never limited her choice of media, and practiced as a painter, sculptor, performance artist, and writer. Ringgold had her first one-person show in 1967 (Spectrum Gallery), and numerous other exhibitions followed, including a major survey at The Studio Museum in Harlem (1984) and a 25-year retrospective that traveled nationally from 1990 to 1992. Ringgold has received eleven honorary doctoral degrees and many awards, including a Guggenheim Memorial Foundation Fellowship (1987). Since 1985, she has been professor of art at the University of California in San Diego.

236

About the work

Faith Ringgold made her first quilt, *Echoes of Harlem*, with her mother, Madame Willi Posey, in 1980. She was inspired to pursue quiltmaking as a vehicle for her art after hearing her mother's stories of their ancestors, who were slaves trained to make quilts on their plantation. By 1990, the year of her residency at the FW+M, Ringgold had completed a second quilt, Who's *Afraid of Aunt Jemima?*, her first story quilt incorporating both text and image. Her FW+M quilt, *Tar Beach 2*, tells the story of a young African American girl who grows up in Harlem, spending her time outdoors on the rooftops of her urban landscape. The narrative is told through text and image, which are printed with dyes on silk duppioni. Ringgold chose a variety of decorative fabrics to border the quilts, making each quilt in the edition of 24 unique.

In 1991, Ringgold published *Tar Beach* as a children's book (Crown Publishers). It has won over twenty awards, including the Caldecott Honor and the Coretta Scott King award for best illustrated children's book in 1991. Ringgold has since gone on to write other children's books, including *Aunt Harriet's Underground Railroad in the Sky* (Crown Publishers, 1992) and *Dinner at Aunt Connie's* (Hyperion Books, 1993).

Tar Beach 2, 1990 (detail). Acid dyes on bleached silk duppioni, and cotton. 65 x 65 inches (165.1 x 165.1 cm). Edition of 24. Collection of The Fabric Workshop and Museum; Philadelphia Museum of Art; Pennsylvania Academy of the Fine Arts; and the Virginia Museum of Fine Arts, Richmond.

Daddy said the George Washington Bridge was the longest and most beautiful bridge in the world and that it opened in 1931 on the very day I was born. Daddy worked on the bridge hoisting cables. Since then, I've wanted that bridge to be mine.

238

Tar Beach 2, 1990. Acid dyes on bleached silk duppioni, and cotton. 65 x 65 inches (165.1 x 165.1 cm). Edition of 24. Collection of The Fabric Workshop and Museum; Philadelphia Museum of Art; Pennsylvania Academy of the Fine Arts; and the Virginia Museum of Fine Arts, Richmond.

7.
But still he can't join the Union
because Granpa wasn't a member. Well
Daddy is going to own that building
cause I'm gonna fly over it and give
it to him. Then it won't matter that
he's not in their ole Union or whether
he's Colored or a half breed Indian
like they say.

e to go wherever
t of my life.

ee the Union Build-
. He can walk
igh up in the sky
y call him the cat.

8.
He'll be rich and won't have to stand
on 26 story high girders and look down
He can look up at his building going
up. And Mommy won't cry all winter
when Daddy goes to look for work and
doesn't come home. And Mommy can
laugh and sleep late like Mrs Honey
and we can have ice cream every
night for dessert.

Next I'm going to fly over the ice cream
factory just to make sure we do.

Tonight we're going up to Tar Beach.
Mommy is roasting peanuts and fry-
ing chicken and Daddy will bring
home a watermelon. Mr and Mrs
Honey will bring the beer and their old
green card table. And then the stars
will fall around me and I will fly
to the Union Building.

10.
I'll take Be Be with me. He has threatened
to tell Mommy and Daddy if I leave him
behind.
I have told him it's very easy, anyone
can fly. All you need is somewhere to
go that you can't get to any other
way. The next thing you know, you're
flying among the stars.

THE GOODIE GOODIE ICE CREAM FACTORY

Tim Rollins and K.O.S.

About the artist

Tim Rollins, American, born 1955, lives in New York City

In 1981, Tim Rollins was recruited by Intermediate School 52 in the South Bronx, New York, to start a program for adolescents who had been labeled by their school as learning-disabled or emotionally handicapped. Rollins established the Art and Knowledge Workshop, and Kids of Survival (known as K.O.S.) emerged from this interdisciplinary program. Rollins himself earned a BFA from the School of Visual Arts in New York City (1978) before attending New York University for graduate school in art education. The Art and Knowledge Workshop is composed of junior and high school students from the South Bronx, and some of the longstanding members of the group now attend universities around the country. The group studies literary texts together, discovering their own contemporary and personal interpretations, and then collaborates to make new art based on their responses. They have addressed books such as Franz Kafka's *Amerika*, Aeschylus' *Prometheus Bound*, and George Orwell's *Animal Farm*. Their work has been the subject of many museum exhibitions, including a web-based project at Dia Center for the Arts in New York (1997), and solo shows at The De Young Memorial Art Museum in San Francisco (2000), the Berkeley Art Museum (1998), and the Hirshhorn Museum and Sculpture Garden, Washington, DC (1992).

240

About the work

Tim Rollins and K.O.S. first participated in the FW+M's residency program in 1989, making two projects—a t-shirt, entitled *By Any Means Necessary* and based on the autobiography of Malcolm X, and *Scarlet Letter* shirt, a white dress shirt emblazoned with an embroidered "A" and based on the Nathaniel Hawthorne novel.

In 1997, the group returned to the FW+M, undertaking a limited edition multiple, titled *Invisible Man (after Ralph Ellison)* and based on the novel of the same title. In an exhibition that same year at the FW+M, they also presented a new painting from a series based on Harriet Jacobs' autobiography, *Incidents in the Life of a Slave Girl*. This young woman's account of being born and raised as a slave in the South before the Civil War includes her eventual escape from an abusive master and describes seven years of hiding in a small garret in her grandmother's house. The painting by Tim Rollins and K.O.S. combines actual pages from the book, which cover the surface of a canvas, and a delicate overlay of vertical bands of brightly-colored satin ribbons. The colors of the ribbons were selected by K.O.S. to express "the colors of joy," a reference to a passage from Jacobs' book when the narrator glimpses the brilliant, festive colored ribbons worn by local Christmas revelers from the window in her grandmother's attic.

During their second residency in 1997 and later in 1999, Tim Rollins and K.O.S. led educational workshops for middle and high school students using *Incidents in the Life of a Slave Girl* as inspiration for the group's discussion and collaborative art project; the later workshop was held at the FW+M and sponsored by the Philadelphia Arts in Education Partnership.

Incidents in the Life of a Slave Girl (After Harriet Jacobs), 1997 (detail). Satin ribbons and book pages on linen. 64 x 52 inches (162.56 x 132.08 cm). Collection of the artists.

XVI

...es at the Plantation

XIX

The Children S...

XXIV

The Candidate for C...

Incidents in the Life of a Slave Girl (After Harriet Jacobs), 1997. Satin ribbons and book pages on linen.
64 x 52 inches (162.56 x 132.08 cm). Collection of the artists.

Ugo Rondinone

About the artist

Swiss, born 1963, lives in New York City

Born in Brunnen, Switzerland, in 1963, Ugo Rondinone's early artistic formation included a short stint working with the performance artist Hermann Nitsch and his Orgies Mystery Theater. Rondinone attended Vienna's Hochschule für Angewandte Kunst from 1986 to 1990. He came into prominence in Europe in the early 1990s with installations that explored the contrasts between natural and artificial environments, and combined live actors, sound, painting, photography, and video. Rondinone has had solo exhibitions at museums such as the Kunsthalle Zurich, the Centre d'art contemporain in Geneva, and P.S. 1 Contemporary Art Center in New York. Rondinone represented Switzerland at the XXIII Bienal São Paulo in 1996 and the 6th Istanbul Biennial in 1999. His work has also been included in thematic exhibitions such as *Let's Entertain* at the Walker Art Center in Minneapolis (2000); *L'autre Sommeil* at the Musée d'art moderne de la ville de Paris (1999); and *Conversation Pieces II* at the Institute of Contemporary Art in Philadelphia (1996).

244

About the work

Lowland Lullaby is an interactive visual and sound installation in the form of a stage onto which gallery visitors can walk. The piece was first exhibited at the Swiss Institute in New York, as part of a collaborative installation between Rondinone, Swiss artist Urs Fischer, and spoken-word poet John Giorno. Forty speakers embedded throughout the floor played Giorno's reading of his poem "There Was a Bad Tree." This provided a platform for Fischer's drawings and sculpture, which dangle from the wall and lean onto the platform, contributing to an environment of flux and unrest.

Rondinone's stage, created in collaboration with the FW+M, is made of 100 individual wood sections, hand-printed using black and white car paint in a repeat design. Through a grid of curving lines, the two-dimensional pattern perceptually suggests a three-dimensional undulating space. To protect the pattern, the entire surface was coated with the highest-grade polyurethane, designed for use on buses and airplanes. Using relatively simple means (plywood, speakers, hand-printed paint), Rondinone's installation investigates the construction and interaction of physical, visual, aural, and social spaces.

In this as well as his other works, Rondinone has used vibrant patterns and bold imagery—in the form of targets, clowns and neon signs—to translate conflicted psychological states into environments that provoke corresponding moods in the viewer. Elizabeth Janus, writing in *Artforum*, describes the "parallel realities" he creates as "filled with fantasy, angst, monotony, and despair . . . closer to the truth than we'd care to admit" (*Artforum*, No. 3, November, 1998).

Lowland Lullaby, 2002 (detail). Installation at the Swiss Institute, New York, 2002. Hand-printed automotive paint and polyurethane on wood. Dimensions vary with installation.

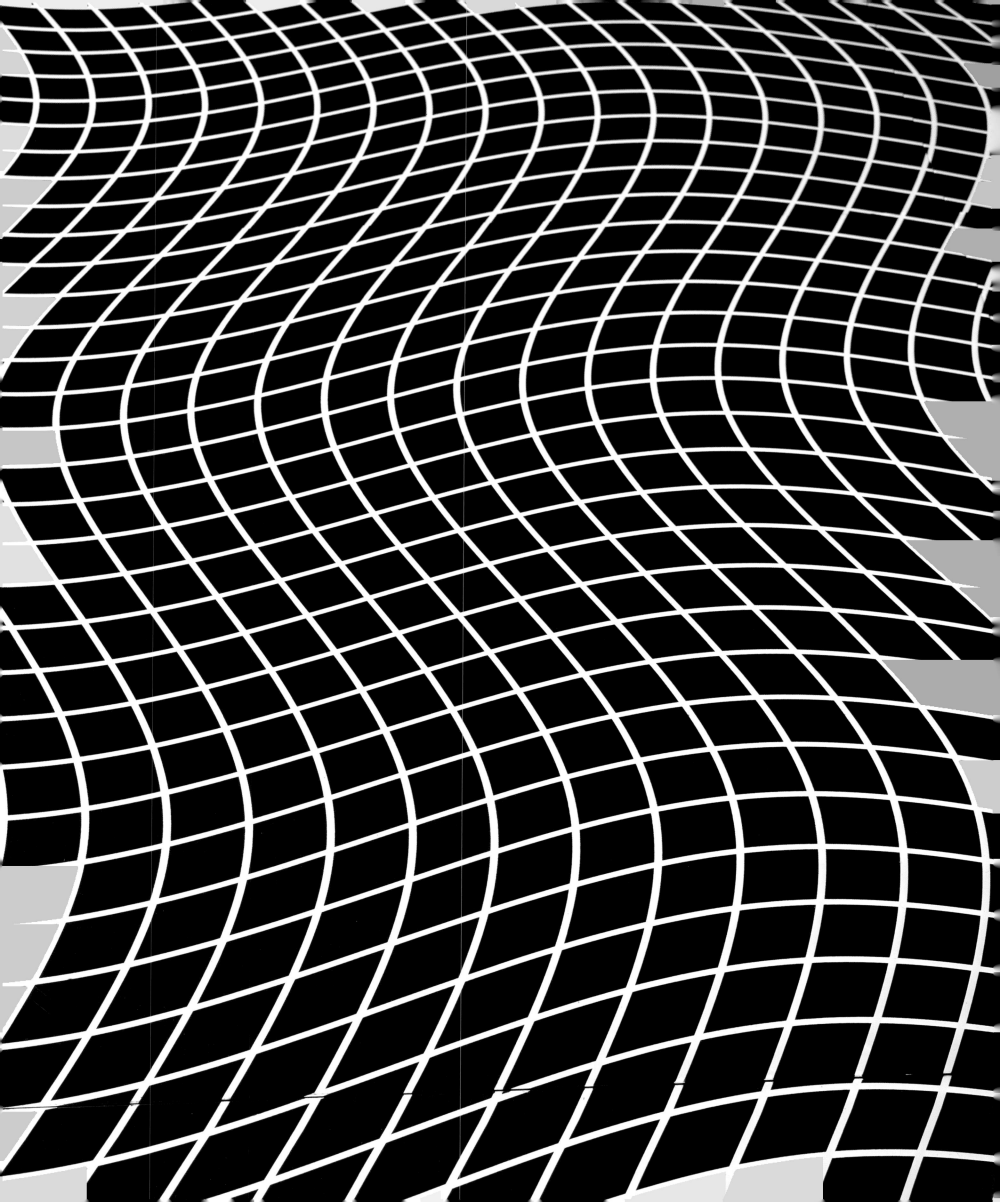

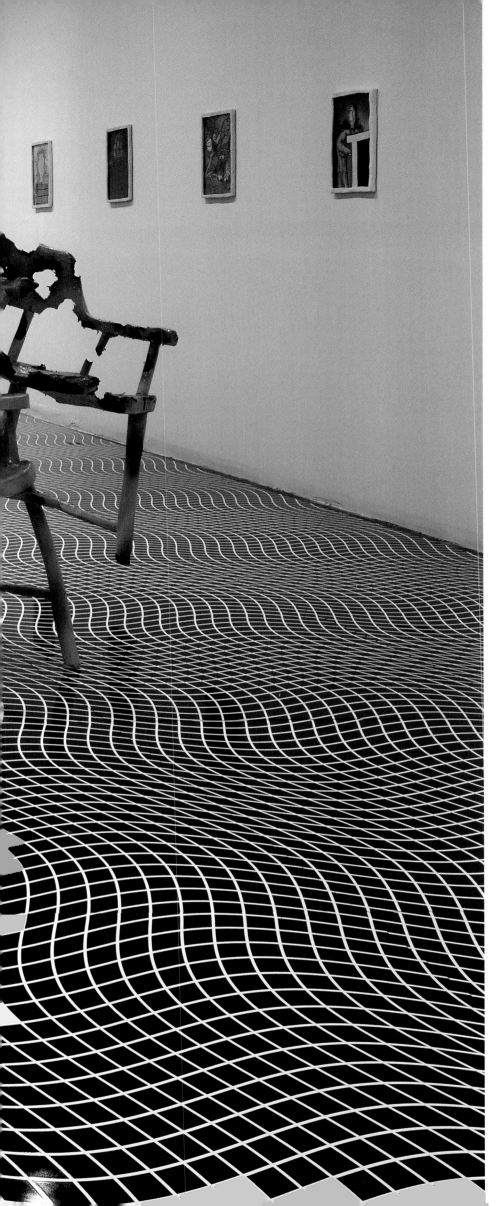

Lowland Lullaby, 2002. Installation at the Swiss Institute, New York, 2002. Hand-printed automotive paint and polyurethane on wood. Foreground: Swiss artist Urs Fischer's *Untitled* sculpture. Dimensions vary with installation.

Nancy Rubins

American, born 1952, lives in Topanga, California

About the artist

Nancy Rubins studied at The Maryland Institute College of Art in
Baltimore, earning a BFA in 1974 before completing a MFA at
the University of California in Davis (1976). She is known for her
architectural-scale indoor and outdoor sculptural work, made from
unlikely objects such as airplane parts, water heaters, and trailers.
Rubins' work has been shown in solo exhibitions at the Miami Art
Museum (1999), the Museum of Modern Art in New York (*Projects*
series, 1995), the Venice Biennale (*Aperto*, 1993), and The Drawing
Center in New York (1991). Her project with the FW+M, *Mattresses
and Cakes*, was included in the Whitney Biennial of 1995. She has
been the recipient of numerous awards including a Rockefeller
Foundation Travel Award (1993) and The Louis Comfort Tiffany
Foundation Award (1991).

About the work

Mattresses and Cakes is a monumental ceiling installation combining objects that are, in many ways, strange bedfellows. A tangle of 59 mattresses and 299 Entenmann's cakes comprise the sculpture, and the overall effect is both humorous and aggressive.

To create the piece, Rubins and the FW+M salvaged old mattresses from thrift stores and the Salvation Army, and bound each with a metal strap using an industrial strapping machine. Rubins then bundled them together to form an abstract sculpture, with rolled ends of mattresses jutting out into space and bulbous clusters weighting the piece in all directions. This feat of engineering (for all of its weight, the sculpture is suspended off the ground) was then smeared with cake so the patterned surfaces of the mattresses mixes with clumps of sweet junk food. This combination of recycled debris and mass-produced food from our excessive consumer culture is typical of Rubins' artistic vocabulary. She has acknowledged the sprawling development and wasteful consumption of Southern California as an influence, but as the art critic Peter Schjeldahl has written about her work, it is not sculpture that lingers solely on politics. Discussing the formal qualities of her 1995 *Airplane Parts*, he wrote:

> The work's enthralling details serve a formal end like that of the flung paint in a Jackson Pollock, giving an inch-by-inch reality check to an overwhelming sublimity. You can do with Rubins' piece the art-loving dance of near and far, looking at it from a distance and up close by turns . . . The rewards won't stop. ("Airfill," *The Village Voice,* February 14, 1995*)*

Mattresses and Cakes, 1993 (detail, right).

Mattresses and Cakes, 1993 (following pages). Mattresses and cakes. 156 x 216 x 156 inches (396.24 x 548.64 x 396.24 cm). Collection of the artist.

Beverly Semmes

American, lives in New York City

About the artist

Beverly Semmes attended the Boston Museum School at Tufts University, earning her BFA in 1982. After studying at the New York Studio School for one year (1983–1984), she attended Yale School of Art, where she completed a MFA in 1987. Semmes has employed sculpture, photography and film, and is best known for her oversized garments, primarily dresses, which she alters by elongating the arms and hem length to extend to the floor, encouraging the excess fabric to billow in pools of sensuous material. There is a surrealistic tone to much of Semmes' work, and even when offering cultural critique, her works have a humorous edge. Since her first major one-person exhibition at P.S. 1 Contemporary Art Center in Long Island City, New York, in 1990, Semmes' work has been shown in other solo shows at the Wexner Center for the Arts in Columbus, Ohio (1997); the Hirshhorn Museum and Sculpture Garden in Washington, DC (1996); and the Museum of Contemporary Art in Chicago (1995).

About the work

After creating a first residency project with the FW+M in 1997—a mechanized, gigantic black cat made from crushed velvet, called *RISEANDFALL*—Beverly Semmes returned in 2000 to investigate a new form and material. Entitled *Watching Her Feat*, the dominant visual cue in this installation and exhibition of the same name is the color of bright, fluorescent yellow.

Sewn from rip-stop nylon and stuffed with biodegradable peanuts, the forms of *Watching Her Feat* are gigantic mounds made from overlapping and wound tubes of yellow fabric. A window to the outdoors is covered with red translucent fabric tubes, and the interplay of the warm glow of the red against the sensory-overload of the fluorescent yellow creates a total environment of color. An attendant, dressed in the same electric fabric, sits in a single chair in the middle of the installation of feces-like mountains, adding one interpretation to the mysterious title: perhaps a stand-in for the artist herself, the attendant keeps watch over Semmes' creative feat.

Semmes exhibited this fabric installation in conjunction with a series of videos, which offered a visual pun to the show's title through their literal portrayal of the artist's feet shot from her own vantage point. Filmed in different settings and with various manipulations to her feet (band-aids in one, Vaseline in another), the videos depict the artist watching her feet as they traverse water, walk along boards of a deck, or make their way through pools of purple fabric.

Watching Her Feat, 2000 (detail). Fabric, polyester filling, and attendant. Dimensions vary with installation. Collection of the artist.

Watching Her Feat, 2000. Fabric, polyester filling, and attendant. Dimensions vary with installation. Collection of the artist.

Yinka Shonibare

British, born 1962, lives in London

About the artist

Yinka Shonibare was born in London and grew up in Nigeria, where his family moved when he was four years old. He returned to London at the age of 17 to study at Goldsmith's College, University of London. Shonibare's interest in the longlasting and pervasive effects of colonialization is evinced in the sculptural tableaux for which he has become known. *Nuclear Family*, for example, is an arrangement of headless figures clothed in finely detailed Victorian fashions, made not from historically-accurate fabrics, but from African kinte cloth. The kinte cloth, too, is not what it seems; through the complex web of colonial-era trade, the wax-printed fabric was actually manufactured in Holland and only later shipped to West Africa, where it was adopted and has now become synonymous with traditional African textiles. Shonibare's work was the subject of a major retrospective at the Studio Museum in Harlem in 2002, and other one-person shows include those organized by the Tate Britain in London (2001), The Andy Warhol Museum in Pittsburgh (2001), the Victoria and Albert Museum in London (2000), and the Art Gallery of Ontario in Toronto (1997).

About the work

While not new to fabric as an artistic medium, Yinka Shonibare had the freedom during his residency at the FW+M to create custom print designs for the textiles that would clothe figures in a new installation. Titled *Space Walk*, the installation ventures into the new frontier of American exploration—space. A man and woman—dressed in brightly-colored space suits, and wearing backpacks and helmets—float near a half-scale fiberglass and wood copy of the Apollo 13 shuttle. Pioneers of space, the couple refashions concepts of expansion, exploration, and potential colonization.

Shonibare designed four new fabrics for *Space Walk*. Based on the Dutch wax-printed batiks he has often used in previous work, the new designs recreate a batik patterning not through the traditional wax method, but through silkscreen printing. Two batik designs were created—one based on a traditional batik drip patterning, the other on a grid—and they were used as background for the printed textiles. The handmade quality of the prints was emphasized by printing the repeat pattern off-register; in other words, with each printing of the design, the silkscreen was allowed to move so the patterns do not align perfectly. The dominant motifs—drawn from the late 1960s and early 1970s music tradition produced in Philadelphia, known as the "Philly Sound"—are layered on the batik background. The artist borrowed images, text, and photographs from record albums of such period bands as The Intruders, Three Degrees, The O'Jays, and contemporary singer Jill Scott. Shonibare made a master drawing, which was then transferred to silkscreens for printing. Characteristic of Shonibare's work, the colors of the textiles are vibrant oranges, turquoises, and reds, another reference to the Dutch wax fabrics on which the designs are based.

Space Walk, 2002 (detail, right).
Space Walk, 2002 (following pages). Fiberglass (England), silkscreen print on cotton sateen and cotton brocade (USA), and plastic (England). Dimensions vary with installation. Edition of 2.

Gary Simmons

American, born 1964, lives in New York City and Los Angeles

About the artist

Gary Simmons grew up in New York City and upstate New York. He attended the School of Visual Arts in New York, where he earned his BFA in 1988, before moving to California to study at The California Institute of the Arts in Valencia (MFA, 1990). He first became known for his "erasure" drawings, in which he applied blackboard surface to walls, drew an image with chalk and then partially erased it with his hands. His 1993 wall drawing for the Whitney Biennial, *Wall of Eyes*, is a monumental example of this signature technique. Simmons' work has been presented in many one-person exhibitions, including a major exhibition in 2002 at the Museum of Contemporary Art in Chicago that traveled to SITE Sante Fe, New Mexico, and The Studio Museum in Harlem, New York. The Saint Louis Art Museum (1999), the Museum of Contemporary Art in San Diego (1997), and the Hirshhorn Museum and Sculpture Garden in Washington, DC (1994) have also presented solo shows of Simmons' work.

260

About the work

Step in the Arena (The Essentialist Trap) is a quarter-scale boxing ring that ruminates on the themes of boxing, dance, and the spectacle of entertainment—especially those forms of entertainment in which black men are valued for their prowess and grace. Simmons also brings music into the fold, borrowing a portion of the title—*Step in the Arena*—from the title of a song by the hip-hop group Gangstarr, in which the world of young black men is depicted as a dangerous battleground.

The floor of the ring is canvas printed with a dance instruction pattern, and tap shoes are hung from the ultrasuede-covered ropes. Simmons sees these elements as related to boxing in the way that great boxers like Muhammad Ali literally danced around the ring, using this graceful movement to evade their opponents and triumph in "battle." The printed pattern is smudged—in a style reminiscent of Simmons' erasure drawings—suggesting movement and the flurry of feet. The dance diagram shows step-by-step instructions for a waltz, a dance that emphasizes the class distinction between social dancing and the world of boxing, while the tap shoes recall the common practice of young urban kids marking their territory by throwing their sneakers over telephone wires.

Step in the Arena (The Essentialist Trap) was included in the exhibition *Black Male: Representations of Masculinity in Contemporary Art*, curated by Thelma Golden for the Whitney Museum of American Art in New York (1994). This groundbreaking exhibition examined the stereotypes and myths of the African American male in contemporary culture.

Step in the Arena (The Essentialist Trap), 1994 (detail). Wood, metal, canvas, ultrasuede, pigment, ropes, shoes, and taps. 85 x 120 x 120 inches (215.9 x 304.8 x 304.8 cm). Collection of Whitney Museum of American Art, New York. Gift of Peter Norton Family Foundation.

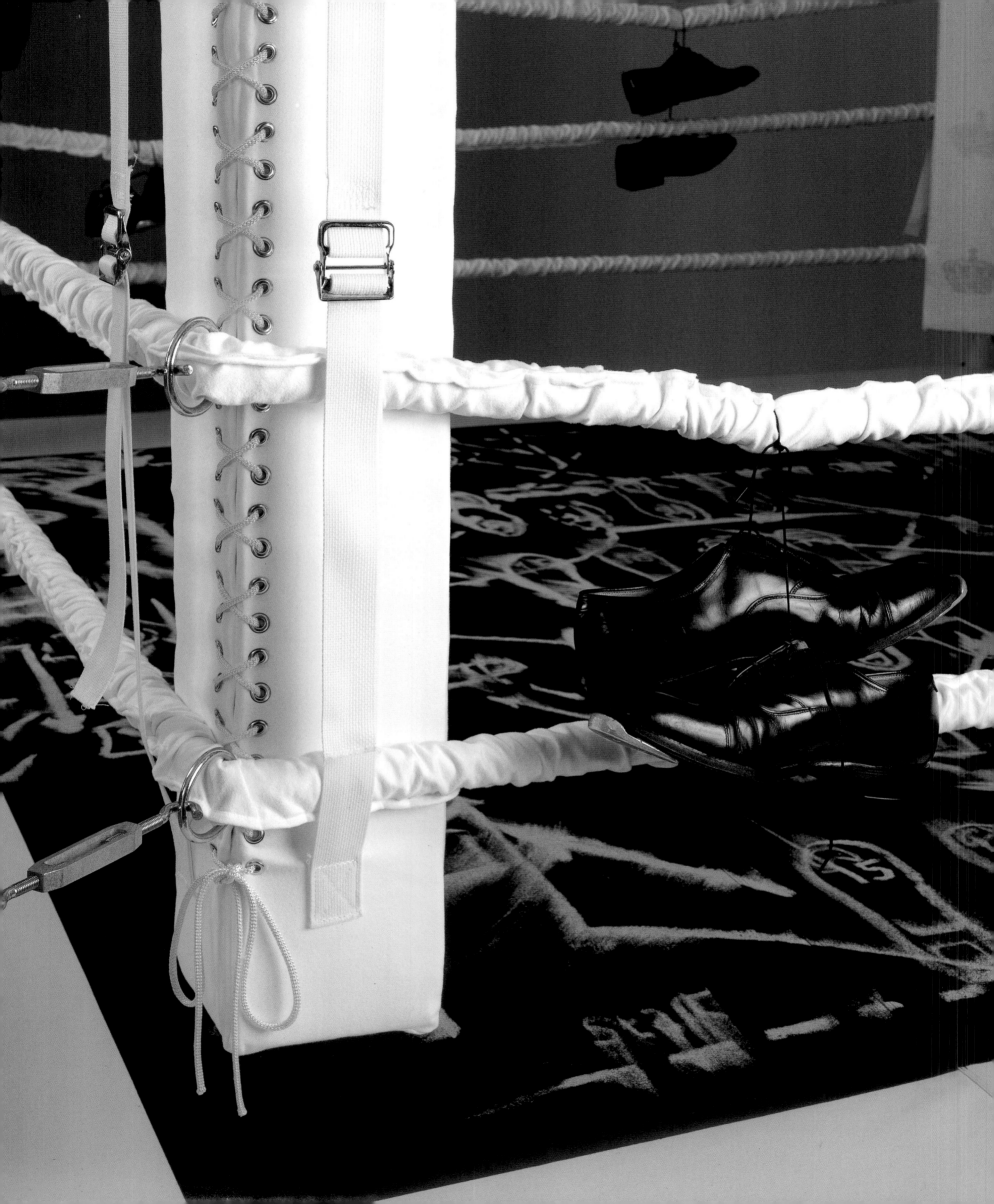

Step in the Arena (The Essentialist Trap), 1994. Wood, metal, canvas, ultrasuede, pigment, ropes, shoes, and taps. 85 x 120 x 120 inches (215.9 x 304.8 x 304.8 cm). Collection of Whitney Museum of American Art, New York. Gift of Peter Norton Family Foundation.

Lorna Simpson

About the artist

American, born 1960, lives in New York City

Lorna Simpson was born in Brooklyn and continues to live in New York City. She studied photography as an undergraduate, earning a BFA from the School of Visual Arts in New York (1982), before going on to the University of California in San Diego for her MFA in Visual Arts (1985). Simpson's photography, sculpture, and film projects are grounded in her conceptual orientation to art, and she cultivates each medium to best express the content of individual works. Simpson is known for her text and photography works, which critique the cultural and historical contexts that give meaning to images and language. Her work has been the subject of many solo exhibitions: Whitney Museum of American Art, New York (2002); National Gallery of Women in the Arts, Washington, DC (2001); Walker Art Center, Minneapolis, MN (1999); and the Wexner Center for the Arts, Columbus, OH (1997). She was a finalist for The Hugo Boss Prize in 1998 at the Solomon R. Guggenheim Museum, and in 1990 she was awarded The Louis Comfort Tiffany Award.

264

About the work

Standing in the water is a room-size multi-media installation comprising video, sound, and a silkscreen printed industrial felt floor sculpture. The dominant motif is water, and each of the installation's components resonates with attributes of and associations to water. Simpson described her intention for the piece: "I wanted the viewer to experience the power of being mesmerized by the water, stopped dead, standing in the water. So I don't want the title to refer to a religious experience, but really to the body and this experience of confronting water in all its meanings" (*Lorna Simpson: Standing in the water*, brochure from Whitney Museum of American Art at Philip Morris, New York, 1994). Simpson's interest in probing psychological states of mind, and her ongoing investigations of race and identity lead to an interpretation of this piece as an environment evoking the great distance through water of slaves from Africa to the United States and elsewhere, known as the Middle Passage.

Simpson brought a photograph of waves from the scientific text *An Album of Fluid Motion* to her first meeting at the FW+M. This wave would become the central pattern for the silkscreen print on felt, with five screens needed to handprint the repeating image on the 14-foot panels. The 1-1/2-inch thick felt was then carved to accommodate glass panels etched with the image of untied shoes. This project represents Simpson's first work using industrial felt, a material she would go on to explore in many other sculptural and photographic works.

The accompanying video and audio bring other senses into the installation's meditations on water. The audio track projects gentle sounds of water's many movements—dripping, pouring from a spigot, a person climbing out of a bathtub—while two small video screens show water in motion. On the lower monitor, repeating images of waves combine with text describing common water sounds, while the upper monitor depicts a water pitcher with text taken from newspaper stories detailing incidents relating to water.

Standing in the water, 1994 (detail). Pigment on wool felt, etched glass, video monitors, and audio track. Three panels: 1 $\frac{1}{2}$ x 172 x 52 inches (3.81 x 436.88 x 132.08 cm) each.

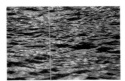

Standing in the water, 1994 (left). Pigment on wool felt, etched glass, video monitors, and audio track. Three panels: 1 ½ x 172 x 52 inches (3.81 x 436.88 x 132.08 cm) each.

Video stills from *Standing in the water*, 1994 (above).

Kiki Smith

About the artist

American, born 1954, lives in New York City

Kiki Smith was born in Nuremberg, Germany, and returned home with her family to South Orange, New Jersey when she was one. She grew up in a creative household led by her parents, the sculptor Tony Smith and her mother, Jane, an opera singer and actress. Smith attended Hartford Art School for a year in the early 1970s; during the late 1970s she moved to New York City and began working with Collaborative Projects, Inc., an arts collective. Her first solo exhibition was in 1982 at The Kitchen in New York, and it firmly established Smith's interest in the human body, especially the female form. Since this exhibition, Smith's work has been shown widely at museums such as Kunstmuseum in Bonn, Germany (2000), the Carnegie Museum of Art in Pittsburgh (1998), the Museum of Contemporary Art in Los Angeles (1996), and the Lousiana Museum of Modern Art in Humlebaek, Denmark (1994).

268

About the work

Kiki Smith approached her residency at the FW+M as an opportunity to explore a traditional textile form, the blanket. Drawing on the well-established tradition of American weaving on Jacquard looms, Smith designed a wool coverlet, which the FW+M fabricated in conjunction with a small weaving company in western Pennsylvania. The Jacquard loom produced a double-woven blanket in which the imagery and colors pictured on the front are seen in reverse on the back. After weaving, the blankets were put through a fulling mill—an industrial device equipped with hundreds of needles that grab and fluff the fibers—to soften the coverlets and slightly blur the imagery.

Titled *Familiars*, Smith's coverlet depicts a benevolent scene of a woman surrounded by a menagerie of animals with snowflakes or stars dotting the sky above. Reminiscent of a fable, the scene is repeated twice on the blanket—a technical limitation of the weaving process that was used by Smith to accentuate the reflective nature of the text woven above the women and their flocks. "I see the moon, and the moon sees me" are the words from a nursery rhyme. The idea of reflection, or doubling, also highlights a fable's inherent "function" as a mirror image of behavior, from which one can learn something new. The word "Familiar" is woven below the scene, a reference to a familiar as a spirit, often embodied in an animal, that extends protective powers over a person. Smith has said that she was drawn to the idea of these animals as a concert of witches, acting as a conduit to the spirit world. The subject of animals has been a consistent theme in Smith's work since the mid-1990s when she began moving away from the body as the sole subject of her artistic explorations.

Familiars, 2001 (detail). Wool. 83 x 54 ½ inches (210.82 x 138.43 cm). Unlimited edition.

Familiars, 2001. Wool. 83 x 54 ½ inches (210.82 x 138.43 cm). Unlimited edition.

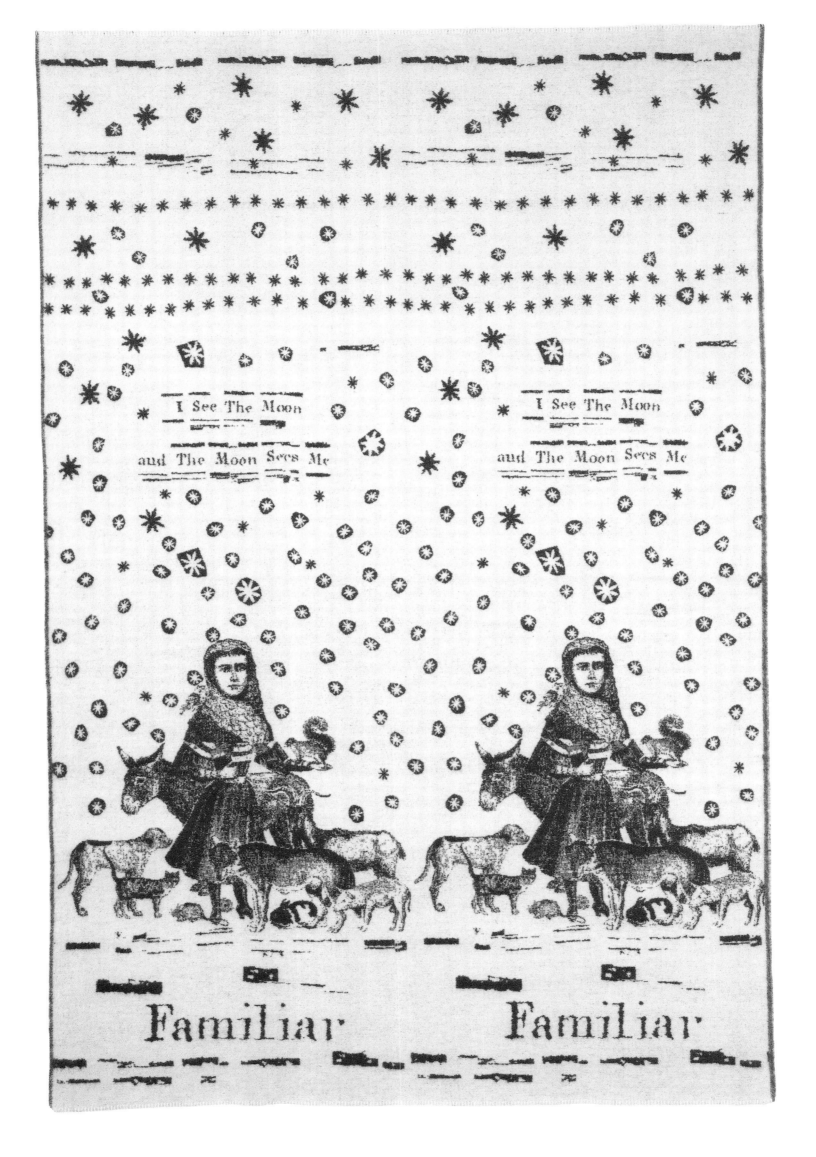

Jana Sterbak

About the artist

Canadian, born Czechoslovakia 1955, lives in Montreal and Barcelona

At the age of thirteen, Jana Sterbak immigrated to Canada with her family after Czechoslovakia was invaded by the Soviet Union. She earned her BFA from the Université Concordia in Montreal in 1975. Thematically, Sterbak's sculptural work focuses on the individual and is characterized by dark humor, as in her highly regarded *Vanitas: Flesh Dress for an Albino Anorectic* (1987). Constructed from sixty pounds of raw flank steak sewn into a dress, the sculpture slowly hardens into leathery material alluding to the deterioration of the body. Sterbak's work has been the subject of many exhibitions in North America and Europe, including a solo show at the Museum of Contemporary Art in Chicago (1998); a European traveling show with venues in Spain (Fundació Antoni Tàpies, 1996), England (Serpentine Gallery, 1996) and France (Musée d'Art Modern de Saint-Étienne, 1995); and a *Projects* exhibition at the Museum of Modern Art, New York (1992).

About the work

Oasis is Jana Sterbak's investigation into the psychological and physical limits of the self within the spiritual and technological realities of our day. Its title suggests a safe haven, and its tent-like form is an enclosure large enough for a person to occupy. Fabricated from knitted stainless steel filaments, *Oasis* is modeled after the idea of a Faraday Cage, a 19th century sealed metal structure used in scientific laboratories to block lower frequency electromagnetic waves. In today's culture, this would include blocking waves from cell phones, televisions, and radios. As a space of retreat from the technology that surrounds us, yet created from a technologically advanced metal fiber, the symbolism of Oasis darts between poetry and science.

Sterbak and the FW+M extensively researched conductive fibers currently in production that would satisfy the artist's aesthetic sensibility, functionally perform the capabilities of a Faraday cage, and have the tensile strength to hold their shape. Experimentations were conducted with handwoven copper, nickel-plated Kevlar, and silver-plated knit nylon before settling on knitted stainless steel, which was developed in Belgium for use in industry.

After Sterbak selected a final form for the tent from the many experimental shapes modeled at the FW+M, a small three-dimensional prototype was given to FTL Happold in New York, an engineering and design firm that specializes in tensile structures. With the aid of their form-finding computer programs for tensile structures, FTL Happold generated a blueprint for the tent's exoskeleton and a pre-stressed pattern for the knitted stainless steel skin. Based on this pattern, the FW+M then sewed the knitted steel into the tent form.

Computer-generated form-finding models for *Oasis*, FTL Happold, New York (right).
Oasis prototype, 2000 (following pages). Stainless steel, wool, and nylon. 119 x 158 x 122 inches (302.26 x 401.32 x 309.88 cm).

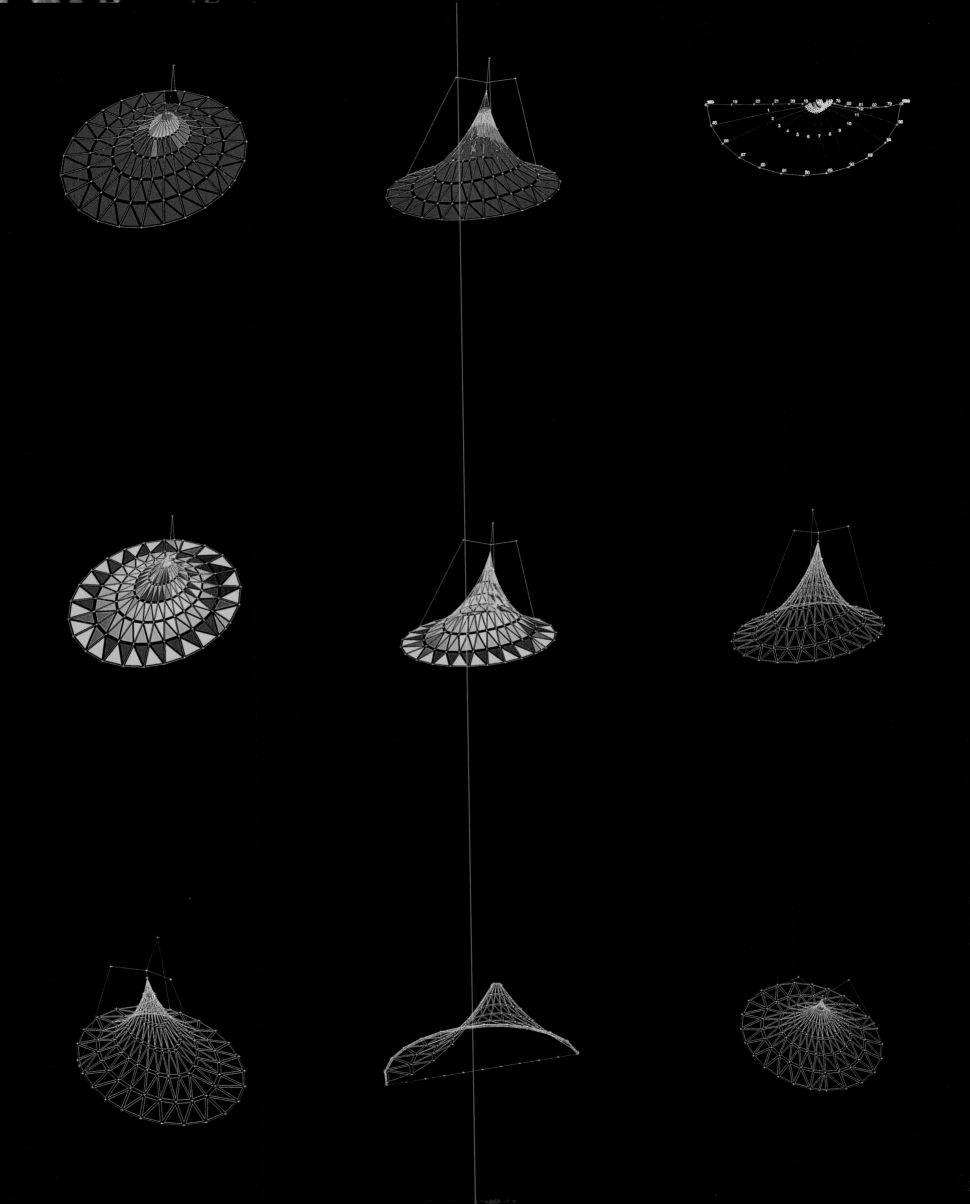

Robert Storr

About the author

American, born 1949, lives in New York City

Robert Storr is an artist and critic, and a senior curator in the Department of Painting and Sculpture at the Museum of Modern Art, New York. His exhibitions at MoMA include *Gerhard Richter: Forty Years of Painting* (2002), *Tony Smith: Architect, Painter, Sculptor* (1998), and *Willem de Kooning: The Late Paintings, The 1980s* (1997). From 1991 to 2000, he coordinated the *Projects* series of exhibitions focusing on contemporary art at MoMA, curating shows of new work by artists such as Ann Hamilton, Bruce Naumann, Tom Friedman, and Art Spiegelman. Among his many publications is the forthcoming *Intimate Geometries: The Work and Life of Louise Bourgeois* (Timken/Rizzoli). A contributing editor at *Art in America* since 1981, Storr writes prolifically on contemporary art and criticism in art journals and exhibition catalogs. Storr earned his BA from Swarthmore College and his MFA from the School of the Art Institute of Chicago. He is a professor at The CUNY Graduate Center and at Harvard University. Storr is a member of the Artist Advisory Commitee of the FW+M.

". . . Five Potato, Six Potato, Seven Potato, More!"

It is common practice when serving on a jury or assuming any other position in an art world context where the work of colleagues or institutions is evaluated to begin with full disclosure of prior involvements that might influence one's judgment. It seems only proper that I do so here, as well. At a minimum the exercise will prove that I do have a bias—and a strong one—in favor of what The Fabric Workshop and Museum has done and is doing. Beyond that, though, it may help to illustrate the range of the Workshop's activities in a more vivid way than an ostensibly "disinterested" description would. Finally, given that pleasure and discomfort are closely allied in every aesthetic experience that leaves its mark, the account I am about to offer will usefully qualify the feel-good assumptions of most testimonials.

Over the years, I have been to The Fabric Workshop and Museum numerous times to see exhibitions, and to peek behind the scenes in order to catch a glimpse of what is being made or is about to be made. On one such visit, I looked around a corner to discover a clear gelatinous carpet molded in the form of labyrinthine entrails, as if a classic modernist stripe painting had been brought low in every sense. A work of 1995 by Mona Hatoum (pp. 128–133) called *Entrails*, this domestic booby-trap—imagine stepping on such a glowing "unwelcome" mat of intestines—triggered exactly the simultaneous "Wow!" and "Ugh!" referred to above. Similarly "under foot," though one would never tread on it, was Mike Kelley's (pp. 150–155) *Lumpenprole*, made four years earlier, though I saw this piece at his 1994 retrospective at the Whitney Museum of American Art in New York and not in Philadelphia. Kelley's habit of mixing the nasty and the too nice is not just for effect, and it is certainly not intended for "balance." Rather the linkage is there so that when people are upset by what he shows them, their brains as well as their guts turn over. In this case creepy, possibly creeping shapes are hidden by a heavy, off-puttingly wholesome knitted rug that does more or less the same thing to formalist painting of the 1960s as Hatoum's piece does while reminding us that taste is not just a matter of common sense attraction or repulsion, but also a product of primal appetites and fears repressed or reinforced by the class

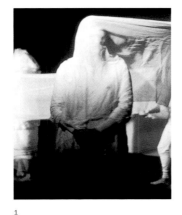

1, 2. Performance of *She Lost It* at
the FW+M, 5 December 1992.

taboos. Meanwhile, another trip to Cherry Street was timed to the 1994 exhibition of
Felix Gonzalez-Torres (pp. 106–113), an artist whose work had never ceased to amaze
me, and, in the utter simplicity and poignant delicacy of the curtains he made for this
occasion, did so once again. Of the artists who came fully into their own in the 1990s,
Gonzalez-Torres had the subtlest as well as fiercest understanding of individual desire,
social self-delusion and the fragility of all things human, coupled with the surest aesthetic
touch. This combination of qualities convinced me then—and I remain convinced—that
he is the well to which generations of artists will go to plumb ideas.

But I have gotten ahead of myself, or rather skipped "myself" and the personal
involvements I had promised to mention. They are of two kinds. The first is ownership.
On the table next to the couch in my living room sits a galvanized aluminum box with
the letters AHDI punched through the top (figs. 5, 6). They stand for Ann Hamilton
(pp. 122–127) and David Ireland (pp. 142–145), and, along with the box itself, the
contents constitute the artists' collaboration for The Fabric Workshop and Museum.
On one side of the partitioned interior is a pale gray granular ball, a "dumb ball" as
Ireland calls them, since it is made by tossing a lump of wet cement from hand to hand
while thinking about nothing (fig. 4). Thinking of something, in particular thinking too
hard about what one was doing as the lump passed between one's palms would not
only inhibit the maker's reaching the contemplative state that the rhythmic manufacture
of the ball renders accessible, but would ruin the ball itself. For the ball is not formed
like a sculpture modeled to match an ideal mathematical perfection. Rather it forms
itself, and thereby approaches an ideal that is, so to speak, completed in the "perfect"
absent-mindedness of the person who fashions it. "Zen-ball" would aptly describe the
object but an explanatory title of that kind would spoil the experience of holding it,
calculating its weight, its circumference, its equilibrium and its residual asymmetry.
It would in effect make it the symbol of an idea or system of ideas rather than the
manifestation of a way of being in which "thoughtlessness" counts for everything.
"Dumb ball" is better then, and the practice of tossing it casually while my mind wan-
ders—like a kid tossing a baseball—but not so casually that it falls—which would likely
crack it and any toe or floorboard that it landed on—roughly replicates the process by

3

4

3. Jerry Gorovoy, Louise Bourgeois, Jean-Louis Bourgeois, and Robert Storr on the evening of the performance of *She Lost It* at the FW+M, 1992.

4. David Ireland in process making *Dumb Ball*, 1998.

which the sphere was created. Thus Ireland's unassuming little mass exerts a small, entirely mental gravitational pull on the larger mass—the body—which it "orbits." The pang that this beautifully plain and otherwise benign thing gives rise to is this: when handling it one does not regret the ball's failure to precisely reproduce its Platonic paradigm—on that score Ireland's approximation, different in each example of the edition, seems infinitely preferable—but one does somehow wish that one could reach into a box of forever moist matter and delight in making such a ball from scratch. In that sense, art always makes the possessor envious of the practitioner, and Ireland's having playfully diminished the distance between the two to the extent that he has only makes that which remains more tantalizing, and sweetly saddening.

In the compartment on the other side of the box sits—or is nested—a ball made of long, wiry strands of brown, black and silvery horsehair. This too is sculpture for the hand, though, by conventional definitions, it is just barely sculpture at all. Like Ireland's only less so, Ann Hamilton's ball has a certain heft, being heavier than it looks, and denser as one palpitates it, than the externally loose bundling of the hairs suggest. Although a descendant of Meret Oppenheim's fur-lined teacup, this soft but assertively hirsute whirlwind avoids the obvious sexual innuendo of its Surrealist precursor, but lacks nothing of its uncanny sensuality. Indeed where Oppenheim's sculptural bon mot has become a look-don't-touch museum piece, Hamilton's spongy object insists upon being squeezed. First, being coarser than the human kind, the bunched hair can be slightly disconcerting, at times even repellent. Second, the more one indulges in the temptation despite this impediment, the looser the ball becomes, so that one is quickly made aware that repeated satisfaction of this haptic urge will eventually undo the source of one's compulsion. In the meantime stray ends multiply and change its configuration like a bun on the back of a woman's head from which all the pins have shaken free, except, once again, that there is nothing silky about the hairs that have been bound together, and a good deal that is unsettling.

Paired in this manner Hamilton's ball and Ireland's ball represent two extremes of tactility, two of weight, and two locations on the continuum of inherently formless materials taking shape, or, having briefly taken it, losing it again. And so, on a given morning or evening, I dip into the box, choosing one or the other—but seldom picking up both—and feel and think along the intersecting lines of which each of these eloquently simple spheres is a point. I must admit, therefore, to a certain dependency that AHDI has instilled in me, and the reader will have to decide if it has prejudiced me in the other things I have so say.

After ownership, the second of my "conflict of interests" regarding The Fabric Workshop and Museum is participation. In 1992 Louise Bourgeois (pp. 52–59) was asked to do a project there, and she in turn asked me if I would be willing to take part in a performance piece she was planning. By that time I had worked on and off with Bourgeois for over a decade, and knew enough to be sure that the invitation was not only a test of loyalty in the ordinary way that long term association with her frequently demands, but a special challenge in which my assigned role would have its own symbolic importance in the piece and for our relationship. As it stood, I had recently finished my first major exhibition at the Museum of Modern Art, and was on to the second. Consequently I was very busy and unable to see her once or twice a week as I had done for the ten previous years. Although Bourgeois had been included in that debut effort, she felt neglected. And as I knew, sooner or later she would get even, though humor was usually her weapon of choice.

The theme of the performance was abandonment, as spelled out in a long, gauze banner she had made at the Workshop. It was printed in red with the text of a simple parable about a husband who leaves his wife at home too often, too long, so that when he finally comes back all he finds in the chair she was sitting in when he departed is a tiny pea. Other recruits for the event included Mark Setteducati, a magician and long-time friend of Bourgeois; Sean Kelly, the dealer who read to the audience in a rich and measured voice; Virgil Marti (pp. 194–197), a young artist—and former student of mine at the Tyler School of Art whose installation *For Oscar Wilde* created for a site-specific exhibition at the Eastern State Penitentiary in 1995 was made with the assistance of The Fabric Workshop and Museum—Sarah Vanderlip, another young artist who I knew, and several more who I did not. In sum it was a typically Louisian version of the extended—and interestingly dysfunctional—family.

With the exception of Kelly and Setteducati, all the performers were instructed to dress in their underwear over which were buttoned or hung various skirts and jackets embroidered in red thread with other texts, for example, "Fear makes the world go round." It does, of course, and while the artist's original plan had been for us to wear nothing underneath these garments, fear—coupled in my case with concern that the unwarned public not be exposed to a middle-aged man with nothing to hide but nothing to show off either—overruled her wishes. Conceptually turning the tables on her old friend Marcel Duchamp, Bourgeois has more than once enjoyed playing "the bride who strips the bachelors bare" in works performed in public as well as in private. For instance this particular form of ritual humiliation was the basis for her 1978

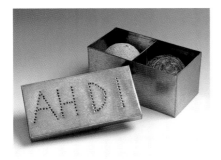

5   6

5, 6. Ann Hamilton and David Ireland,
Untitled, 1994. Handmade, galvanized
tin box; hair ball; dumb ball.
Box dimensions: 4 $\frac{1}{2}$ x 4 $\frac{1}{2}$ x 8 $\frac{3}{4}$
inches (11.43 x 11.43 x 22.23 cm).
Edition of 80.

performance piece, "A Banquet and Fashion Show of Body Parts," for which she enlisted an assortment of art world figures, including several art historians whose nakedness she sheathed in sheer latex costumes with protruding breast and phallic forms hanging off in all directions. Clearly she had something of the same sort in mind for us, but no one would take the bait.

As things turned out, the performance was wild enough, and to achieve her whimsical revenge Bourgeois made certain that collectors, curators, and other notables were invited to this comic spectacle, including the president of the Museum of Modern Art where I work. And so on the appointed night, as the audience shuffled into the performance space at the Workshop, I stood on the stage with a wooden ball and iron chain on my leg and the entire banner with the fable of the woman and the pea wrapped around my head and torso so that I looked like a giant Q-Tip. No one, I assumed, could tell who I was, but just before things started, a voice in the muffled noise around me said, "I know you're in there, Rob." No doubt mischievously prompted by the person responsible for my mummification, it was MoMA's President. As awkward as the situation was, I had to laugh, trying as I did so to ease my discomfort with the thought that she must be laughing too. In the event, Kelly read the story of the lonely wife aloud while slides of Bourgeois prints from the 1940s flashed on the screen and Setteducati wheeled out a table on which he performed his tricks (fig. 2). After that everyone else came out in their costumes and did their various bits of theatrical business to the sound of throbbing disco music. As the reading of the text concluded, I was moved over and slowly spun around—risking my loss of balance, which is one of Bourgeois' signature metaphors—until the gauze had been rewound onto the bodies of two other performers, freeing me to step forward in my ill-fitting union suit and present to the darkened room the green pea clutched in my fist (fig. 1). Then stage lights off, house lights on, and enthusiastic applause for the artist who never left her safe haven near a pillar twenty feet back from the action. So if you ask again what attachments I have to The Fabric Workshop and Museum, I would now add that they are emotional as well as aesthetic; the fond memory of being a willing pawn in a favorite artist's game at the cost of the kind of "dignity" people in my profession can benefit from shedding.

If all of what has preceded seems to ramble, that is not such a bad thing. The make-it-up-as-you-go-along aspect of this text is in harmony with the follow-your-hunches programming of the Workshop itself. In the final analysis, it is the quality of those hunches that matters. Above all their "rightness" has had to do with finding artists who are willing to experiment, and providing them the means they require, be it textiles, horse

hair, cement, rubber, calla lillies—materials used by those so far mentioned—or scavenged mattresses and richly frosted layer cakes, the "mediums" for Nancy Rubins (pp. 248–251) eponymous *Mattresses and Cakes* (1993). This latter project is one of the Workshop's most extraordinary efforts to date in which Baroque extravagance for form and color meets the funk of the gutter and the garbage dump, once more connecting visual marvels to sensual discomforts of other sorts.

Since it would be impossible in a short essay to encompass the full variety of projects The Fabric Workshop and Museum has sponsored over the past 25 years, I have chosen first-person narration as a sorting device, but several things ought to be clear from this otherwise arbitrary cross-section. First, the Workshop has broadly and vigorously expanded beyond its initial, self-imposed technical limitations to create work out of virtually anything its participating artists can think of. Second, it has moved beyond the concept of the object to embrace space-and-time based work from site-specific installations like Marti's and Rubin's, to performances like Bourgeois's, even as it continues to produce multiples that are, in the original spirit of that movement, well within the reach of ordinary people. In all these fields, meanwhile, it has distinguished itself as a practical innovator. In short, The Fabric Workshop and Museum's scope is as wide as contemporary art itself, and its role is that of a patron of some of the liveliest of talents active today. All in all something to celebrate!—which I do every time I pick up a ball from my galvanized box and flip it back and forth, or recall with a smile and a twinge my appearance on stage in too-tight long-johns with a pea in the cup of my hand.

Richard Tuttle

About the artist

American, born 1941, lives in New York City and Abiquiu, New Mexico

Richard Tuttle earned his BA from Trinity College in Hartford, Connecticut (1963). Following his studies, he worked in New Mexico as an assistant to painter Agnes Martin. Tuttle's first solo exhibition was in 1965 at the Betty Parsons Gallery in New York, and since that time his work has been shown in hundreds of one-person and group exhibitions. Early important exhibitions include a 1972 *Projects* series installation at the Museum of Modern Art, New York (1972), and a 1975 show at the Whitney Museum of American Art, New York. More recently, Tuttle's work was the subject of an exhibition at the Institute of Contemporary Art, Philadelphia (2002), and was included in the Venice Biennale in 1997 and 2001. He is best known for his sculptural works, which find their originations in Minimalism and are marked by his use of unusual and often humble materials.

About the work

In 1978, and again nearly twenty years later in 1997, Richard Tuttle collaborated with the FW+M to create new projects using fabric. Occurring as they did at such different phases of the artist's career, not to mention different periods of the FW+M's history, his works are interesting to compare.

During his first residency, Tuttle embraced the silkscreen printing process and the idea of fabric to make a series of clothing—*Shirts* in 1978 and *Pants* in 1979. Functional in nature, these projects rely on the ability of silkscreen printing to repeat endlessly. The dramatic gesture of the simply designed *Pants* is accentuated by the broad lightning bolt pattern and the elongated length—they extend beyond the feet of their wearer, so that long trains of printed fabric limit motion. These projects were the costumes for a performance in 1979, in which members of the Pennsylvania Ballet danced.

Tuttle's 1997 project, *The Thinking Cap*, also utilizes the silkscreen printing process and maintains a connection to conceptual fashion, yet instead of a shape connecting to the body, this more recent work focuses on the mind. Slight and peculiarly shaped with four protruding arcs, the small cap is clearly not intended to be worn. In his 1998 exhibition at the FW+M, Tuttle displayed *The Thinking Cap* on another collaborative project, entitled *24*—a minimal sculptural table. It seems an offhanded placement, yet the table overlooks 20th century design paradigms much in the same way the cap ignores the scale and material of "serious" sculpture.

The Thinking Cap, 1998 (detail). Pigment on cotton, and stainless steel. 12 x 8 ½ x 7 ½ inches (30.48 x 21.59 x 19.05 cm). Edition of 5.

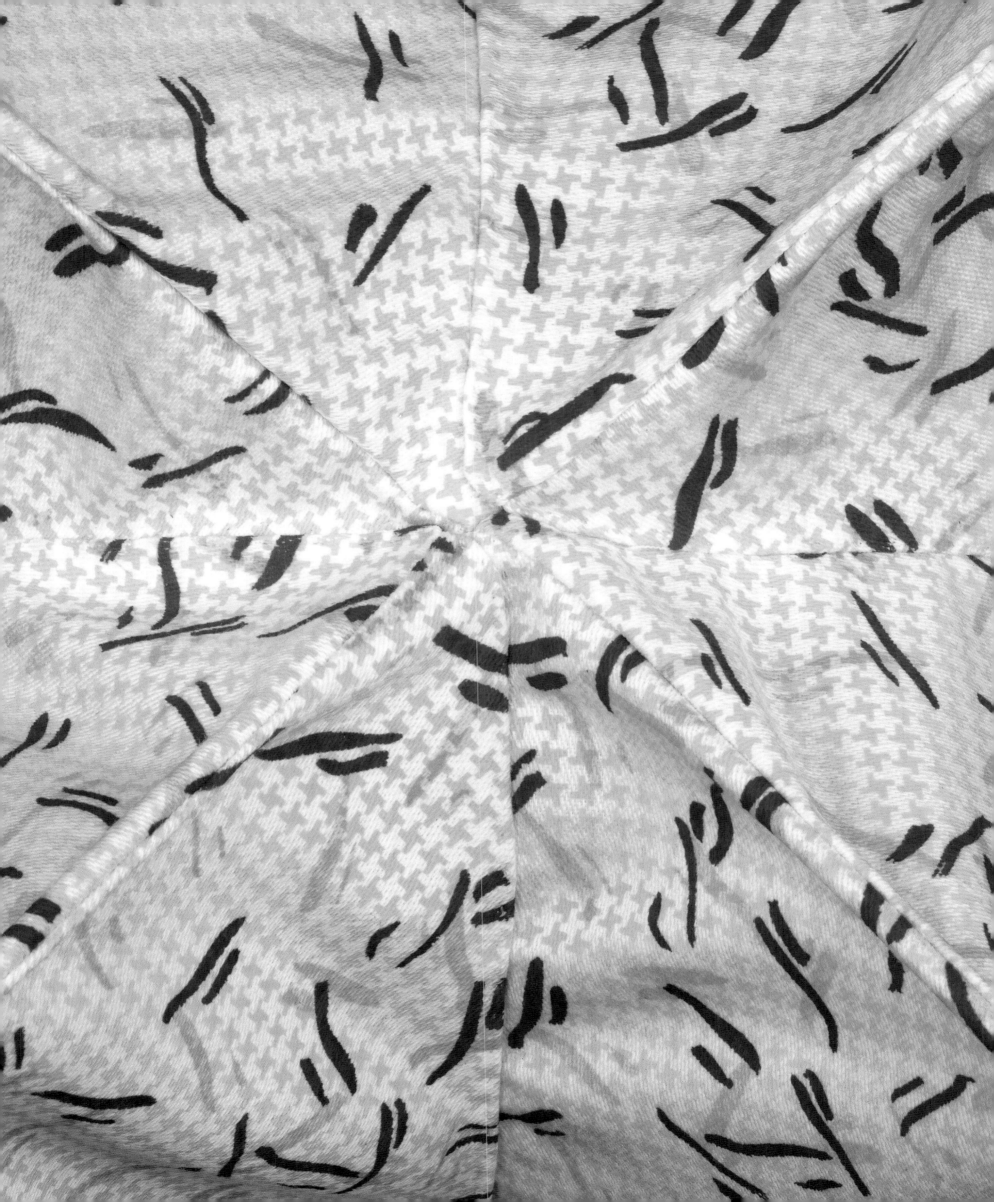

The Thinking Cap, 1998 (left). Pigment on cotton, and stainless steel. 12 x 8 ½ x 7 ½ inches (30.48 x 21.59 x 19.05 cm). Edition of 5.

24, 1998 (left). Pine. 24 x 24 x 24 inches (60.96 x 60.96 x 60.96 cm). Edition of 8.

Pants, 1979 (above). Pigment on bleached cotton muslin. 72 x 26 inches (182.88 x 66.04 cm).

Venturi, Scott Brown and Associates

About the artist

Robert Venturi, American, born 1925, lives in Philadelphia

Denise Scott Brown, American, born Zambia 1931, lives in Philadelphia

Robert Venturi and Denise Scott Brown have been practicing architecture, writing critical architectural theory and teaching together since the mid-1960s. Their award-winning work has influenced new generations of architects and designers, and includes building projects such as the Seattle Art Museum, a new wing for the National Gallery, London, Gordon Wu Hall at Princeton University, as well as early works such as Robert Venturi's Vanna Venturi House in Philadelphia (his mother's residence) and the façade for Best Products in Oxford Valley, Pennsylvania. Their theoretical writing has been critical to the development and understanding of postmodern theory in architecture, and includes *Complexity and Contradiction in Architecture*, and *Learning from Las Vegas*, which was written with their colleague Steve Izenour. Their four decades of architectural and design work was the subject of a 2001 exhibition organized by the Philadelphia Museum of Art, with additional travel to the Museum of Contemporary Art, San Diego, and The Heinz Architectural Center at the Carnegie Museum of Art, Pittsburgh.

About the work

Robert Venturi and Denise Scott Brown worked collaboratively with the FW+M from 1980 to 1982 to create several new fabric designs. Their longtime associate, Steve Izenour—a principal with Venturi, Scott Brown and Associates from 1969 until his death in 2001—returned in 1993, first to design a floor plan for the FW+M's new home at 1315 Cherry Street, and later to create a graphics and signage program to direct visitors to exhibition galleries and other public areas.

The design inspiration for *Grandmother* (1983) came from an old tablecloth belonging to the grandmother of an associate of Venturi and Scott Brown. They modified the tablecloth's floral print and added an overlay pattern of dashes. Venturi has described the initial design idea: "We wanted a pattern . . . that was explicitly pretty in its soft, curvy configurations and sweet combinations of colors, and represented as well something with nice associations, those of flowers. By juxtaposing the two patterns, the dashes and the grandmother-tablecloth, we achieved design involving dramatic contrasts of scale, rhythm, color, and association, and one that is usable in many ways" (VSBA Archives, project statement, July 19, 1990).

In 1998, Steve Izenour updated the firm's 1982 prototype for *Flowers* fabric, which was originally developed from the façade design for Best Products. Izenour modified the abstracted floral design—changing the colors and scale, and fabricating them from a rigid plastic material called Sintra board—and arranged the resulting large-scale, free-floating flowers on a sea of mint green for the stairway connecting the FW+M's fifth and sixth floors.

Grandmother, 1983. Pigment on cotton sateen. Width: 56 inches (142.24 cm). Collection of The Fabric Workshop and Museum; Philadelphia Museum of Art; and the Montreal Museum of Fine Arts.

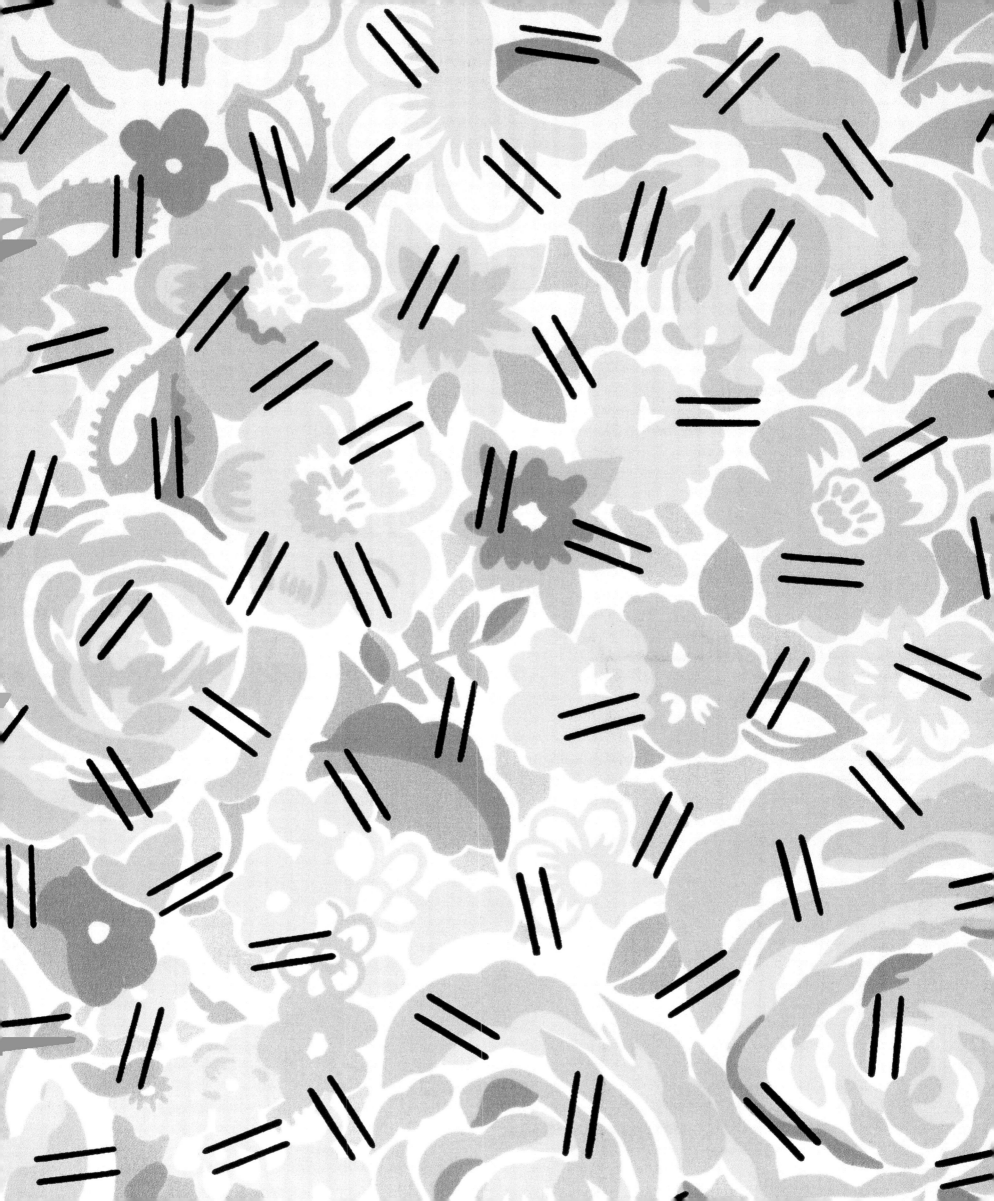

Stairway at The Fabric Workshop and Museum, designed by Steve Izenour, 1998. Sintra board and wall paint. Dimensions vary with installation.

Exhibition of Steve Izenour's work at The Fabric Workshop and Museum, 2001.

Bill Viola

About the artist

American, born 1951, lives in Long Beach, California

Bill Viola earned his BFA from Syracuse University in 1973. He is regarded as a pioneer and leading artist in the field of video art. In addition to his selection as the representative from the United States at the 1995 Venice Biennale, his work has been the subject of many major museum exhibitions including a 25-year retrospective organized by the Whitney Museum of American Art in 1997 (with a tour including the participation of the Los Angeles County Museum of Art, Stedelijk Museum in Amsterdam, Art Institute of Chicago, among others). In 1989, Viola received a John D. and Catherine T. MacArthur Foundation award; previous awards include fellowships from the Rockefeller Foundation (1982) and the Guggenheim Memorial Foundation (1985). He has been awarded honorary doctoral degrees from Syracuse University (1995), California College of Arts and Crafts (1998), and Massachusetts College of Art (1999).

About the work

The Veiling was one of five video and sound installations that Bill Viola created to occupy the five rooms of the United States Pavilion during the 46th Venice Biennale in 1995. Working in collaboration with the FW+M, Viola created a system of nine sheer scrims that are hung parallel to one another and catch the light from video projections positioned on either end. Images of a man and a woman can be seen slowly walking toward each other, passing through the scrims, merging at the center, and then moving apart again. This ghostly action becomes hypnotic, repeating over and over. Like much of Viola's work, *The Veiling* has a dream-like quality, and suggests the multiplicity of experience that exists both in our own thoughts and our understanding of our interaction with another human being.

In 1995, the FW+M exhibited *The Greeting*, the final video Viola created for the 1995 Venice Biennale. The richness of the color and detail of *The Greeting* is accentuated by the slow movement of the figures, a group of three women who approach one another until two embrace. Inspired by a sixteenth-century Italian masterpiece by Jacopo Carrucci da Pontormo depicting The Visitation, the video was recorded on high-speed 35mm film and then elongated to twelve times its original length. This simple sequence is mesmerizing to behold, as the nuances of gesture and the drape of flowing fabric are exaggerated by the filming technique.

The Veiling, 1995 (detail). Video/sound installation, including two channels of color video projections from opposite sides of dark gallery through nine scrims suspended from the ceiling, two channels of amplified mono sound, and four speakers. 138 x 264 x 372 inches (350.52 x 670.56 x 944.88 cm) (ideal room dimensions). Private collection.

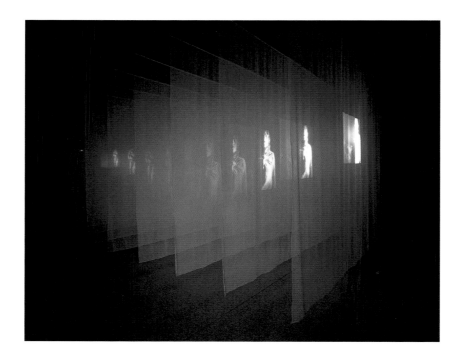

The Veiling, 1995 (above). Video/sound installation, including two channels of color video projections from opposite sides of dark gallery through nine scrims suspended from the ceiling, two channels of amplified mono sound, and four speakers. 138 x 264 x 372 inches (350.52 x 670.56 x 944.88 cm) (ideal room dimensions). Private collection.

The Greeting, 1995 (right). Video/sound installation, including color video projection on large vertical screen mounted on wall in darkened gallery, and amplified stereo sound. 168 x 258 x 306 inches (426.72 x 655.32 x 777.24 cm) (ideal room dimensions). Collection of Modern Art Museum of Fort Worth, Texas; Kunstmuseum Basel, Switzerland; De Pont Foundation for Contemporary Art, Tilburg, Netherlands; and the Whitney Museum of American Art, New York.

Carrie Mae Weems

About the artist

American, born 1953, lives in New York City and Syracuse, New York

After completing a BA at the California Institute of the Arts in Valencia, CA (1981), Carrie Mae Weems continued on to graduate school, earning a MFA from the University of California, San Diego, before studying folklore at the University of California, Berkeley. Known for her integration of photography and text, Weems has focused her work on universal themes such as relationships and family, while simultaneously commenting on social, cultural, and historical realities. She is one of the leading artists to emerge from a period in American art focusing on identity politics. Her work has been the subject of frequent exhibitions, including a traveling exhibition organized by Williams College (2000); a one-person show at the Whitney Museum of American Art at Philip Morris, New York (1998); and a *Projects* show at the Museum of Modern Art, New York (1995). In 1998, The Fabric Workshop and Museum, working with independent curator Mary Jane Jacob, organized an exhibition of Weems' work for *DAK'ART*, an international biennial of contemporary art in Dakar, Senegal.

About the work

Carrie Mae Weems retells the biblical story of Adam and Eve in *The Apple of Adam's Eye*. Using a folding screen as her form, Weems worked with the FW+M to silkscreen print a central image of a shrouded woman flanked by side panels depicting a decorative, serpentine vine. Gold text is elaborately embroidered and reads: "She'd always been the apple/Of Adam's Eye" (front panels) and "Temptation my ass, desire has its place, and besides, they were both doomed from the start" (on reverse).

The central figure shields herself, yet also reveals part of her body. There is sexual tension in this work, which Weems has acknowledged: " . . . there is . . . great desire, seduction, sexual charge and a point to be made—you know, stuff that makes the world go round" (*Projects: Carrie Mae Weems*, Museum of Modern Art, New York, 1995). Weems continued on to say that this work is about "how both men and women are accomplices in their own downfall, in their own oppression, in their own victimization." The sculpture—like much of Weems' work—undulates between the larger social implications between the sexes and a very intimate, interpersonal interaction.

Weems often exhibits *The Apple of Adam's Eye* with the wallpaper *Looking High and Low*. The pattern comes from the end sheets of George Bernard Shaw's 1933 book, *Adventures of the Black Girl in Her Search for God*, which introduces race to the retelling of the creation myth.

The Apple of Adam's Eye became a central element in Carrie Mae Weems' exhibition at the FW+M in 1993, and in subsequent exhibitions including *Ritual & Revolution*, her 1998 exhibition for the Dakar biennial exhibition, which has traveled extensively.

Looking High and Low (wallpaper), 1993. Pigment on paper. Width: 26 ½ inches (67.31 cm).

The Apple of Adam's Eye, 1993 (this page, front; facing page, back). Pigment and silk embroidery on cotton sateen, and Australian lacewood. 73 x 81 x 1 ¾ inches (185.42 x 205.74 x 4.45 cm). Edition of 5.

Temptation my ass, desire has its place, and besides, they were both doomed from the start.

Rachel Whiteread

About the artist

British, born 1963, lives in London

Rachel Whiteread was educated at Brighton Polytechnic (1982-85) and the Slade School of Art (1985-87) in London. She is best known for her major public art projects such as *Judenplatz: Place of Remembrance*, a Holocaust memorial in Vienna (2000); *Water Tower Project* (1998), a full-scale cast of the interior of a water tower made from translucent resin and installed on a rooftop in New York's SoHo neighborhood; and *House* (1993), a full-scale concrete cast of a row house in London's East End. Her work has been exhibited widely throughout the world, with recent one-person exhibitions at the Solomon R. Guggenheim Museum, New York (2002); Serpentine Gallery, London (2001); the Tate Gallery, London (1997); and the Reina Sofia, Madrid (1997). In 1997, Whiteread was selected to represent her country at the Venice Biennale.

About the work

Like much of Whiteread's sculpture, *Untitled (Felt Floor)* is a sculptural casting of negative space, in this case a wooden floor. Often focusing on objects from domestic interiors, Whiteread is interested in the associations these ghost-like negative spaces have to our lived experience. She makes spaces that are usually hidden—such as the underside of chairs—visible and viable as three-dimensional form, thereby assuring that these ordinary yet hidden voids are brought to our consciousness. In effect, Whiteread summons presence from absence.

The FW+M identified an industrial manufacturer of high-grade felt, and brought this company into the project as a collaborator. The process of creating *Untitled (Felt Floor)* involved several labor-intensive steps. First, a pine floor was built in six sections; a negative rubber mold was made of each section, into which positive rubber molds were cast. These positive rubber forms were pressed into resin-bonded sand to form molds in which bronze positives could be cast. The resulting bronze plates were placed on top of three-inch thick blocks of industrial felted wool, impregnated with resin, and placed in a heated press. Under the weight of the press, the surface of the white wool absorbed the impression of the pine floor form, while the heat cured the resin, ensuring that the embossed design would be permanent. The full sculpture is made of eighteen units, or three impressions each of the original six wooden floor sections. The resulting image is extremely subtle, and under subdued lighting, can look like an unadorned, white Minimalist sculpture. The image becomes apparent with the slightest shift in lighting, however, and the impression of a wooden floor appears in a ghostly state.

Untitled (Felt Floor), 1997 (detail, right).
Untitled (Felt Floor), 1997 (following pages). Resin-impregnated wool felt. Eighteen units: 3 x 18 x 54 inches (7.62 x 45.72 x 137.16 cm) each. Overall dimension: 3 x 108 x 162 inches (7.62 x 274.32 x 411.48 cm). Private collection.

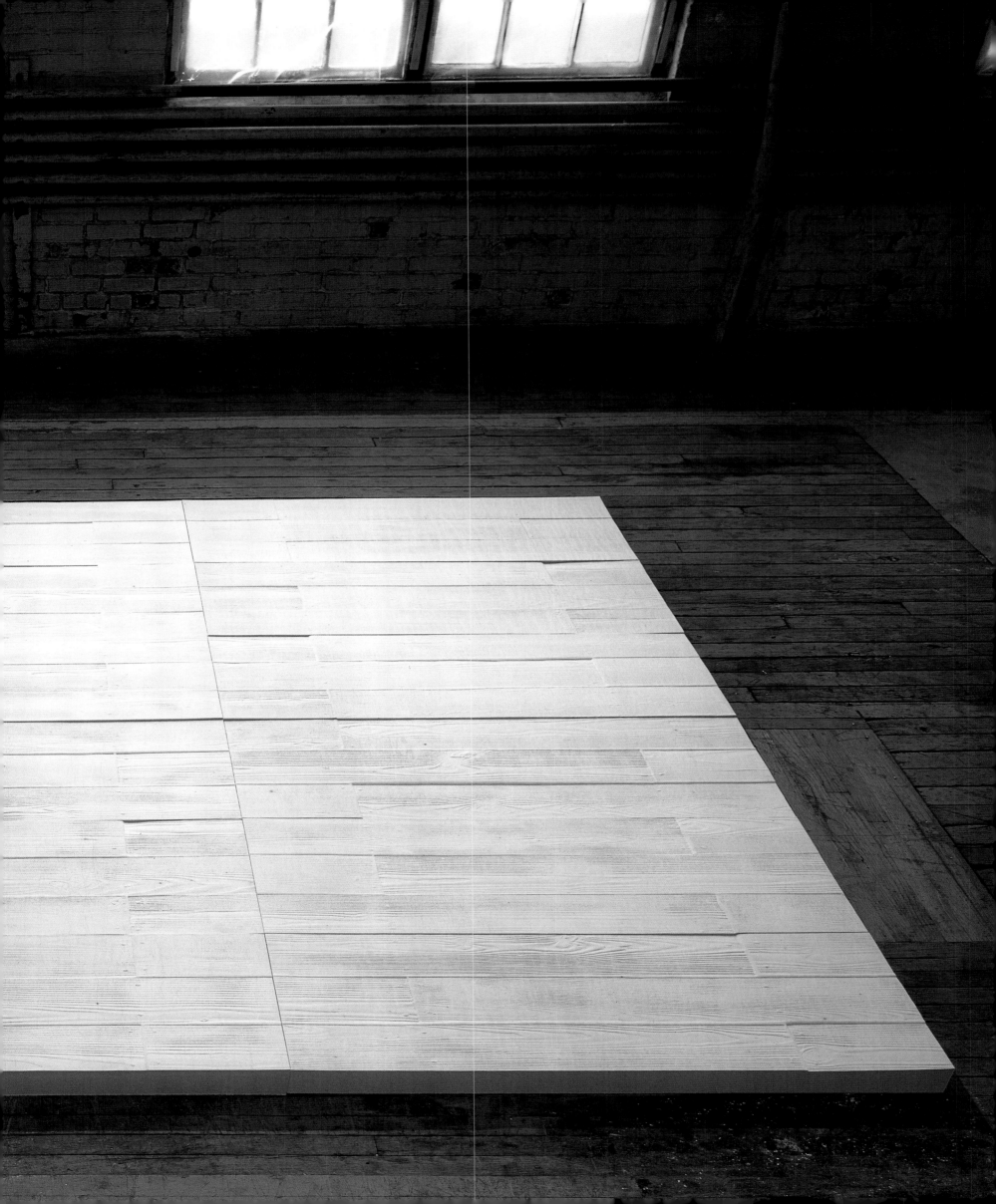

Yukinori Yanagi

Japanese, born 1959, lives in Tokyo, Japan and New York City

About the artist

Raised in Fukouka, Japan, the prefecture nearest Korea, Yukinori Yanagi grew up with an awareness of the existence of a foreign country and a culture different than his own. After studying art at Musashino Art University in Tokyo, and receiving both a BA and a MFA in painting (1985), Yanagi moved to the United States and completed another MFA at Yale University (1990). One of the first Japanese artists to critique his nation's social and political systems, Yanagi is perhaps best known for his project *Ant Farm*, in which a series of national flags made from colored sand are eventually blurred and mixed by a colony of ants. Yanagi's work has been the subject of one-person exhibitions in the United States, Japan, and Europe: Hiroshima City Museum of Contemporary Art (2000); The Queens Museum of Art, New York (1995); and Naoshima Contemporary Art Museum, Kagawa, Japan (1992). He was selected to participate in the 2000 Biennial at the Whitney Museum of American Art, New York.

302

About the work

Over the course of several years, Yukinori Yanagi made a series of works in collaboration with the FW+M. In 1995, he created *The Forbidden Box*, an installation of two large-scale Iris inkjet prints depicting the mushroom cloud created by the explosion of the atomic bomb in Hiroshima. Yanagi selected the image from a 1946 Japanese newspaper. Printed on sheer fabric, the panels are embellished with the words of the Japanese constitution's Article 9, which renounces the nation's ability to wage war and was originally drafted by General Douglas MacArthur after the end of World War II. The MacArthur version is printed in English on the rear panel, while the Japanese version—which is written in a much more conciliatory tone—and its English translation can be found on the front panel. The juxtaposition of the two texts allows for a comparison of the cultural differences between the United States and Japan.

Below the billboard-size prints, Yanagi placed an open lead box with the words "Little Boy"—the name of the bomb—inscribed on the lid. The box is a reference to a Japanese folktale called *Urashima Taro*, taught in elementary schools from the time of imperial rule up until World War II. Urashima Taro was a fisherman who achieved immortality by rescuing a turtle from a group of cruel children. Taro eventually goes to live with a sea goddess in an underworld palace; when he misses his home, the sea goddess gives him a box that will allow his return to the palace as long as he does not open it. Taro opens the box, releasing a great cloud of white smoke that turns him into an old man.

In 1997, Yanagi created a limited edition multiple, *Loves Me/Loves Me Not*, which is a smaller version of his 1994 sculpture *Chrysanthemum Carpet*. In the center of the deep red carpet is an impression of a chrysanthemum, the Japanese imperial crest, with its petals—made from brass—torn off and scattered across the surface. Also woven into the carpet is the text "s/he loves me" and "s/he loves me not," written in the languages of countries once dominated by Japanese imperial rule. With this piece, Yanagi confronts a Japanese myth that a homogenous people were united as one during the emperor's reign.

Loves Me, Loves Me Not, 1997 (detail). Wool with jute backing, and brass. 144 x 96 inches (365.76 x 243.84 cm). Edition of 7.

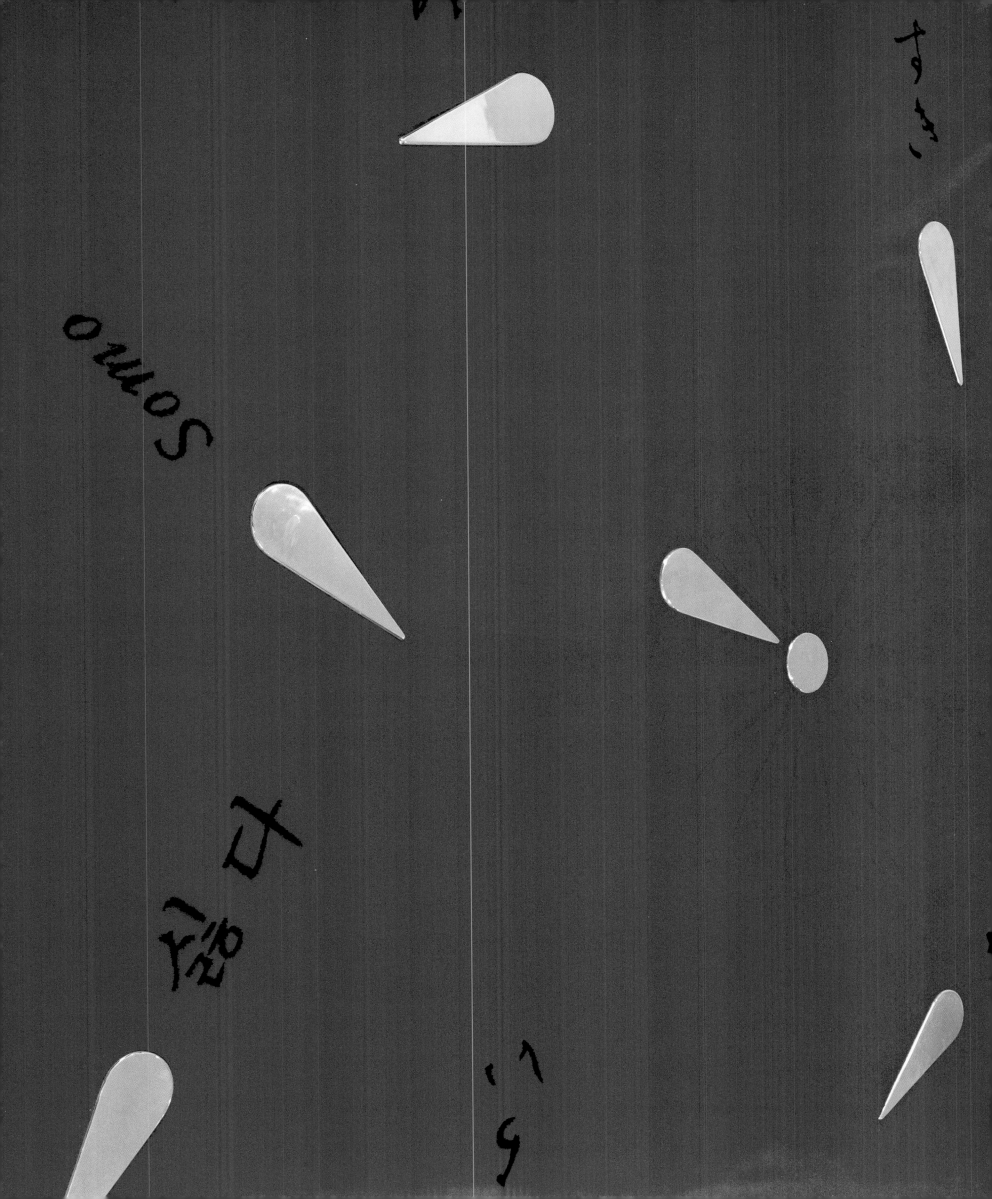

Loves Me, Loves Me Not, 1997 (above). Wool with jute backing, and brass. 144 x 96 inches (365.76 x 243.84 cm). Edition of 7.

The Forbidden Box, 1995 (right). Iris and silkscreen print on ninon voile, lead, and wood box. Two panels: 204 x 115 inches (518.16 x 292.1 cm). Box: 24 x 36 x 24 inches (60.96 x 91.44 x 60.96 cm). Edition of 2.

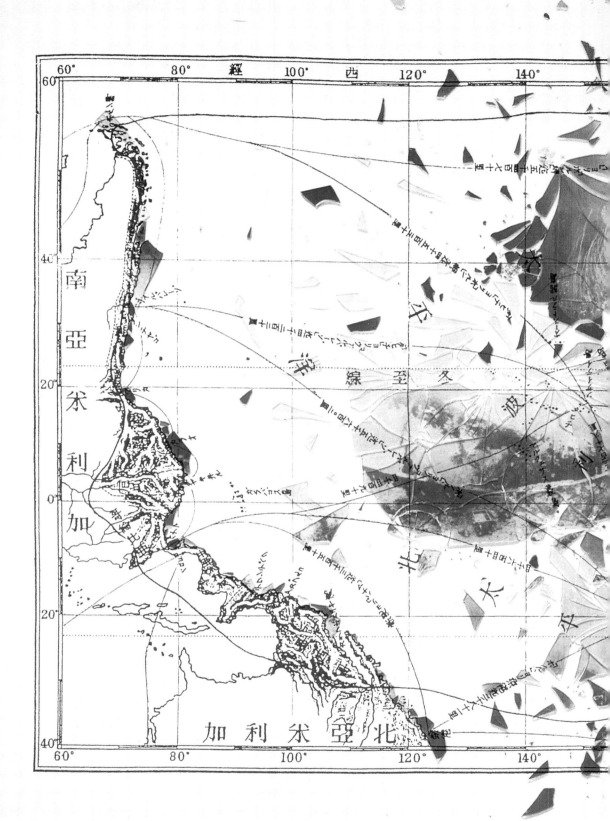

Pacific-Shattered Blue, 1997. Pigment on muslin, screenprint on glass, and plywood. 83 ½ x 118 x 3 ¾ inches (212.09 x 299.72 x 9.53 cm). Collection of the artist.

The Fabric Workshop and Museum
History, Mission, and Programs

History and Mission

The Fabric Workshop and Museum (FW+M) is a distinct institution, the only non-profit arts organization in the United States that commissions today's cutting-edge artists to collaborate in creating new work in fabric and other unconventional materials. Equally unique, the FW+M has always included the public in its unusual creative enterprise, with open studios that invite visitors to witness the evolution—from conception to completion—of challenging works of art. Experimental from its inception in 1977, the FW+M has maintained its core spirit of innovation for 25 years. At the same time, it has evolved into an influential, internationally-acclaimed contemporary art museum with a significant permanent collection, the fruits of a quarter century of artistic experimentation in a range of media.

FW+M founder Marion Boulton Stroud began with an ambitious vision. The Fabric Workshop would be an amalgam: one part avant-garde arts laboratory, modeled after such ateliers as Gemini G.E.L., which encouraged artists to experiment with untried techniques and media; one part design collaborative, akin to William Morris' late 19th century textile studios at Merton Abbey or the late 20th century Scandinavian collective Marimekko, both of which set high aesthetic and technical standards for useful, everyday objects; and one part educational center, a training ground for underserved students that would encourage creative expression while providing solid technical and vocational skills. The last was a natural outgrowth of Stroud's successful artistic leadership of an inner-city art education program, Philadelphia's Prints in Progress.

Twenty-five years later, that unusual fusion has yielded results beyond what even Stroud could have imagined. At first, the FW+M gave artists and students the opportunity to explore and expand the possibilities for silkscreen printing on fabric, resulting in works such as Roy Lichtenstein's *Untitled* shirt (1979), Scott Burton's *Window Curtains* (1978), and Robert Kushner's *Hawaiian Punch* cape (1977), which was used in one of Kushner's outrageous fashion shows. Quickly, the parameters of experimentation broadened as each artist's residency introduced unexpected new applications for artmaking with fabric, such as Kim MacConnel's *Bamboo Curtain* fabric made partly with Mexican roller painting brushes (1978); Michael Singer's *Untitled* flocked dirt series (1983); Robert Morris' *Restless Sleepers/Atomic Shroud* (1981), which used a human skeleton as a printing tool; and Ken Little's *Bread Couple*, *Buck and Doe* suit and dress (1988) made from U.S. one-dollar bills. Collaboration with FW+M project coordinators—skilled technicians, textile artists and sculptors in their own right—provides a key component in each artist's residency, and makes such daring material exploration possible. And with close to twelve artist's residencies every year, the number of new artworks

quickly grew into an exciting permanent collection, which is exhibited regularly in the FW+M galleries and traveling exhibitions. An active loan program also ensures that collection works are seen in art museums around the world. In 1996, the institution formally added the word *museum* to reflect the significance of its collections, as well as the FW+M's commitment to preserving and presenting the more than 5,500 objects in its care.

Taken as a whole, those objects form a vital historical record of the major art movements of the late 20th century, from Pop and Minimalism to Pattern & Decoration and site-specific installations. Indeed, as the artistic vanguard moved into interdisciplinary and installation work, the FW+M responded by expanding artistic operations to accommodate works of greater scale and technological complexity. A substantial supporter of minority artists, the FW+M also now has one of the leading collections tracing the theme of multi-culturalism since the late 1980s, including works by Mel Chin, Renée Green, Hachivi Edgar Heap of Birds, Glenn Ligon, James Luna, Gary Simmons, and Carrie Mae Weems. And while the fine arts collection is international in scope and influence, more than 80 regional artists are included, making the FW+M an invaluable resource and networking center for the area's arts community.

The FW+M's unique emphasis on fabric as a medium for experimentation has had a profound impact on artists and public alike. Artists selected for residency, forced to rethink their accustomed approach to materials and, in many cases, working collaboratively for the first time, have often created breakthrough work at FW+M. During her residency, Lorna Simpson, for example, created her first work in industrial felt, a material that became the focus of many future investigations. Jim Hodges, after learning the basics of sewing in collaboration with staff, created his first large-scale silk flower curtain. This project became the first in a signature series of works for Hodges. For the FW+M's visitors, the medium of fabric—familiar and domestic—instantly makes even the edgiest art accessible.

As such, the FW+M has been instrumental in redefining craft and design and integrating them into mainstream contemporary art. The institution continues Philadelphia's long legacy as a leader in the fields of international contemporary crafts, architecture, design, and art. Like the great modernist collections in the region—notably the Barnes Foundation's modern "masters" and the Philadelphia Museum of Art's comprehensive collection of Marcel Duchamp—the FW+M has stimulated artistic explorations that challenge established boundaries while engaging a broad general audience in the exciting forms, new materials, and ideas of contemporary art.

Programs

The Fabric Workshop and Museum is the rare organization involved in all aspects of the creative process, from conception through production—and beyond, with exhibition, public education, and preservation integral to the FW+M's mission. Ambitious in scope, the FW+M achieves its goals through the following programs:

Artist-in-Residence Program

Each year, the FW+M invites 10–12 artists to create experimental new work in untried media. Emerging and established; regional, national, and international; painters, sculptors, architects, designers, conceptual and installation artists, and even performance and video artists, collaborate with the FW+M's staff of printers and technicians, redefining the boundaries of fabric as an artistic medium in the process. A significant part of the residency, the interaction with staff—who bring creative innovation and a wide range of technical abilities to the collaboration—often leads artists to take their work in exciting new directions.

Apprentice Training Program

High school, college, and post-graduate students learn all aspects of silkscreen printing on fabric in the FW+M's professional studios. Students design and print their own fabric yardage, assist staff in producing artist residency projects, actively participate in the FW+M community and its educational and exhibition programs, and finish the 12-week term having acquired new tools for artistic expression and empowerment.

Exhibitions

Centered on work created in the Artist-in-Residence Program, the FW+M's exhibitions of innovative contemporary art range from solo shows to provocative thematic exhibitions. Guest curators are invited to provide fresh perspective and reinterpretations of new and past residency works. An active publications program complements the exhibition series, with monographic catalogues on artists published annually.

Permanent Collections

The more than 5,500 objects in the FW+M's collections cover the major art movements of the last 25 years, with significant works by such diverse artists as Doug Aitken, Louise Bourgeois, Sam Gilliam, Felix Gonzalez-Torres, Ann Hamilton, Reverend Howard Finster, Marie-Ange Guilleminot, Anish Kapoor, Robert Morris, Louise Nevelson, Claes Oldenburg, Jorge Pardo, Yinka Shonibare, Kiki Smith, Richard Tuttle, Robert Venturi and Denise Scott Brown, and Bill Viola. In addition, the FW+M's holdings include an unprecedented collection of materials documenting resident artists' creative process. Photographs and videos recording the stages of each project, as well as the actual materials used and the sketches and prototypes made, are available for loan and research. These archives significantly enhance the permanent collections, offering an extraordinary, in-depth view of how works of contemporary art develop, both conceptually and technically.

Education Programs

Education is the guiding principle of all FW+M programming. The FW+M designs its extensive roster of lectures, tours, and technical workshops to engage audiences of all ages and backgrounds in the challenging ideas and techniques of contemporary art. School groups and other visitors to the FW+M are invited to see artists in action in the FW+M's open studios and have the chance to ask resident artists questions while they work. Through traveling exhibitions and presentations in schools, the FW+M brings its unique perspective on contemporary art out into the wider world.

Board of Directors, Staff, and Funders

Former staff

Annette Alexander
Ingrid Bachmann
Nancy Miller Batty
Steven Beyer
Grace Bishko
Michelle Bregande
Yane Calovski
Christine Cook
Treya Cooper
Helen Cunningham
Betsy Damos
Matthew Drutt
Christian Fahlen
Ann Freeman
Carl Fudge
Megan Granda
Stephen Griffin
Kathy Halton
Charlotte Herring
Elizabeth Hopkins
Roby Isaac
Ed James
Barbara Johnson
Marie Keller
Barbara Kelly
Brigitte Kraus
Chris Kronthaler
Alexandra Kudrjavcev-
  DeMilner
Betty Leacraft
Maria Lee
René Lego
Kristen Leida
Susan Leonard
Dana Levy
Shanna Linn
Cassandra Lozano
Susan Maruska
Merrill Mason
Laurie McGahey
Alexis McGlynn
Elizabeth McIlvaine
Kelly Mitchell
Katie Morita
Lucy Michels Morris
Maritza Mosquera
Jennifer Nelson
Robin Nemlich

Cynthia Porter
Marc Robinson
Annabeth Rosen
Marianne Schoettle
Richard Siegesmund
Elizabeth Spungen
Mika Tajima
Stephanie Tyishka
Sarah Vanderlip
Pamela VanderZwan
Karen Wagner
Emily Wallace
Barbara Woodall

Major Funders

The Arcadia Foundation
American Craft Council
The Barra Foundation
California Tamarak
  Foundation
E. Rhodes & Leona B.
  Carpenter Foundation
Louis N. Cassett Foundation
The Claniel Foundation
Dolfinger-MacMahon
  Foundation
The Fidelity Charitable
  Gift Fund
Independence Foundation
Institute of Museum and
  Library Services
LLWW Foundation
Mid-Atlantic Arts Foundation
The Miller-Plummer
  Foundation
National Endowment for
  the Arts
Agnes and Bill Peelle
William Penn Foundation
Pennsylvania Council on the
  Arts
Pennsylvania Historical and
  Museum Commission
The Pew Charitable Trusts
The Philadelphia Cultural
  Fund
Philadelphia Exhibitions
  Initiative
The Philadelphia Foundation
Philip Morris Companies, Inc.
The PNC Foundation
The Quaker Chemical
  Foundation
The Rosengarten-Horowitz
  Fund
Stockton Rush Bartol
  Foundation
Cynthia Stroud
Andy Warhol Foundation for
  the Visual Arts

Artists in Residence, 1977–2002

Marina Abramović
Vito Acconci
Phoebe Adams
Doug Aitken
Adela Akers
Anni Albers
Jesse Amado
Gregory Amenoff
William Anastasi
Harry Anderson
Laurie Anderson
Edna Andrade
Robert Arneson
Luis Cruz Azaceta
Shelley Bachman
Miroslaw Balka
Ed Baynard
Lynda Benglis
Steven Beyer
Bob Bingham
Robert Blackburn
Barbara Bloom
Ecke Bonk
Jill Bonovitz
Berrisford Boothe
Christine Borland
Louise Bourgeois
Gary Bower
Luchezar Boyadjiev
Moe Brooker
Roger Brown
Chris Burden
Charles Burns
Scott Burton
Mark Campbell
Maria Fernanda Cardoso
Cynthia Carlson
James Carpenter
Rosemarie Castoro
Dale Chihuly
Mel Chin
William Christenberry
David Chung
Nannette Clark
Willie Cole
Robert Colescott
Warrington Colescott
Lillian Concordia
Houston Conwill

Louise Todd Cope
Tony Costanzo
Betsy Damos
Brad Davis
Agnes Denes
Roy DeForest
Richard DeVore
Linh Dinh
Mark Dion
Mark diSuvero
Iran do Espirito Santo
Milena Dopitova
Leonardo Drew
Alan Edmunds
Charles Fahlen
Eiko Fan
Frank Faulkner
Sherry Feldman
John Ferris
Rev. Howard Finster
Terry Fox
Richard Francisco
Helen Frederick
Viola Frey
Tom Friedman
Carl Fudge
James Gadson
David Gilhooly
Andrea Gill
Sam Gilliam
Tina Girouard
Robert Gober
Felix Gonzalez-Torres
Sidney Goodman
Lonnie Graham
Nancy Graves
Renée Green
Rodney Alan Greenblat
Red Grooms
Arturo Guerrero
Marie-Ange Guilleminot
Richard Haas
Dorothy Hafner
Ann Hamilton
Gaylen Hansen
Mona Hatoum
Hachivi Edgar Heap of Birds
Mary Heilmann
Edward Henderson

Marcy Hermansader
Linda Herritt
Jene Highstein
Jim Hodges
Howard Hodgkin
Mei-ling Hom
Rebecca Howland
Eleanor Hubbard
Margo Humphrey
Lydia Hunn
David Ireland
Diane Itter
Steve Izenour
Alfredo Jaar
Luis Jimenez
Hella Jongerius
Narelle Jubelin
Charles Juhász-Alvarado
Fumi Kaneko
Jun Kaneko
Anish Kapoor
Steve Keister
Mike Kelley
Maurie Kerrigan
Michael Kessler
Alexa Kleinbard
Joyce Kozloff
Robert Kushner
Eva Kwong
Rachel Lachowicz
Moshekwa Langa
Marisa Lara
Lee Bul
Lee Mingwei
Stacy Levy
Roy Lichtenstein
Glenn Ligon
Donald Lipski
Ken Dawson Little
Bert Long
Tristin Lowe
Cassandra Lozano
Michael Lucero
James Luna
Lysiane Luong
Phillip Maberry
Kim MacConnel
Martha Madigan
Andrew Magdanz

Maisin Artists of Papua
  New Guinea
Lynn Mandelbaum
Kirk Mangus
Margo Margolis
Tom Marioni
Graham Marks
Virgil Marti
Gabriel Martinez
John McQueen
Jim Melchert
Michael Mercil
Arturo Miralda
Jeffrey Mitchell
Juanita Mizuno
Mineo Mizuno
Renny Molenaar
Jacqueline Matisse Monnier
John Moore
Toshiko Mori
Robert Morris
Matt Mullican
Hiroshi Murata
Robert Murray
Don Nakamura
Joseph Nechvatal
Eileen Neff
Stuart Netsky
Louise Nevelson
Gladys Nilsson
Claes Oldenburg
Pat Oleszko
Michael Olijnyk
Michael Olszewski
Bill Omwake
Dennis Oppenheim
Laura Owens
Jorge Pardo
Izhar Patkin
Sue Patterson
Pedro Perez
Judy Pfaff
Jody Pinto
Keith Piper
J. Morgan Puett
Egle Rakauskaite
Red Roof Design
David Reed
Jacquie Rice

Judy Rifka
Faith Ringgold
Matthew Ritchie
Warren Rohrer
Tim Rollins and Kids of
  Survival
Ugo Rondinone
Alison Rossiter
Nancy Rubins
Alison Saar
Betye Saar
Alan Saret
Wade Saunders
Tad Savinar
Italo Scanga
Miriam Schapiro
Barbara Schwartz
Frederic Schwartz
Vicki Scuri
Warren Seelig
Beverly Semmes
Kendall Shaw
Judith Shea
Yinka Shonibare
Patrick Siler
Gary Simmons
Buster Simpson
Lorna Simpson
Michael Singer
Kiki Smith
Robert Smith
Ned Smyth
Katherine Sokolnikoff
Laurinda Spear
Rudolph Staffel
Pat Steir
David Stephens
Jana Sterbak
Lizbeth Stewart
Will Stokes
Alan Stone
Marjorie Strider
Do-Ho Suh
Paula Sweet
Gregorz Sztwiertnia
Toshiko Takaezu
Lenore Tawney
Anita Thacher
Rena Thompson

Patricia Torres
Richard Tuttle
Marie Tyniec
Susan Van Campen
Pamela VanderZwan
Robert Venturi and
  Denise Scott Brown
Ales Vesely
Carlos Villanueva
Bill Viola
Ursula von Rydingsvard
Yoshiko Wada
Clara Wainwright
Kara Walker
Bill Walton
Phillip Warner
Jeff Way
Carrie Mae Weems
Susan Chrylser White
Rachel Whiteread
Robert Whitman
William T. Wiley
Fred Wilson
Robin Winters
Karl Wirsum
Beatrice Wood
Betty Woodman
George Woodman
Shirley Woodson
Christopher Wool
Yukinori Yanagi
Lily Yeh
Teruyoshi Yoshida
Isaiah Zagar
Claire Zeisler
Martha Zelt
Zhou Miao
Zhou Ziu Fen
Barbara Zucker
Rhonda Zwillinger

Acknowledgments

The Fabric Workshop and Museum would like to extend its deep gratitude for the dedication of the following people, who, in their own unique and wonderful ways, have contributed enormously to the vision of the FW+M.

The Artists-in-Residence, Board of Directors, Artistic Advisory Committee, staff, apprentices and interns

Doina Adam
Gheorghe Adam
Barbara Aronson
Ted Aronson
Ingrid Bachmann
Mei-mei Berssenbrugge
Dilys Blum
Francesco Bonami
Michael Brenson
Denise Scott Brown
Emily Brown
Will Brown
Ellie Burgess
Stewart Cades
Dale Chihuly
Paolo Colombo
Diene Cooper
Lafcadio Cortesi
Helen Cunningham
Arthur Danto
Anne d'Harnoncourt
Ann de Forest
Daniel Dietrich
Drew Dominick
Ed Drummond
Matthew Drutt
Letty Lou Eisenhauer
Helen W. Drutt English
Chuck Fahlen
Noelle Fahlen
Milton Feldman
Russell Ferguson
Margaret Fikioris
Ruth Fine
Annette Friedland
Jack Friedland
Mary Anne Friel
Vivian Gast
Barbara Glickman
Richard Gluckman
Thelma Golden
Lonnie Graham
Jennifer Gross

Richard Haas
Gail Harrity
Ann Hatch
Kathryn Hiesinger
Ulrich Hiesinger
Jim Hodges
Katy Homans
Harold Honickman
Lynn Honickman
Aaron Igler
Mary Jane Jacob
Lauren Jacobi
Charles Juhász-Alvarado
Ron Kanter
Janet Kardon
Tim Kearney
Marie Keller
Emanuel Kelly
Jane Korman
Leonard Korman
Joan Kremer
Ann Lauderbach
Brad Lee
Margery Lee
Gene Lefevre
Dina Levy
Ann Loftus
Martie Lobb
Elsa Longhauser
Bill Longhauser
John Lucas
Martha Madigan
Paula Marincola
Virgil Marti
Merrill Mason
Jay Richardson Massey
Takaaki Matsumoto
Patricia McLaughlin
Lorie Mertes
Harvey Shipley Miller
Kelly Mitchell
Sylvester Moi
Eugene Mopsik
Lucy Michels Morris
Robert Morris
Ellen Bethany Napier
Benjamin Neilson
Ted Newbold

Ann Ollman
John Ollman
Jorge Pardo
Sue Patterson
Agnes Peelle
Bill Peelle
Lisa Phillips
J. Randall Plummer
Conny Purtill
Ned Putnam
John Ravenal
Larry Rinder
Ana Rosa Rivera
Christina Roberts
Walter Robinson (Buddy)
Anne Rorimer
Laura Rosenthal
Mark Rosenthal
Patsy and Karl Rugart
Ella Schaap
Katherine Schade
Paul Schimmel
Innis Howe Shoemaker
Richard Siegesmund
J. Patterson Sims
Merve Smucker
Katherine Sokolnikoff
Will Stokes, Jr.
Ann Percy Stroud
Cynthia Stroud
W.B. Dixon Stroud
Charles Stuckey
Clint Swingle
Susan Lubowsky Talbott
Mark Thompson
Emily Todd
Ella King Torrey
Thanh X. Tran
Marcia Tucker
Phillip Unetic
Dianne Perry Vanderlip
Sarah Vanderlip
Pamela VanderZwan
John Wesley Vaso
Robert Venturi
John Vinci
Yoshiko Wada
Jace Wagner

Karen Wagner
Carla Washinko
Barbara Westman
Ann Wetzel
Candyce Wilbur
Amy Wilkins
Graydon Wood
Sally Wood
Tetsuya Yamada
Samuel H. Young

In memory of
Roger Brown
Scott Burton
Felix Gonzalez-Torres
Diane Itter
Steve Izenour
Roy Lichtenstein
Lallie Lloyd
Louise Nevelson
Michael Quigley
Italo Scanga
Carl Shaw
Robert Smith
Philip Warner
Louis Williams
Claire Zeisler

Index of Artists

Colophon

This book was composed principally in the Franklin Gothic font family using QuarkXPress, and typeset at Matsumoto Incorporated, New York. All images were scanned and separated into four process colors. The book was printed in Itabashi, Tokyo, Japan at Toppan Printing, on Kinfuji 157 g/m^2 stock, and Smythsewn bound.